5.00

The Ultimate
QUILTING
Book

The Ultimate
QUILTING
Book

*Over 1,000 inspirational ideas
and practical tips*

BARNES
&NOBLE
BOOKS
NEW YORK

First published in 1999 by Collins & Brown
64 Brewery Road
London N7 9NT
A member of **Chrysalis** Books plc

1 3 5 7 9 10 8 6 4 2

ISBN: 0-7607-4762-8

Editorial Director: Sarah Hoggett
Editors: Catherine Ward, Ian Kearey, Corinne Asghar, Claire Waite, Mandy Lebentz
Design Manager: Alison Lee
Designers: Liz Brown and Axis Design

Printed in China

*HALF TITLE PAGE: This early version of the Fans pattern made in
about 1910 is pieced from bright-colored fabrics on a black
background. The fans are outline-quilted, while the
black background is worked in diagonal lines that meet
the chevron pattern used on the wide border.*

*TITLE PAGE: A fabulous Mennonite Irish Chain quilt has blocks
of alternating red and green stripes as the "blank" areas between
the yellow and red double chains, and a beautifully pieced chain
border. Each square of the chains is quilted with a diagonal line
in each direction, and the background is stitched in concentric
circles radiating out from every intersection.*

Contents

INTRODUCTION

Enjoying a beautiful quilt is the ultimate aim of the quiltmaker. On the pages that follow, you will find inspiration, ideas, and instructions for making your own, as well as a wealth of fascinating historical detail.

This Sampler quilt made in Pennsylvania in about 1865 has 85 different blocks, many of them unique, set on point. The simple beige geometric print used to make the sashing, which is necessary to define each block, also forms the outer border.

Introduction

QUILTMAKING HAS PROVIDED PLEASURE to countless needleworkers for centuries, and the skills of patchwork, appliqué, and quilting have been handed down through generations in most of the world's cultures. Creating a beautiful quilt is a challenge and luckily, enormous numbers of quiltmakers have risen to meet it.

On the pages that follow are several hundred quilted, appliquéd, or pieced items that fall into the broad category of "quilt." Many of them are antiques, in some cases nearly two hundred years old. Some of them have just begun their life and may someday become heirlooms. The variety is immense, enough to whet the appetite and imagination of anyone interested in making – or just simply looking at – quilts.

Because by far the majority of old quilts – certainly those made before about 1970 – are patchwork, one whole section of this book is devoted to examples of the main types of pieced work. There is a separate section on the most important patchwork techniques, together with a selection of easy-to-follow projects.

Quilts that are deemed important because of the quilting itself are much rarer than patchwork ones, as are fine examples of antique appliqué quilts. However, beautiful examples of both survive, and they are featured in their own section, with another section devoted to quilting and appliqué techniques and projects.

Patchwork and quilting most likely developed from necessity, the former allowing the most economcial use of scarce textiles by joining scraps together to make larger pieces of fabric. Quilting may have arisen from the need to make thick clothes or covers for warmth, and padding for protection on the battlefield. Appliqué is probably purely decorative.

Quilts used as bedcovers date from about the fourteenth century – the earliest known example is from Sicily – but quilted garments and household textiles are much more ancient. Historical evidence from paintings and carvings has revealed the use of quilted clothing from as long ago as ancient China and ancient Egypt – the latter from the First Dynasty in about 3400 BC – and fragments of quilted cloth still exist from the Middle Ages in Europe. The word "quilt" – spelled "quylt" or "twylt" – was used in various forms before the thirteenth century. Quilted armor was worn by medieval soldiers under their chain mail for comfort, protection, and sometimes warmth, and European women in many areas wore quilted petticoats for warmth and modesty for several generations,

OPPOSITE AND ABOVE: This beautiful blue and white Double Feathered Star quilt is a fine example of the best of all three quiltmaking skills: the pieced double stars are patchwork, the folk-art motifs in the square spacer blocks and around the border are appliqué, and the entire piece is blended and secured with quilting of the highest order. Each of the plain, diamond spacer blocks is quilted with a different motif, and the floral patterns that predominate elsewhere, such as the leaf and branches in the triangular spacers around the edge, are beautifully wrought. Made in about 1865 in New York, the piece is initialed at the bottom "C/E.B".

including the one in which the first European settlers arrived in North America.

By the seventeenth and eighteenth centuries, quilted clothing was highly fashionable, first in Europe and then in North America, and the skills were widely known and practiced. This technical expertise went with the colonists wherever they settled, and their knowledge of stitching, together with their necessarily frugal habits, no doubt helped many to survive the harsh, unfamiliar climate and privations of life in an alien land.

In the nineteenth century, the methods used to make quilts were being applied to decorative bedcovers on both sides of the Atlantic, and the quilt as we generally think of it today came into its own. A cottage industry grew up in the North of England making beautiful

ABOVE: *Made in about 1900, this borderless quilt has, instead of the usual quarter-circle Fans, fully open versions in magenta, blue, and green with a red center. Each fan and its blades is blanket-stitched around the edges.*

LEFT: *The quintessential hexagon pattern, Grandmother's Flower Garden, is made from scraps cut and placed with the utmost care on a cream background. Made in about 1840, it has a chintz strip as the border and is beautifully quilted between the hexagon blocks with running feather.*

quilts, mainly to sell, and it spread from its roots in Country Durham and Northumberland to various parts of North America as new immigrants attempted to escape poverty and persecution.

The crowning achievements of so-called Durham quilting were beautiful wholecloth quilts and strippies, which required relatively large pieces of fabric. Such textiles were a luxury in newly settled areas of North America, where the nearest store might be several days away and the cost would be prohibitive. The English method of using scraps of fairly small size cut into geometric shapes and joined into full-size quilts had also arrived on North American shores with the early colonists. The settlers had, of necessity, to reuse and recycle even small scraps of a resource as valuable as

ABOVE: *An Amish Basket of Chips quilt, made about 1915, in Lancaster County, Pennsylvania – somber yet glowing colors. The liveliness of the basket blocks turned on point and set with dark teal, also used to bind the piece, makes a highly desirable quilt.*

RIGHT: *A 1920s Diamond in the Square – Amish quilting at its best. The center diamond is filled with a feathered wreath, and the setting triangles closely worked with crosshatching. The two red borders are stitched with pumpkin seed, and the wide outer border shows lovely swoops of running feather looping into the corner squares and out again.*

ABOVE: An1850s Massachusetts sampler quilt: 24-point compasses, pieced corner squares, hexagon, flying geese, and a floral vine appliqué on the outer border.

fabric. On the frontier, there was the added complication of very little storage or working space. So pioneer stitchers developed a system for making blocks of patchwork that could be completed and set aside until there were enough for a whole quilt. Such blocks were easy to transport if the family moved around, and if friends and neighbors got together to help, a quilt could very quickly be put together and quilted at a quilting bee. Block patterns became a tradition in their own right, and the variety of patterns based on blocks is virtually infinite.

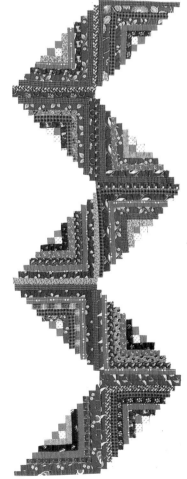

The use of appliqué to create household textiles is documented from the eighteenth century. Almost as soon as printed fabrics from the East, particularly India, began to be imported into Europe, they were cut into shapes and applied to less expensive background fabrics to make them more economical to use. Because appliqué lends itself to curved and intricate shapes, it is often used in non-geometric designs and to create quilts that tell a story or include people. Needlewomen of the mid- to late-eighteenth century (and most were women) are responsible for some of the most beautiful examples of appliqué quilts, including the group known as Baltimore album quilts, which were made mainly in Maryland in the 1840s and 1850s. Appliqué took a back seat to patchwork and even quilting in the twentieth century, but it is still a technique favored by many quilters, especially those who value hand stitching.

In many ways, quilting itself is the overriding aim of the quiltmaker. Most

RIGHT: *This lovely 1930s quilt is a Seminole piece, made from plain strips interspersed with pieced ones in three typical patterns. The colors are less characteristic – they are more pastel than the hues usuallly found in Seminole work. A quilt with this many seams would be difficult to quilt with any but the simplest of patterns.*

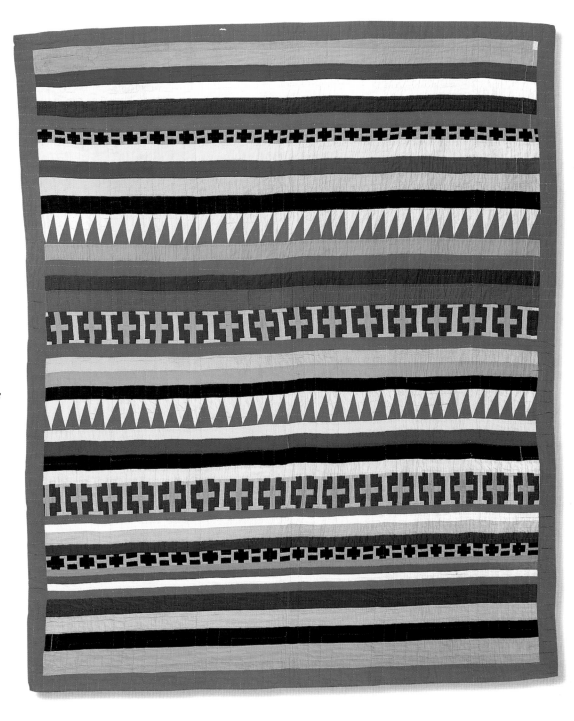

OPPOSITE: *Made in New York in about 1970, the fabrics in this album quilt are luxurious, mainly silk and velvet. It is an outstanding example of high-quality appliqué. The squares are joined edge to edge and heavily embroidered, both along the joining seams and in the blocks.*

people find hand quilting the hardest aspect of quiltmaking to execute well. Like so many other skills, it comes only with practice. The hand quilting found on a vast number of old quilts attests to the amount of time spent by the quiltmakers. They just sat and stitched, and the beauty of the quilts they produced shows how worthwhile their efforts were.

For today's stitchers, making a quilt has become a leisure activity. Few make an entire quilt by recycling material. Most of us who make quilts do so because it gives us great pleasure to handle fabric, work with color, design patterns and texture, and make the stitches. This book is intended to provide ideas and inspiration as well as technical backup to anyone who likes making quilts.

CLASSIC QUILTS:
Patchwork

THE CLASSIC PATCHWORK quilts on the following pages represent only a tiny, and eclectic, selection of the wonderful pieces made since the use of two layers of fabric stitched to an inner batting began. They can be used as inspiration or simply enjoyed as objects of great beauty.

This Light and Dark Log Cabin, made by the author in 1999, is a miniature quilt. The strips are only half-an-inch wide worked on a foundation backing.

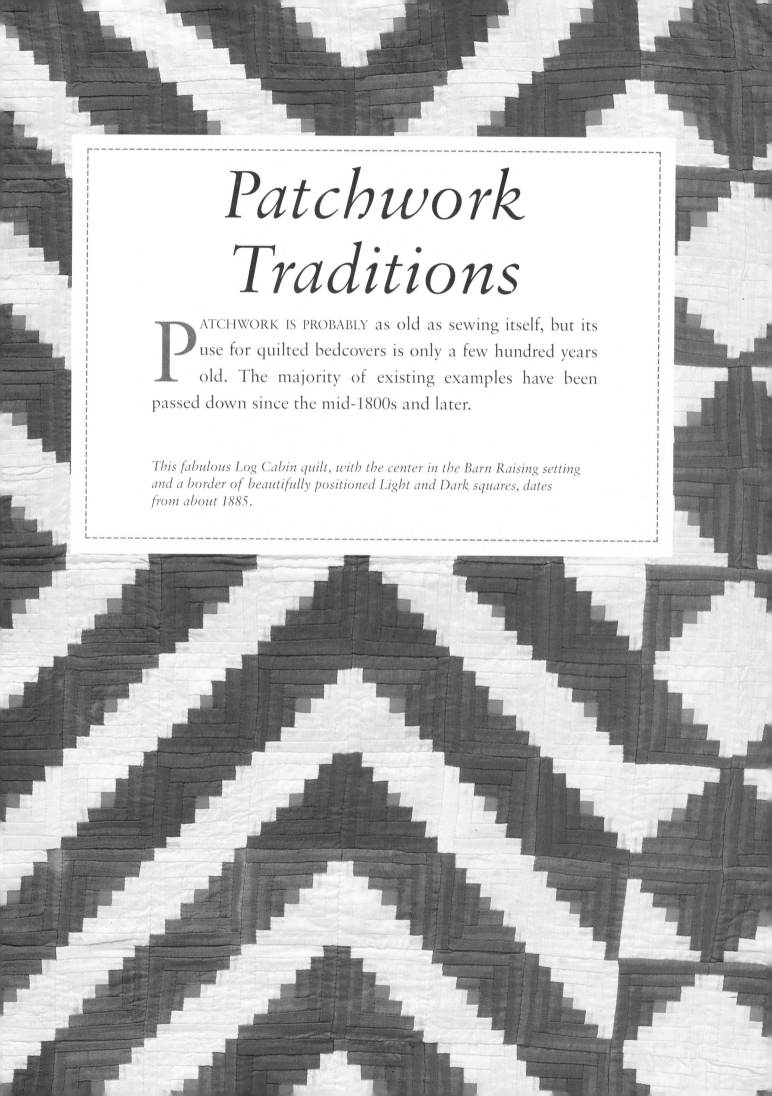

Patchwork Traditions

PATCHWORK IS PROBABLY as old as sewing itself, but its use for quilted bedcovers is only a few hundred years old. The majority of existing examples have been passed down since the mid-1800s and later.

This fabulous Log Cabin quilt, with the center in the Barn Raising setting and a border of beautifully positioned Light and Dark squares, dates from about 1885.

LEFT: *This red and white Strippy quilt, made in about 1883 in Wear Head, County Durham in the Northeast of England, has an unusual thick-and-thin design of wide strips of Turkey red cotton, alternating with narrow cream and red ones. The beautiful quilting is worked along the length of each strip, with a running diamond pattern on the white strips and hammock and double hammock on the red ones.*

BELOW: *The cream, beige, and gray shading of the vertical strips is interspersed with orange and lavender blue, while the horizontal areas are made from beautifully blended blocks of color.*

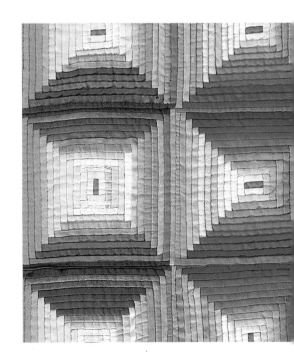

Patchwork quilts had become popular in Europe by the seventeenth century, and the techniques, carried to the New World by colonists who braved the unknown, the elements, and the vast distances, were very useful for recycling scarce materials. The skills were passed from generation to generation, and when the pioneers pushed westward to settle in the newly acquired lands west of the Mississippi, the making of quilts from any available scraps of material went with them.

The European quiltmakers of the same time were making wholecloth and strippy quilts, but the settlers had little access to the large pieces of fabric needed for such bedcovers and limited space in which to work or to store them. The development of block patchwork was a way of assembling enough pieces to eventually make an entire quilt, and it allowed the maker to use scraps as they became available from other sewing projects. As people developed new patterns and passed them along to friends and neighbors, the idea of blocks spread, and by the late 1800s, the techniques had crossed back to Europe. Block patchwork found less favor in the Old World, where patchwork made from scraps tended to be worked using the English, or paper-piecing, method, and by the end of the century, quiltmaking in Europe had declined dramatically, due to the availability of machine-made bedspreads and comforters. By the 1930s, the traditions of quiltmaking in Britain in particular

BELOW: This beautiful quilt of many colors, made in about 1875, is a Courthouse Steps variation of the traditional Log Cabin pattern. The red center of each block is a narrow strip, instead of the more usual square.

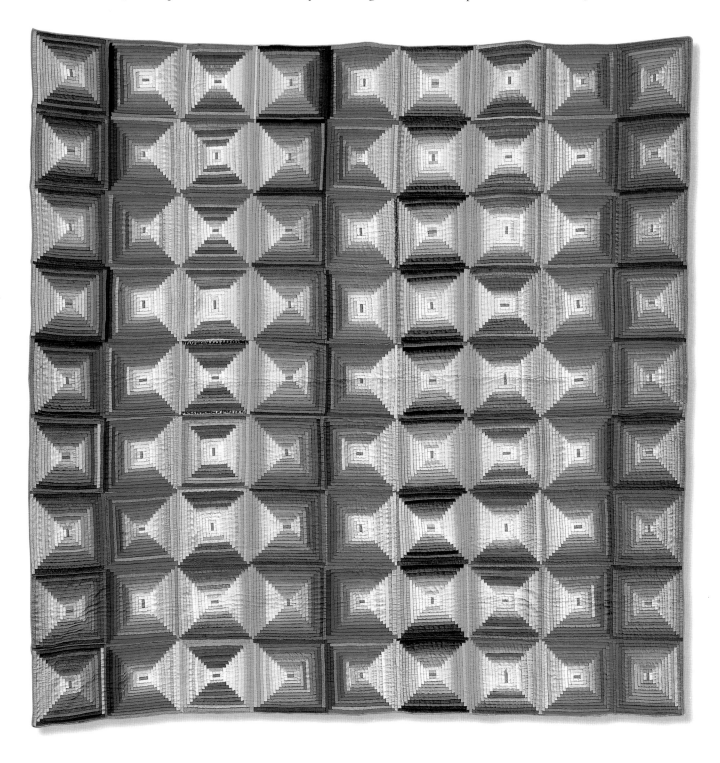

had all but disappeared, but in the early 1950s the technique of quilting, and with it the skills of quiltmaking in general, were rescued, thanks in large measure to one woman, Durham County quilter Amy Emms, who began by teaching, in local evening classes, the fine stitching that she had learned as a girl.

In North America, too, the techniques of making quilted bedcovers began to vanish under the emancipation of women who flocked to the workplace after the two world wars of the twentieth century and the advent of easily available and reasonably priced substitutes for most everyday needs, including quilts.

ABOVE: Red calico print is used for the eight-point stars in the center and corners, and combined with navy calico in the larger Sawtooth Star and border in this medallion-style crib quilt made in Pennsylvania in about 1885.

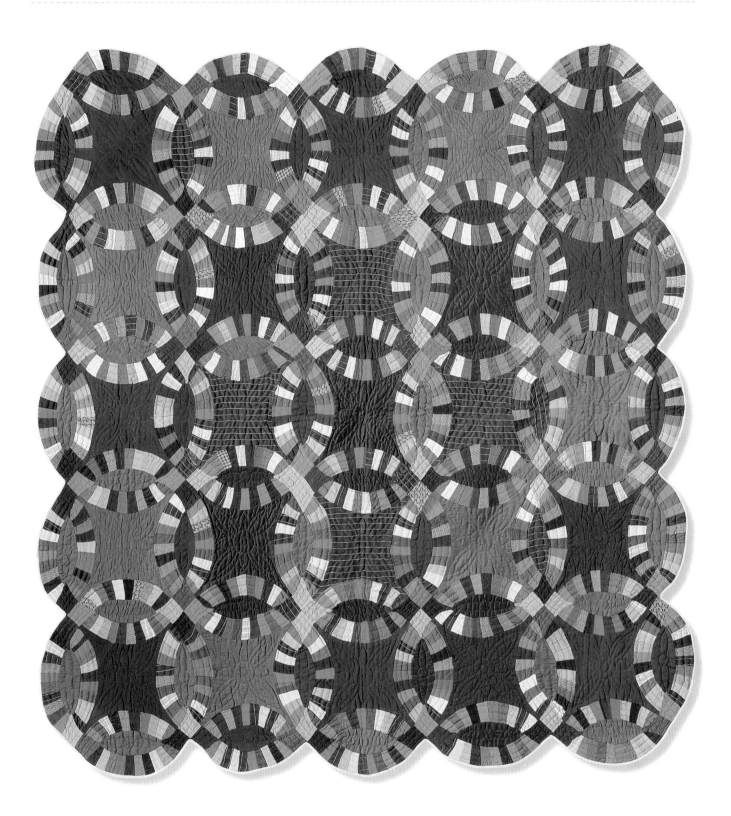

By the 1970s people – among them textile artists and historians – had discovered the beauty – as opposed to the utility – of quilts and began to reintroduce the patterns and the skills of the quiltmaker to a wider public. Today, making quilts is no longer a necessity, as there are other options for covering beds, However, although people have many calls upon their time, patchwork and the making of quilts and other quilted items is still enjoyed, both as a pastime and profession, by millions of people – men as well as women – throughout the world.

ABOVE: The scrappy rings of this Amish Double Wedding Ring quilt, made in the Midwest in about 1925, are set around charcoal gray and black. Four striped centers form a cross in the center.

Strips and Squares

S TRAIGHT SEAMS ARE, of course, easier to stitch than
curves or angles, and many traditional patchwork
patterns are based on straight-sided shapes with
right-angled corners, such as squares and rectangles,
together with strips.

*This beautiful early twentieth-century red and cream Streak of Lightning
quilt embodies the simple effectiveness of patchwork created from
strips and squares.*

Strips and squares are thought to be the basis for the oldest patchwork patterns, and certainly squares, rectangles, and strips of fabric are the easiest shapes to join together since they are all stitched using only straight seams.

Simple patch patterns exist in every civilization, made from squares and rectangles, and both strips and the so-called strings, or uneven strips, of fabric, like those left over nowadays from sewing projects, have formed the basis for putting together large pieces of textile materials that can be used as they are or cut into different shapes and rejoined into more intricate patterns. Joining long seams by hand is a tedious process, but with the advent of the sewing machine in the mid-nineteenth century, strip piecing became a time-saving way to assemble a quilt more quickly and more accurately.

Many of the most familiar traditional patchwork designs are made mainly, or even exclusively, from strips. The first of

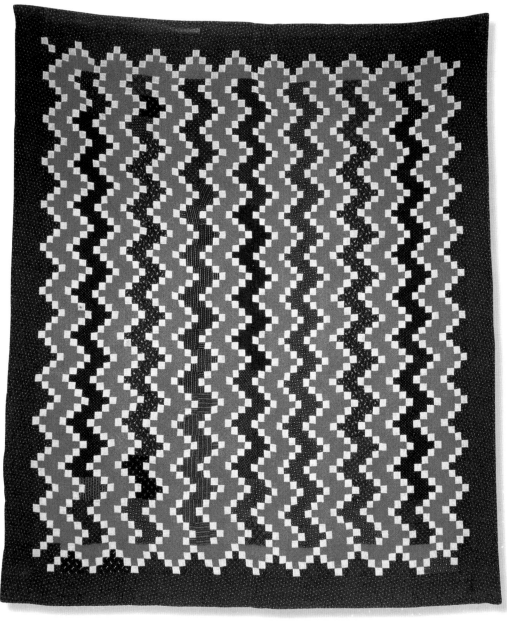

LEFT: *This cotton quilt from about 1890 is from the same collection as the version of this pattern that is shown on pages 24–5, but what a different impact it has. Made in three colors, with three different shades of blue included as well, it is a quintessential example of the quiltmaker's art. Note the places in some of the blue streaks, as well as in the border, where a different fabric has been used.*

these is the Strippy, traditionally from the North of England, which consists of vertical strips of fabric of alternating color. This pattern is thought to have been the inspiration for the Amish Bars design, in which alternate strips are enclosed by one or more wide borders.

Log Cabin, one of the world's favorite quilt patterns, consists of rows of strips sewn around a center square, usually in alternating arrangements of light and dark colors. Bricks, or Steps, in innumerable variations are pieced from squares or rectangular strips, and Rail

ABOVE: Squares at their simplest – rows and rows of them – in a checkerboard of blue and white. The white frames that occur at intervals act as a border in this quilt from about 1910.

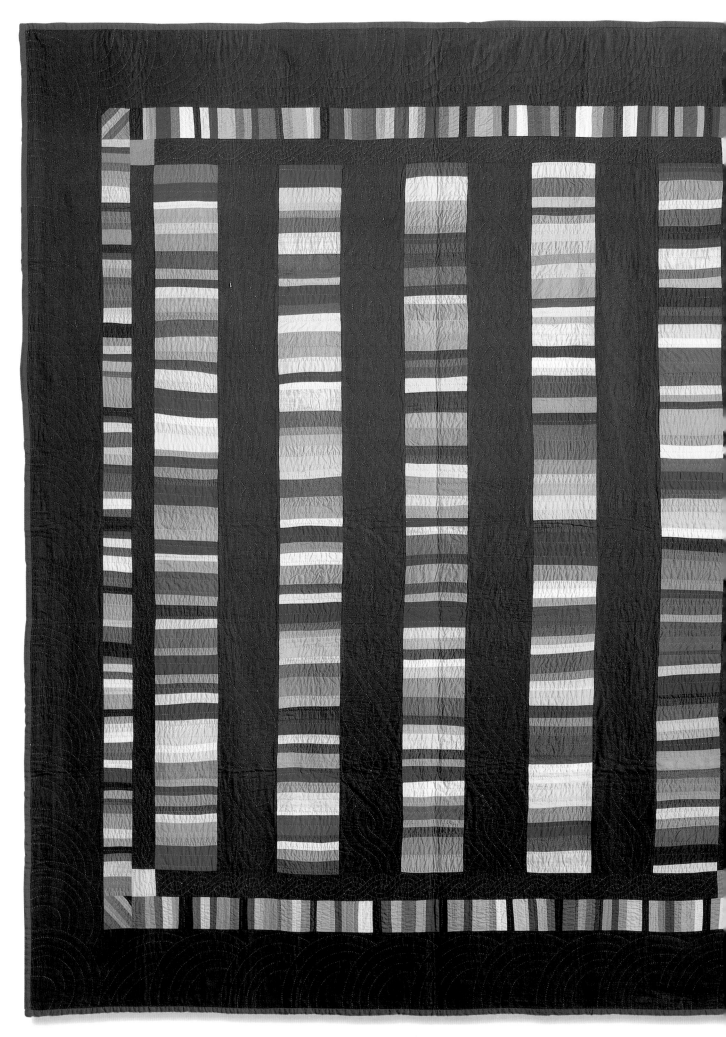

LEFT: *This Amish Roman Stripe, made in the 1970s, is a superb example of a scrap quilt. The stripes are assembled from random sizes and colors, and set off by the black alternating rows and inner border. The corner squares on the inner black border link the outer striped rows to the middle border.*

RIGHT: *This Courthouse Steps variation of the traditional Log Cabin pattern was made of wool challis and cotton in about 1850. The brown center squares are somewhat larger than those usually found with strips of this width. The outer green binding is the same width as each of the three borders.*

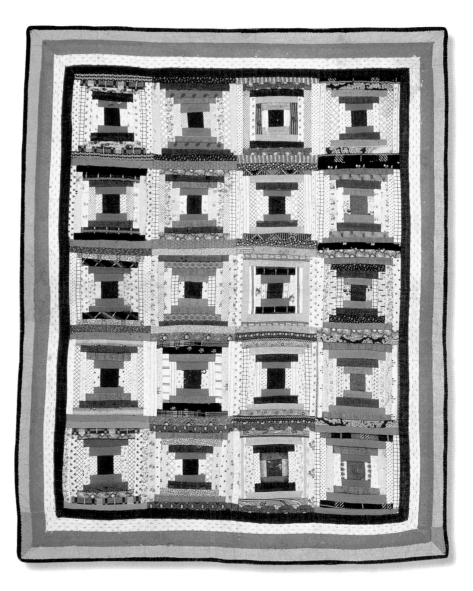

Fence and its Basketweave variation are also fashioned from rectangular strips.

One version of the pattern called Roman Stripe consists of strip-pieced fabrics cut into right-angle triangles and joined to a plain triangle of the same size to make a square block; another, which is commonly known as Chinese Coins, is made from lengths of horizontal strips that are alternated with long plain strips.

Strips are also widely used in the tradition of the African-American quilters. Many of the quilts created bear a relationship to their roots in Africa – the tradition of Ghanaian weaving in particular. Some of the most vibrant of these quilts are made from strings instead of straight strips, and their uneven edges give a liveliness to the piece that is hard to beat.

Patterns devised by women of the Seminole tribe in Florida in the early 1900s are doubly strip-pieced. Not only are they assembled by piecing strips together; these strips are then cut apart, usually at a sharp angle, and then stitched together again to create bands of pieced fabrics in bright colors that are used to make garments and bags.

The variety of possible patterns based on squares is vast. From simple one-patch designs like Postage Stamp, to Four-Patch or Nine-Patch blocks, to vast Sunshine and Shadow quilts, squares and strips are well-known, well-loved, and well-used by quiltmakers.

Log Cabin

L OG CABIN PATCHWORK takes its familiar name from the construction of pioneer houses on the frontier. Rough logs were laid on top of each other, horizontally, around the center of the building, in the same way that the fabric strips are placed in rows around the center square, which is traditionally red to signify the hearth.

RIGHT: *Made in Ohio between 1870 and 1880, this richly colored Log Cabin quilt is set in the Straight Furrows design. The red, orange, yellow, and cream silk and silk taffeta fabrics shimmer softly along the diagonal rows. These are made more pronounced by the use of the same brown material for one half of each block set against the multicolored rows of the other half.*

OPPOSITE: *This beautiful wool challis quilt, made in Pennsylvania between 1865 and 1875, is set in the traditional Light and Dark design. The strong contrasts between the paler shades and the dark areas are extremely effective.*

The Log Cabin block is perhaps the design most often used to teach beginners the rudiments of strip-piecing. Its simple construction and amazing versatility have made it perennially popular since it first began to be widely used in the 1850s and 1860s. Its origins, however, go back much further. Jean Dubois has traced a very early example from the 1820s to Mary Morgan, an Englishwoman who later emigrated to the American South. Perhaps her Barn Raising design provided the inspiration for all that followed.

Tradition, however, relates the pattern to President Abraham Lincoln, the country's most famous resident of a log

cabin. The design was certainly very popular during the period just before and after the Civil War, which may be related to the great man's time in office, but may also have something to do with the fact that the pattern is easy to cut and stitch, while remaining one of the most versatile of all quilt designs.

Because it uses narrow strips, traditionally left over from dressmaking projects and not wide enough to be useful for much else, Log Cabin was favored, not just in the little houses on the prairies, but also in the chic townhouses of the post-Civil War cities. Whereas the frontier quiltmakers would have had access mainly to cotton and wool fabrics, and even used flour and feed sacks, towns-women on both sides of the Atlantic were more likely to have had pieces of the expensive silk and velvet material used for elegant evening dresses available to them. Many beautiful examples of Log Cabin quilts survive in collections, and on beds, throughout the quilt-collecting

RIGHT AND ABOVE:
This dramatic piece from Pennsylvania displays the quintessential Streak of Lightning setting for a Log Cabin quilt. Made in black and white with red squares, it dates from about 1890, but its effect is startling and entirely modern.

LEFT AND BELOW: Another Streak of Lightning, also made in Pennsylvania but earlier, in the 1880s, has a completely different feel to it. It uses five different plain colors, with the blue/purple and black 'logs' acting as the dark shade and red and brown, neither one very pale, as the light. The scrappy border is pieced from thin strips of blending colors.

world to provide inspiration for the quiltmakers of today.

Log Cabin blocks are almost always constructed with a strong light and dark contrast, and the standard block divides diagonally. The way the finished blocks are arranged, or set, determines the secondary pattern that results from the color variation. Without a good contrast, these setting designs are lost. Log Cabin blocks are usually set square, which creates a diagonal pattern in the quilt. If the blocks are set on point, however, an unusual, but nevertheless very attractive, square or rectangular pattern emerges.

There are four standard settings for Log Cabin quilts, but here again there is a wealth of fascinating and intriguing variations that create a completely different look. The main sets are called Light and Dark, with four dark areas side by side so the light areas are also juxtaposed; Straight Furrow, with its evocation of plowed fields and country lanes creating diagonal stripes running across the quilt; Streak of Lightning, which makes strong zigzag lines; and Barn Raising, in which the blocks are arranged as concentric bands of diamond-shaped color. Barn Raising is also known as Sunshine and Shadow, especially in the Amish quilting tradition, where Log Cabin is widely used in plain solid colors.

There are two basic ways to construct a Log Cabin block. The traditional method, the way used most often before the advent of rotary cutting and modern strip piecing, is to stitch the wrong side of the center square to the right side of a square of backing fabric – muslin or something similar –

and then sew each strip in turn, right-side down, to the base square around the center square, and then to press it, right-side up, before adding the next strip. This method stabilizes the strips and provides an extra layer if warmth is an issue. It is ideal for use with thin

RIGHT AND BELOW: This unusual variation of the Barn Raising setting has the effect of overlapping layers, built up from a Light and Dark center. The corners are also set as Light and Dark. Made in Pennsylvania or New York state in about 1885, it has blocks made mainly from the same fabrics and arranged in the same order in each layer.

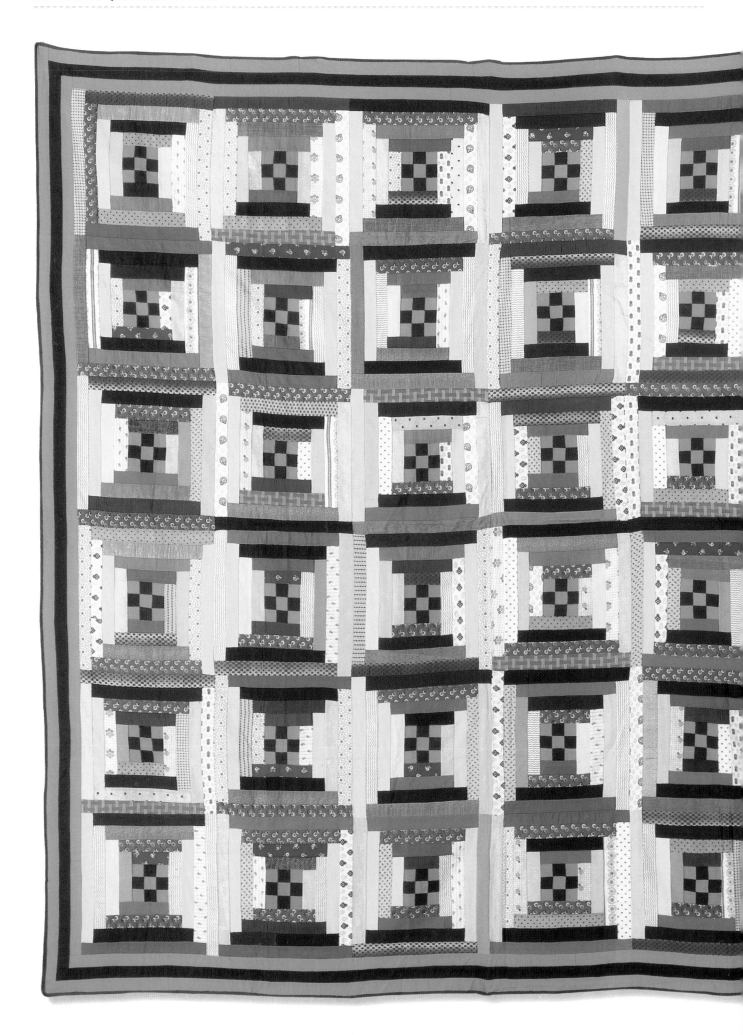

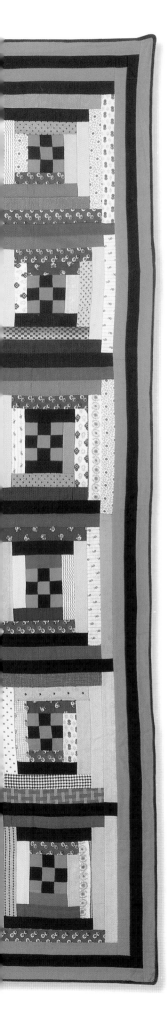

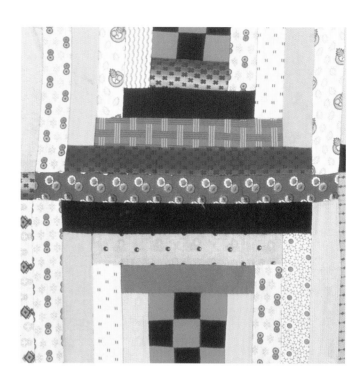

LEFT AND RIGHT: This wonderful Log Cabin 'Chinese Lanterns' quilt is unusual in several ways. It is made from wool challis; it has nine-patch 'eyes,' or center squares, in a red and black checkerboard pattern; and the same two colors are used to make the narrow triple-banded border. But it does evoke its name – the 'strings' of light-colored 'lanterns' positively glow with warmth and beauty.

or fine fabrics, and for those of different weights, but it is very difficult to quilt, except by tying.

The other method involves cutting straight strips and adding them to the center square, one by one with the right-sides together. This works best on strips that aren't too narrow – at least 1½ inches (38mm) – and if the block is thin enough to be quilted in the traditional way.

There are a number of variations of the standard Log Cabin block, with evocative names like Chimneys and Cornerstones, in which a square is added to the end of each strip to make a diagonal line of squares through the block; Courthouse Steps, in which strips are put on opposite sides of the center in turn; Chevron, or Corner, Log Cabin, with the beginning square not in the middle but in one corner; and Off-center or Asymmetrical Log Cabin, in which half of the strips are narrow and the other half wider. The result is a visual curve that can look stunning.

Many other shapes can be used in place of the center square, including diamonds, hexagons, pentagons, and even irregular straight-sided figures.

Pineapple blocks are constructed in a similar way, but strips are placed at the corners and along the sides of the center square to make an eight-sided figure.

Nine-Patch

THE NINE-PATCH is one of the simplest of all quilt blocks, consisting of nine squares arranged three-by-three. At the same time it is also one of the most versatile blocks; the number of variations is practically limitless. Nine-patch blocks can be assembled from individual squares or square units, or they can be strip-pieced using two different arrangements. A huge number of traditional patchwork patterns are based on the nine-patch block.

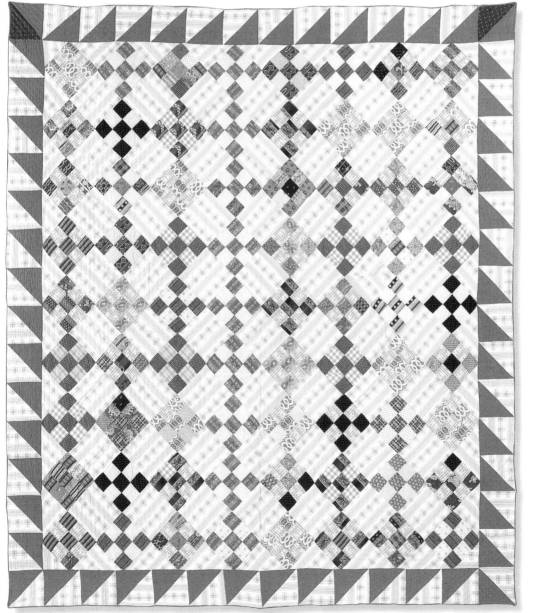

LEFT AND ABOVE: In this Nine-Patch quilt from about 1865, the scrappy blocks, in mainly brown and pink with bits of blue, have been turned on point and alternated with pink and cream striped print to give a soft feel to the piece. There are touches of yellow here and there that give it a lift, and the whole quilt is enclosed by a large-scale sawtooth border in the same pink used for the plain squares combined with a newly introduced green.

Nine-patch blocks can be made into more complicated patterns just by creating a double nine-patch. They can be turned on point to give a dramatic feel, and can be joined into strips and used as sashing or borders, or combined with plain strips in Amish Bars or Strippy quilts. The 'chain' in Single Irish Chain is formed from setting nine-patch blocks with large plain square blocks. Complex geometric combinations of smaller squares or triangles can be joined together to make many familiar patchwork patterns, among them Maple Leaf, Ohio Star, Friendship Star, Shoofly, Churn Dash, Jacob's Ladder, and Card Tricks.

ABOVE: *Soft pinks and browns are used in this quilt from about 1845. These Nine Patches, turned on point, are fashioned from a large center square with side strips and corner squares, and are sashed with a blue check fabric.*

Four-Patch

THE FOUR-PATCH BLOCK is probably the simplest of all pieced patchwork to make. It consists of four squares joined in pairs, and like most patchwork, relies for its effectiveness on a strong contrast between light and dark color.

The Four-Patch may be straightforward to make, but it provides the basis for a great many well-known patterns.

The basic block is assembled by joining two sets of squares and then joining the rows, or strip-pieced. Double Four-Patch blocks also offer an endless source of variety – everything depends on color choice. Like Nine-Patch, the squares in Four-Patch patterns can be subdivided into smaller squares or triangles to provide limitless possibilities.

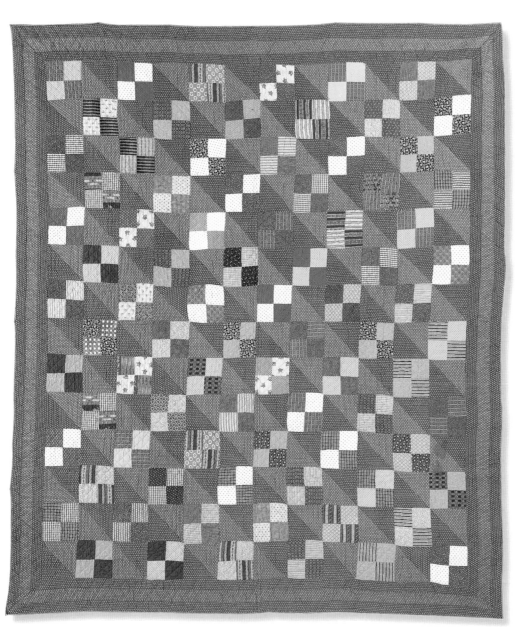

LEFT AND ABOVE: These Four-Patch blocks, probably made from dressmaking scraps, have been alternated with blocks made from a red and a green triangle. When the rows are combined, the quilt becomes a diagonal feast for the eyes. Made in about 1880, it has a border cut from the same red and green fabrics used for the 'background' squares.

OPPOSITE: This is in fact a Double Irish Chain quilt, made in about 1875. Because of the totally random placement of color in the four-patch blocks, it has a completely different feel from conventional Irish Chain examples that use color more rigidly for a more geometric look. The touches of yellow and black against pink are extremely effective.

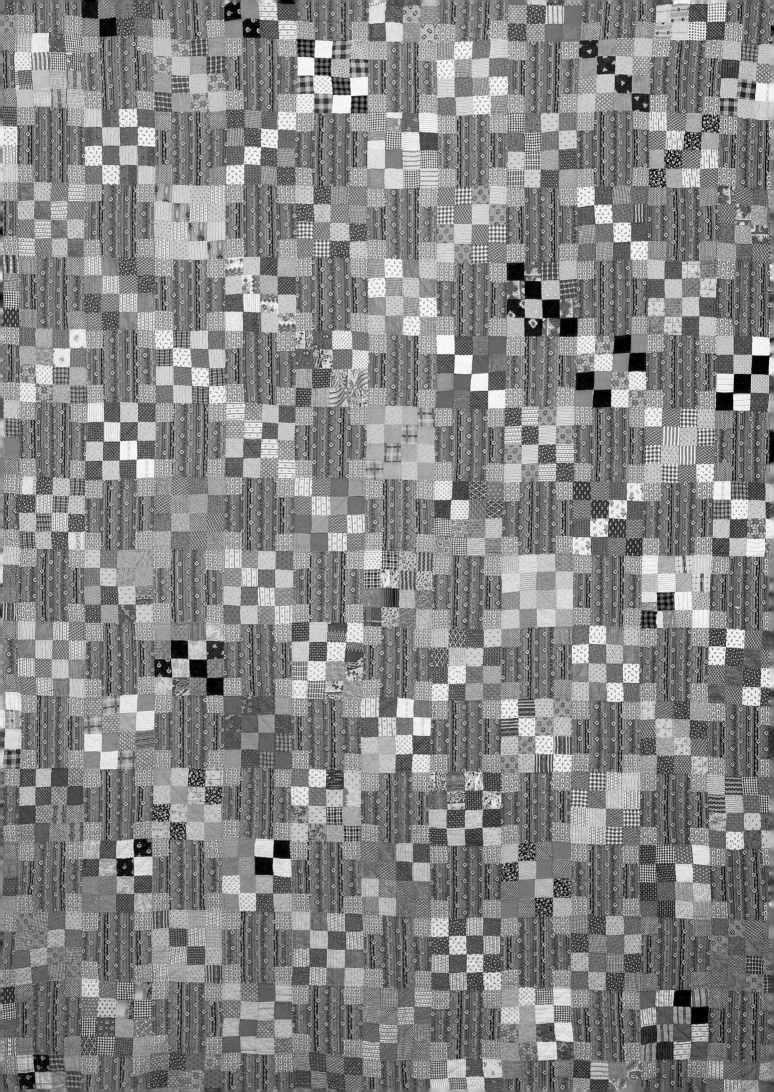

Strips

PERHAPS THE EASIEST WAY to piece a quilt is to sew strips of fabric together. The strips don't all need to be the same width or length. In fact, they don't even need to have straight edges, as can be seen in the example below.

Our earliest ancestors joined strips of hide to make garments, shelters, and household items such as water carriers. Our more recent forbears learned to use woven fabric in similar ways, particularly to make bedcovers to provide warmth and comfort. Primitive quilts were probably made by a variation of string-piecing, in which random strips of unequal length and width were simply

OPPOSITE AND ABOVE: A modern Ohio Amish quilt from the late 1980s is based on a traditional strippy design. This pattern, known variously as Chinese Coins and Roman Stripes, is worked here using small randomly sized solid-color fabrics that were probably scraps.

LEFT: This vibrant strip quilt is attributed to an unknown African-American quilter, who probably made it in the early 1930s. With its random colors and strips of uneven length and width, it is typical of quilts created from fabrics left over from dressmaking or other sewing projects – note that even the red border has been pieced.

sewn together until a piece of fabric of the desired size was created.

At the same time that quiltmaking was growing more sophisticated in the eighteenth and nineteenth centuries, the world was becoming smaller; and migration, particularly from Europe to the New World, meant that traditions of all kinds, including sewing techniques were transferred from place to place.

Strippy quilts, popular in the north-eastern area of England and the borders of Scotland, were made from lengths of fabric about 6–12 inches (150–300 mm) wide stitched together to make up the necessary width for a bedcover, and beautifully quilted with intricate patterns. It is thought that the Amish Bars design originated from strippy quilts carried to North America by English and Scottish settlers.

When the pioneers headed west across the burgeoning United States, they used the available resources to supply their

ABOVE: *Little is known about this unusual round cotton quilt. Experts date it at around 1900, and it is thought to have been used as a baby quilt. Its bold and dramatic colors, the narrowness of the strips used, and its octagonal shape make it a unique example of a strip-pieced quilt.*

needs, and every scrap of fabric, however narrow, became valuable. With the creation of patterns like Log Cabin and Rail Fence, these bits and pieces could be used. As the country became settled and supplies, including fabric, were easier to come by, quilters began to be more creative, creating Spiderweb, Star, and early Op Art designs using narrow strips, as well as pictures and landscapes using unevenly sized pieces.

In the early twentieth century, women on Seminole reservations in Florida began creating designs which were made from strips of bright-colored, unpatterned fabric sewn together lengthwise, cut into strips widthwise or at an angle, and restitched into geometric patterns to make skirts, blouses, bags, and jackets – a technique known as Seminole patchwork which is still practised on a commercial scale today.

ABOVE: *The concentric lines of this blue and white cotton square quilt make it a candidate for the original Op Art influence. Probably made in New York or New Jersey in about 1910, its receding perspective is created by decreasing the width of the strips as they get closer to the small center square.*

Squares

BECAUSE SQUARES are such familiar and geometrically rigid shapes, they are sometimes considered boring. But there is no need for this to be true. Squares can be cut up into right-angle triangles; they can be alternated by color and with other shapes; and they can be turned on point to create a diagonal effect.

The simplest of patterns using squares is often employed in making charm quilts, probably the ultimate in scrap quilts, in which each piece is different and all are joined in a random fashion, or perhaps alternated light and dark. A version of this straightforward design, known as Postage Stamp, is composed, as befits its name, of tiny squares and is often used in miniature quilts. In some full-size historical examples, hundreds or even thousands of minute individual squares

LEFT AND ABOVE: Each block in this Double Square quilt is made up of three seemingly layered 'squares,' although only the central shape is actually a square. Right-angle triangles in a light color have been added to the edges of the middle piece, and another row of larger triangles in the same color as the center square joined to the resulting square. The large square blocks have been turned on point and sashed to create a vibrant quilt in spite of its somewhat sober colors. It has no border, but the careful placement of half-squares around the edges gives the effect of a frame.

have been carefully organized to create amazingly intricate designs. The technique of simply joining the squares into rows and then joining rows was widely used by American quiltmakers during the 1930s, when the Great Depression made frugality both a virtue and also a necessity.

Many so-called Soldier's quilts – those made by mainly British servicemen, including sailors and infantrymen, especially during the nineteenth century – are made from small (or tiny) squares cut

ABOVE: The diamond center of this c.1885 crib quilt from New York state has been pieced from random squares and enclosed by rows of four-patch blocks and squares.

from wool blankets and the heavy, but colorful, uniform fabric of the day and joined painstakingly to make warm field blankets. A surprising number of these quilts – often arranged into geometric patterns of mainly red, blue, black, and yellow – have survived to end up in collections around the world.

Perhaps the most familiar pattern using only squares is Trip Around the World, in which rows of colored squares are joined around the edges of a central shape to radiate out in bands of contrasting hues. This design has been, and still is, widely used by Amish quiltmakers, who call the pattern Sunshine and Shadow and shade the colors from dark to light and back again.

Squares can be used as the basis for the octagonal pattern known as Snowball, in

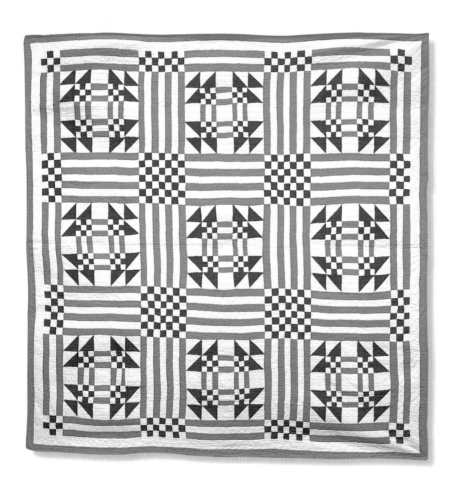

ABOVE AND RIGHT: This patriotic Goose in the Pond quilt gets some of its appeal from the triangular 'geese' in the corners of the blocks, but the 49 small blue and white squares used to make the checkerboards in the corners of the sashing are what sets this piece from about 1915 above the ordinary. The same squares are used in the nine-patch corners in each double nine-patch, that forms the middle of every block.

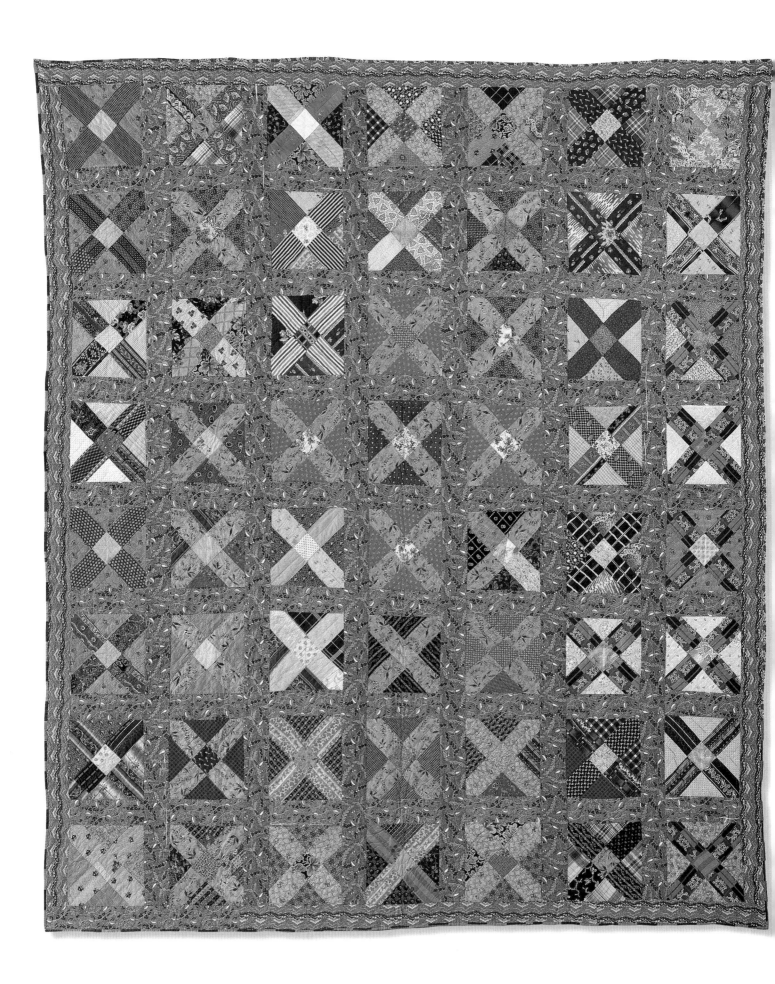

which a small square is placed in each corner of a larger one and stitched in position across the diagonal of the smaller square. The excess triangle is cut away, leaving a seam allowance, and a large square with octagonal corners is created. The same method of joining a small square to the corner of a larger one can also be used to piece a version of Bow Tie, in which four small squares meet in the center of a four-patch block.

Four-Patch and Nine-Patch designs are, of course, based on joining square blocks, many of which are pieced from strips or triangles, and the variety of patterns that can be created as a result is virtually endless – see pages 38–41.

Squares can be made from scraps. They can be positioned at random or sorted into color values and carefully arranged in light and dark patterns. They can be cut from two colors and organized into checkerboards. They can be used as spacer blocks with intricate pieced squares, and they can be quilted or appliquéd to create a unique quilt.

OPPOSITE AND RIGHT:
The Crossroads block contains a small center square set on point inside the larger square that is formed from diagonal strips joined by triangles. In this beautifully conceived example from the 1840s, the placement of the bright red blocks in the middle of the quilt draws the eye in. The indigo fabric used for the sashing picks up the predominant brown and beige color of the quilt, with the blue echoed randomly in a number of the blocks.

Irish Chain

W HILE NO EVIDENCE has been found to show that this pattern originated in Ireland, it has been widely used in the British Isles and North America since the eighteenth century. All of its variations are constructed from two blocks, one intricately pieced from small squares, and the other either a plain square or a very simple pieced block.

Double Irish Chain is probably the best-known version of this family of patterns, but Single Irish Chain is often used in patchwork and quilting classes as a beginner's project. Triple Irish Chain can create a very intricate design with wide diagonal rows, or 'chains,' forming the characteristic pattern.

The pieced blocks are made from small squares and are alternated with simple blocks. This arrangement creates a strong diagonal line that runs throughout the

LEFT: This lovely quilt, made in Northumberland in the North of England in about 1870, is an unusual Single Irish Chain. It uses two sizes of square to create the diagonal chain, with small Turkey red shapes linking larger ones. The triple white and red border provides lots of space for the well-executed quilting.

quilt. In Single Irish Chain, the pieced block is a simple nine-patch block, but more complicated versions use different organizations of squares. The blank areas created by the plain setting squares provide a wonderful space for quilting or applique work to be added.

Fine examples exist, many of them with white or cream plain squares and patterned fabrics for the chains. The design, which provides a good way to use scraps, is also worked by Amish quilters with beautiful contrasts of traditional solid colors throughout.

ABOVE: This Double Irish Chain, which dates from about 1850, uses brown and rust for the chain. The unusual border is covered with flowers of blue and beige print fabrics.

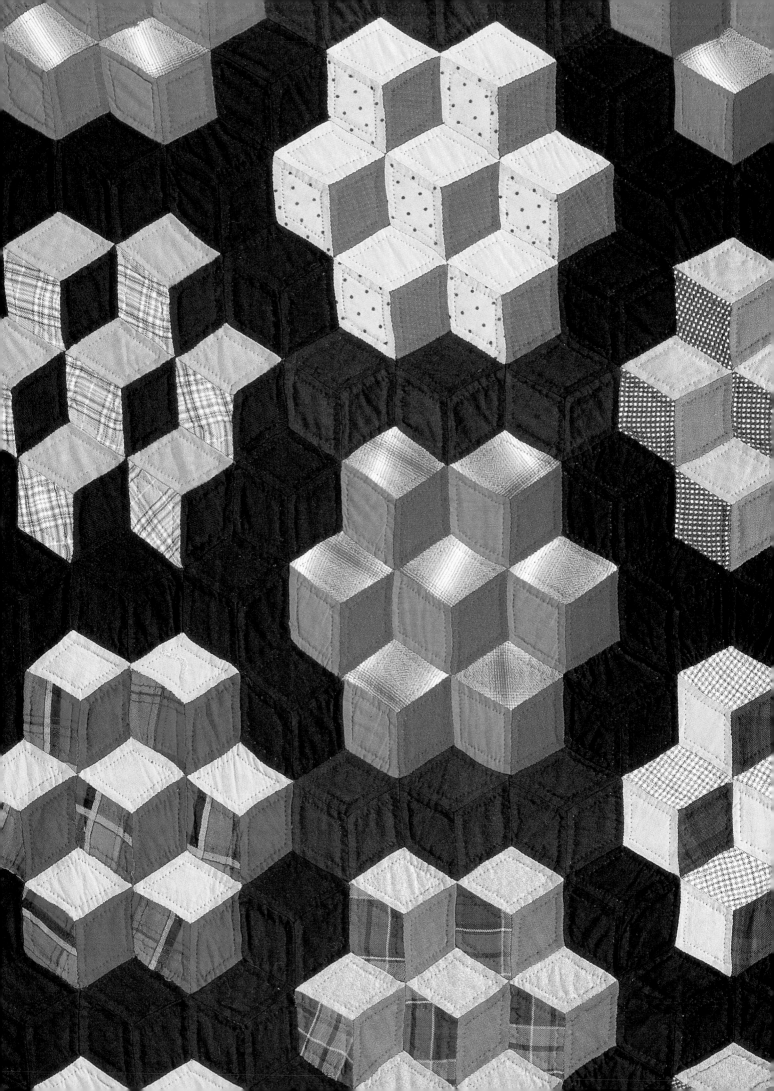

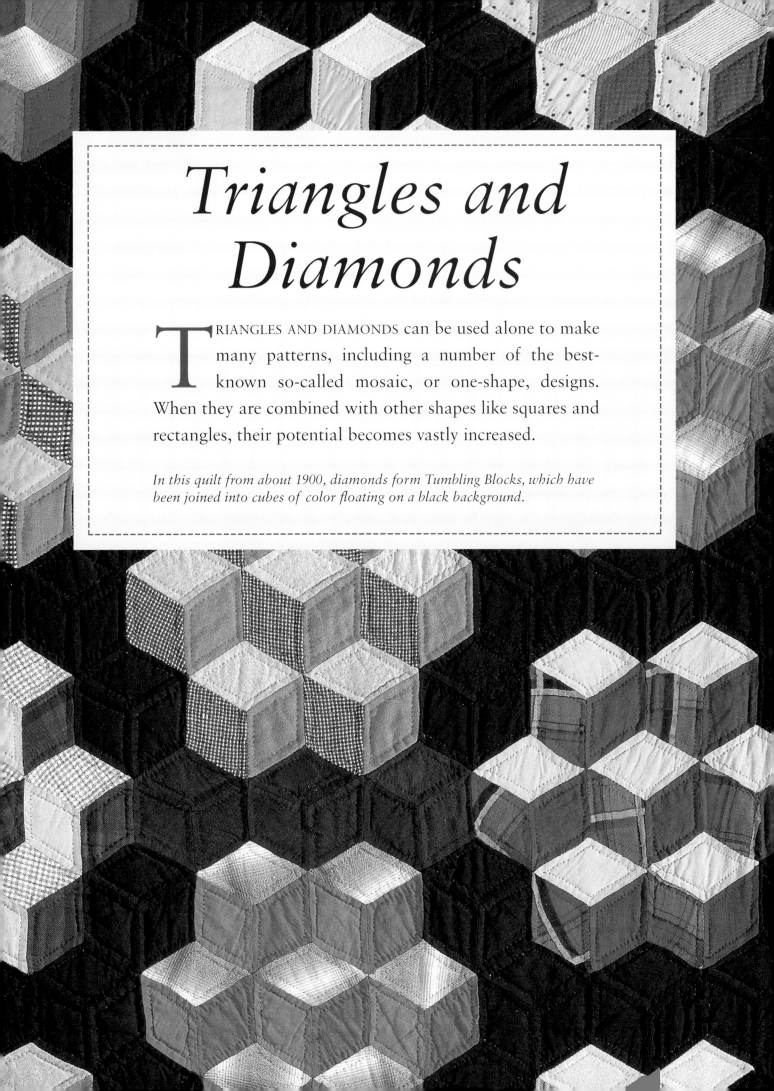

Triangles and Diamonds

TRIANGLES AND DIAMONDS can be used alone to make many patterns, including a number of the best-known so-called mosaic, or one-shape, designs. When they are combined with other shapes like squares and rectangles, their potential becomes vastly increased.

In this quilt from about 1900, diamonds form Tumbling Blocks, which have been joined into cubes of color floating on a black background.

While right-angle triangles can be pieced fairly simply by machine, other types such as equilateral and isosceles, together with diamonds and hexagons, are more easily worked by the so-called English method. The hand sewing of pieces is less popular in our fast-moving world than it once was, since it is time-consuming and doesn't suit fast cutting and stitching techniques very well, although some of the shapes can be stitched by machine. However, the beautiful patterns that are possible when these shapes are used to their best advantage make them very rewarding, and some clever quilters have devised short cuts that can help speed up the cutting-out process.

Equilateral triangles and hexagons both have 60-degree angles, and the diamonds usually found in patchwork have 60-degree angles. When 60-degree diamonds are combined, the color can be arranged so that a hexagon shape emerges, and the block that results can be used in any way that a hexagon can. Isosceles and irregular triangles are also found in patchwork, but they must almost always be cut from a template.

ABOVE: On this star, the stripes have been altered with a paisley motif, probably from the same fabric. The fabric has been used in several stars, each time with a different effect.

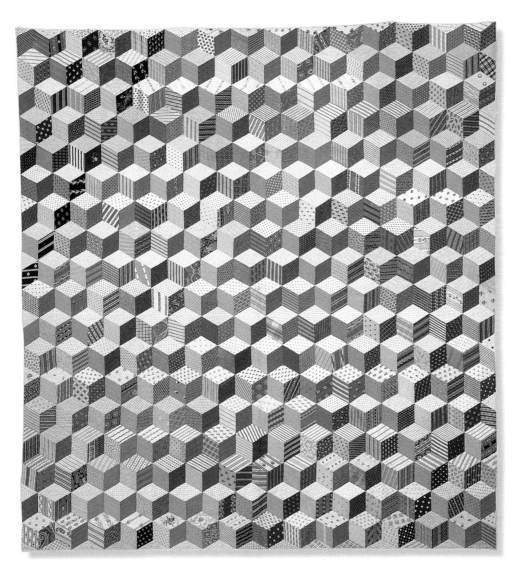

LEFT: The soft colors that make up these Tumbling Blocks have been well-sorted into light, medium, and dark shades, so the randomly placed blocks create a very effective three-dimensional pattern. Made in about 1885 in Pennsylvania, the quilt is, as is often the case, borderless.

RIGHT: This modern-looking quilt was actually made in about 1845 in New York. It is fashioned from two sizes of LeMoyne, or Lemon, Stars, and the use of fabric is outstanding. Many of the stripes are cut lengthwise and create a spiraling effect that gives movement to the design, as does the double zigzag border made from pieced diamonds.

Triangles

ECAUSE SQUARES can be divided into triangles so easily, many patterns, both simple and intricate, are made from right-angle triangles. Most right-angle triangles have two straight-grain edges and only one bias edge, which makes them easier to piece than equilateral, or 60-degree, or even isoceles triangles, which can have only one side on the straight grain.

Right-angle triangles form the basis of a huge number of traditional patchwork patterns, including Pinwheel, Windmill, Broken Dishes, Bear's Paw, Maple Leaf, Bow Tie, Friendship Star, and Ohio Star. Indeed, star-patterns cannot be made without triangular shapes. Many star patterns use right-angle triangles, as do

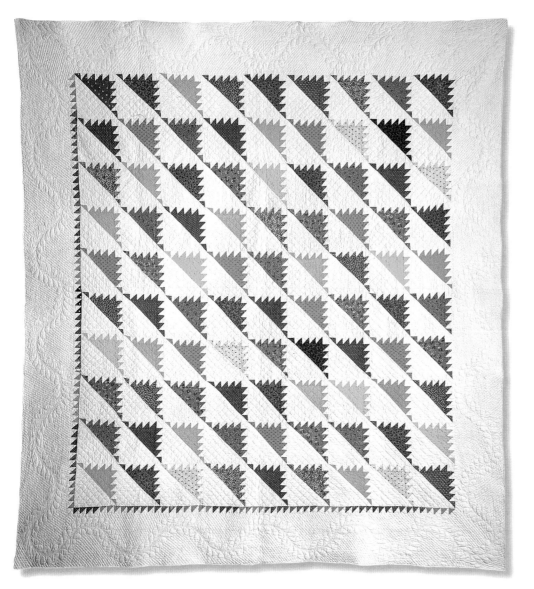

LEFT AND ABOVE: This beautifully worked quilt, called 'Indian Meadows,' dates from about 1865. Thought to have been made in the Maryland-Pennsylvania area, it is created from ninety Sawtooth blocks in a variety of colors. The blocks are set with a random color placement to create strong diagonal lines across the quilt, and the two 'white' edges have been bordered with strips of alternating white and colored triangles to enclose the design.

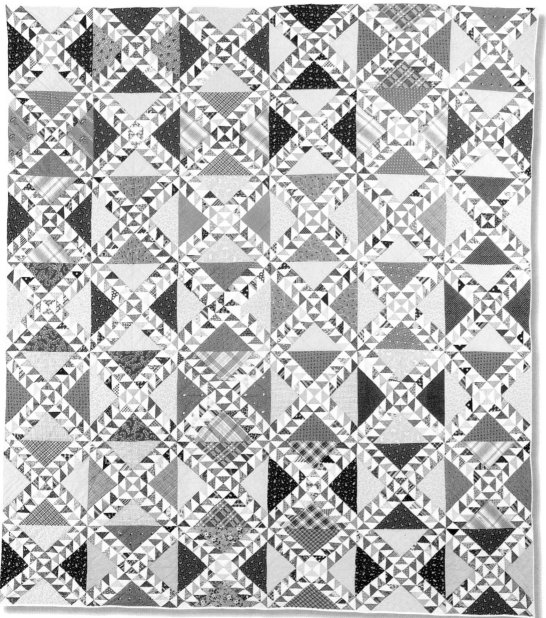

BELOW: *Each block is built entirely of triangles. The border of triangle-squares creates a reversed sawtooth.*

most of the tree patterns like Pine Tree and Tree of Paradise.

Simple but effective Octagon blocks can be created by putting a right-angle triangle in each corner of a large square, while a Snowball variation can be created from nine-patch blocks using squares and right-angle triangles in a similar way to Ohio Star and Shoofly. Sawtooth patterns can be made into blocks, and they are extremely effective as borders both for blocks and for entire quilts.

Flying Geese patterns are made from a right-angle triangle with a smaller triangle placed on each side of the point. These pieces are then stitched together to form strips that can be joined together to make a quilt, or used as sashing or borders. One popular Amish Bars variation is made by alternating strips of Flying Geese with plain strips to create eye-catching patterns.

A number of Baskets patterns can be created by combining right-angle triangles and squares, and many of the well-known naturalistic flower and leaf patterns, among them patterns that create lilies, roses, and tulips, are constructed in the same way, while Snail's Trail and Monkey Wrench are spiraling designs that start with small central squares and are bordered by right-angle triangles of contrasting color. These triangles gradually increase in size to create the distinctive winding effect.

Quilts made from equilateral and isosceles triangles create wonderful, visually stunning, geometric designs such as Thousand Pyramids.

BELOW AND RIGHT: Aptly called 'Crossroads,' the construction of this indigo and white quilt is similar, but not quite identical, to several traditional patterns of the same name. The intriguing pattern is based around a dark square on point in the center of each block, with chevron sashing along each side and light squares at each corner of the sashing.

Diamonds

THE DIAMOND SHAPE, as opposed to the diamond created by setting a square on point, can be used to create some of the most exciting of all geometric patterns. It will have two edges that are not on the straight grain, so careful stitching is of the utmost importance to prevent stretching the piece out of shape.

Some of the patterns based on diamonds can be stitched by machine, but traditionally, diamonds are worked by the paper-piecing method of basting a shape cut from paper to a slightly larger fabric shape. This stabilizes the edges and helps create the precise sharp points that are essential to the effectiveness of the composition. If you cut your papers and your fabric carefully, paper piecing gives

LEFT AND ABOVE: This patriotic Broken Star quilt has the double bonus of being beautifully quilted in the large white spaces. The central star has eleven concentric rings of diamonds that are repeated outside the 'broken' area. The inner border uses the same red, white, and blue diamonds to create a chevron that marches around the quilt to give it an added vibrancy. Made around 1915 in the Ohio/ Pennsylvania area.

LEFT: This woolen quilt uses traditional Amish solid colors and was made in Pennsylvania in 1900–1910, so it is likely that the maker was indeed a member of the Amish community. The quilting is limited to the simple outlining of each diamond shape, and the use of different shades of blue and purple point to a quilt made from scraps left over from dressmaking projects.

your piecing an accuracy that is very difficult to match using a sewing machine, and if you cut the papers from isometric graph paper, your precision should be that much greater.

Tumbling Blocks, or Baby Blocks, is a standard design that uses 60-degree diamonds to create an overall mosaic of three-dimensional effect. It is a pattern that is widely seen in Victorian quilts on both sides of the Atlantic, and it is beloved of the Amish, presumably at least partly because it provides a way to use up small scraps of fabric.

Hexagon Stars can be constructed from six 60-degree diamonds, and hexagons and equilateral (60-degree) triangles can be used interchangeably with 60-degree diamonds to create an interesting visual effect in many mosiac patterns.

BELOW: The Tumbling Blocks pattern is built up using 60-degree diamonds in groups of three shapes of contrasting light, medium, and dark.

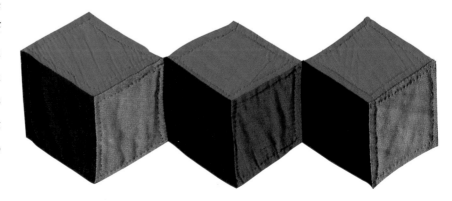

Many of the wonderful traditional star patterns, such as Lone Star, Broken Star, and Star of Bethlehem, are also based on diamond shapes, although these patterns use 45-degree angles to make eight-point stars.

Diamonds offer the quilter an almost infinite range of possibilities for interesting configurations. Working out patterns on isometric graph paper is a useful method of visualizing the way the angles fit together, as well as for checking that the colors are positioned in the most pleasing way. Irregular diamonds are almost never seen in quilt patterns.

RIGHT AND ABOVE: Several thousand diamonds have been joined to create this stunning Blocks pattern, made in about 1800. The three hexagon stars in the center create a triangular shape from which the concentric hexagonal rings of contrasting color radiate. Note the effective use of striped and dotted fabrics in places.

Stars

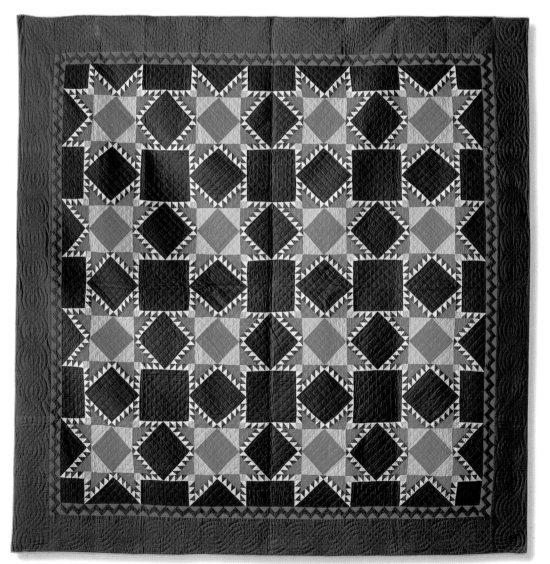

AS ANY QUILT HISTORIAN will tell you, star patterns in all their permutations are the most-often used of all quilt designs. Because stars can have almost any number of points, they are incredibly versatile and lend themselves to endless variation. While some types of star work best in appliqué, a vast choice of patchwork stars is also available.

Perhaps the simplest pieced star is the four-pointed Friendship Star, a nine-patch block made from alternating right-angle triangles around a center square. Another straightforward version of right-angle triangles is the Ohio Star, this time with eight points and made as a nine-patch block. Many simple star

LEFT AND ABOVE: These red and orange Sawtooth Stars with green and white edges are set on a navy background. The red and navy zigzag inner border on this Mennonite quilt made in Pennsylvania in about 1890 looks like a length of giant rickrack. The dark-green border is densely quilted in a multiple cable pattern.

LEFT: *This exuberant Star of Bethlehem was made in about 1885 in Pennsylvania. The corner blocks contain Princess Feather appliqué motifs in the red and green colors that were very popular at the time. Red has also been used to band the star and to make the outer border, which also serves as a binding.*

BELOW: *The evenness of the rows of diamonds attests to the skill of the quiltmakers, as do the triple-headed flower motifs appliquéd in the triangular spaces around the star.*

patterns are made more interesting – and more complicated – by the addition of sawtooth or feathered edges, as shown above left. Feathered, or Feather-edged, Stars occur often on quilts from the late 1800s; they are a clue to the skill of the quiltmaker.

Diamonds with a 45-degree angle are used to make the most familiar star patterns, the Lone Star (also known as Star of Bethlehem or Star of the East), in which colors radiate out from a central diamond shape in rows of contrasting color and finish in points, usually eight, and usually at the edge of the quilt. It was said that a girl who made a Lone Star quilt was destined to remain unmarried, but the pattern was still widely used, perhaps to show off the maker's technical prowess.

The eight-pointed stars used in the Lone Star pattern are based on the LeMoyne Star. Tradition has it that this

ABOVE AND RIGHT: *The lavish appliqué work in the center and around the edges of this Star of Bethlehem quilt from about 1865 is not unique, but it is very beautiful. The colors of the flowers, and in the paisley border, have been carefully chosen to blend in with the diamonds that form the star, and the entire piece represents many, many hours of work.*

pattern was named after the LeMoyne brothers, Pierre and Jean-Baptiste, who founded the city of New Orleans in the early eighteenth century, and that as the design traveled north, the name became corrupted to Lemon Star. If row after row of diamonds is added to a LeMoyne Star, a Lone Star quilt can be made; if squares of a contrasting color are inserted

between the points of a LeMoyne star and new rows of diamonds in the colors of the star are added, a Broken Star, or Carpenter's Wheel, results.

Six-pointed stars can be created from diamonds, too, though the diamonds must have 60-degree angles. Hexagons can be created by inserting the same diamond shapes in contrasting colors

ABOVE: This elaborate Star of Bethlehem from Pennsylvania uses red and green Wild Goose Chase strips for the double border, separated by the same four colors chosen for the diamonds in the star.

LEFT: *This beautiful Ohio Amish Variable Star quilt is unusual in that it is dated: in this case 1905. The stars are turned on point and alternated with dark green, plain square, blocks. The border of Chinese Coins is made, like the rest of the quilt, from wool scraps, and the entire piece is bound in red.*

between the six points and combined to make quilts of stunning complexity and great beauty.

Blazing Star, also known as Mother's Delight, is the name of the pattern most associated with four-pointed stars. Each point is usually constructed from irregular triangles joined on their long sides with the colors alternating. The pieced points are joined on their short sides, and differently shaped triangles can be added at right angles to these four points. The construction of the Blazing Star block usually depends on making templates, but these patterns can be machine-stitched or sewn by hand.

Many of these stars can be constructed from strip-pieced fabrics that have been cut in the appropriate shapes and then joined. Interesting secondary designs result using this method (which also makes effective spiderweb shapes when triangles are cut instead of diamonds).

ABOVE: *The Variable Star block is usually pieced as a nine-patch pattern, but here the blocks have been made so the star is upright with the block itself on point.*

The Mariner's Compass pattern is based on stars, but because of its complexity, this design has been given a section of its own (see pages 74–77).

Five-pointed stars are best reserved for appliqué work rather than classic patchwork, as they are extremely difficult to construct from regular geometric shapes. However, most other star designs are geometric and can be made simply and easily by folding a square of paper and cutting out a pattern.

ABOVE: This Pennsylvania Lone Star from about 1890 is worked mainly in pastels and has many small six-point stars appliquéd to the white background.

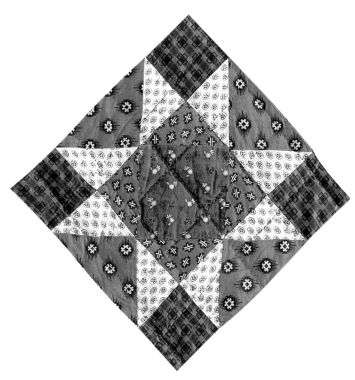

RIGHT, ABOVE, AND BELOW: *The choice of white for the points makes these stars fairly twinkle against their darker backgrounds. The setting squares that alternate with the star blocks are made from an early roller-printed fabric in copper with blue and pink motifs. The red, white, and green 'pillar' print in the border is chintz, which was highly prized and very expensive when this quilt was made in about 1835. The star blocks are again set on point (see page 70).*

Mariner's Compass

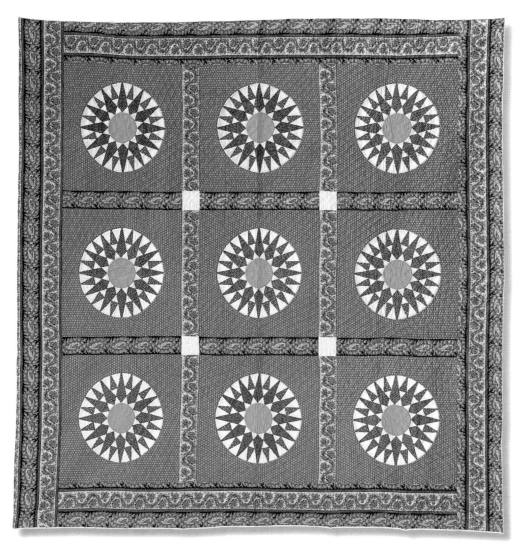

ARINER'S COMPASS is basically a grand and intricate star pattern, one which is a real test of a quilter's skill. The design is characterized by concentric rings of pointed starbursts radiating out from a central circle, often consisting of layer upon layer of different colored fabrics.

The Mariner's Compass pattern has a strong traditional association with the New England coastal area, according to the quilt historian Carter Houck. Understandable, since the pattern looks much like the elaborate compasses used by sailors since the early days of sail and brought to North America on the pilgrim's ships from the late seventeenth century.

Many fine historical examples of these quilts are still in existence – partly, of course, because such elaborate work

LEFT AND ABOVE: This quilt, with nine Mariner's Compass blocks, positively glows with late summer splendor. The sunburst center is surrounded by twelve green points, which are laid over twelve more russet-colored ones, all on a white background. Made in Pennsylvania in about 1870, it contains two paisley-patterned fabrics used for the sashing and the borders.

ABOVE: *The twenty compasses in this c.1865 quilt from Ohio each contain 32 points around a white center circle; four red, four green, eight of pumpkin, and sixteen blue ones. The intricate appliqué border uses the same colors in a flower-and-vine pattern.*

RIGHT: *Made in Ohio in 1845–50, this intricate quilt has a red, white, and blue theme that is emphasized by the unusual stars-and-stripes sashing. The beautiful compasses in simple blue and white have an eight-point star inside the center circle and contain a total of 32 points. The red and blue striped sashing has a blue and white eight-point star at each corner, and there is an inner border and binding of blue and white sawtooth outlining a wide appliqué border showing a green and white vine.*

OPPOSITE: *This intriguing quilt, made in Pennsylvania in about 1860, alternates large compasses with small ones. The center circle and first row of points are the same on all. The small compasses are finished within a yellow circle while the large version has a white background, but is continued with three more rows of points, based on multiples of nine.*

would have been reserved for quilts that were used for 'best', and would have been treasured possessions which were lovingly handed down from generation to generation as precious family heirlooms.

The complexity of the Mariner's Compass design has led modern quilters to experiment with ways of simplifying both the cutting and piecing of these quilts, and many people have found that the pattern lends itself admirably to foundation-paper piecing, in particular.

While it is possible to find Mariner's Compass designs based on a six-point or twelve-point star, most are made in multiples of eight points – some even have ten. To be considered a compass block, the pattern should have at least sixteen points. Many of the most outstanding examples have at least 32, if not 64, points, which become sharper and sharper – and hence more difficult to piece – as the number of points increases.

But the Mariner's Compass is not simply a test of the quilter's technical virtuosity in precision piecing: the most spectacular examples also display an innate flair for design as the points of the compass radiate outward in kaleidoscopic bursts of color.

Representational Blocks

SOME PATCHWORK BLOCKS can be pieced to create a schematic, but nonetheless recognizable, picture. Their names often derive from ordinary household objects (Baskets, for example) or things the quilters saw around them every day (Pine Tree or Schoolhouse).

Made in Holmes County, Ohio, in about 1935–40, this Baskets quilt is made in traditional Midwestern Amish colors, especially its use of yellow.

Representational Blocks

MANY REPRESENTATIONAL BLOCKS are actually a combination of patchwork and appliqué, like these delicate baskets made from pieced triangles and filled with appliquéd flowers. Great ingenuity has been employed by quiltmakers through the years to create realistic representations of a favorite subject.

OPPOSITE: *This fine example of a quilt using a block with piecing and appliqué combined was made in Pennsylvania in about 1860. Each basket is pieced from yellow triangles that have been combined with another color – either red, green, or gray, although one of them includes both red and green. There are two versions of the appliqué flowers in the baskets, one of which is used around the edge of the quilt in place of a border.*

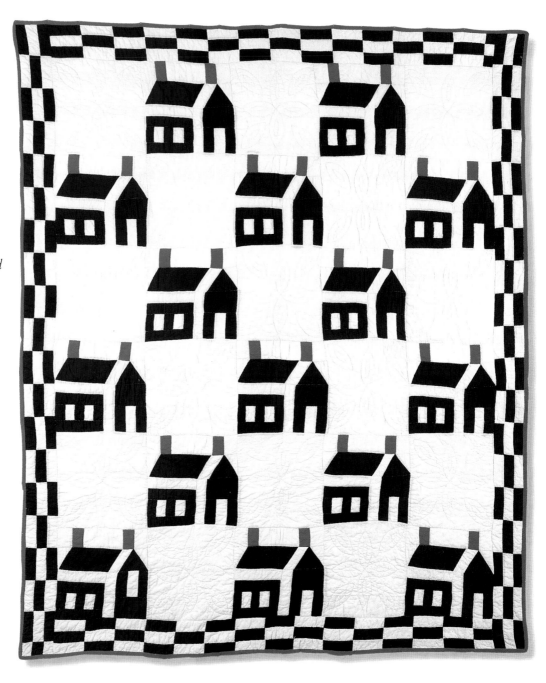

The scope for creating pictures in fabric is limitless, but creating patchwork pictures in repeatable block form provides something of a challenge. Luckily, it is one that seems to have appealed to quiltmakers for many years, and while many realistic patterns, like Sunbonnet Sue and the motifs used in Baltimore Album quilts, are appliquéd instead of pieced, the creativity of traditional blockmakers has left us with a good number of outstanding examples of pieced representational blocks.

Baskets are one of the most favored of these patterns, and there are numerous variations on the theme. Many examples of sampler quilts include a Baskets block. In most versions, the basket itself is fashioned from triangles of various sizes, although parallelograms are sometimes used. Sometimes there is a 'handle' made from right-angle triangles, or the same

ABOVE: *Made in Ohio in about 1920, this House quilt is simple but highly effective. Each navy blue house has two red chimneys, and the background and spacer blocks are white. The blue and white border is pieced in a chain pattern and bound in red.*

ABOVE AND LEFT: *The House pattern must owe much of its popularity to its versatility. In this quilt dated about 1925–30, the multicolored houses have more window panes than can be found in most House patterns. The pink eight-point stars at the corners of the white sashing strips create a secondary pattern like paths joining all the houses together.*

triangles, or diamonds fill the area of the block above the basket to give the effect of a basket filled with flowers. There are many traditional names for these designs: Fruit Basket, Colonial Basket, Tulip Basket, Bread Basket, and even one called Tea Basket. Various basket designs are known by names like Bouquet and Calico Bouquet. Postage Stamp Basket pattern is a four-patch pattern in which each patch is a small basket, and the four pieces are arranged with their handles facing into the center.

One simple Flower Basket pattern is constructed from a triangle set on its point with a rounded appliquéd handle, while a four-patch version called, variously, Basket of Scraps and

ABOVE: These unusual two-story houses worked simply in red and white, and bound in red, were made in about 1910 in either New York or Pennsylvania.

RIGHT AND BELOW: *These highly realistic butterflies are a sublime example of the possibilities offered by a copious scrap basket. Made in Xenia, Ohio, in about 1935, the blocks are arranged with the butterflies' wings on the diagonal. By alternating the direction in which each one is 'flying,' the quiltmaker has created a superb sense of movement. The simple outline quilting, around each block and diagonally through the body, adds to the effect of a flock winging in all directions.*

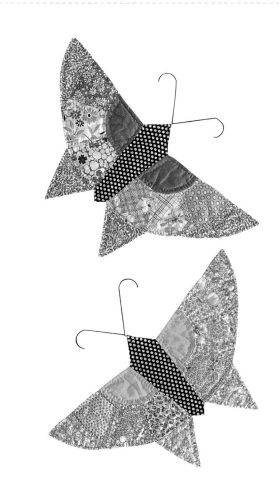

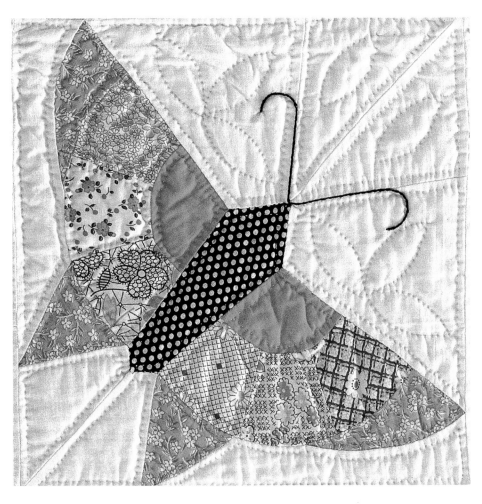

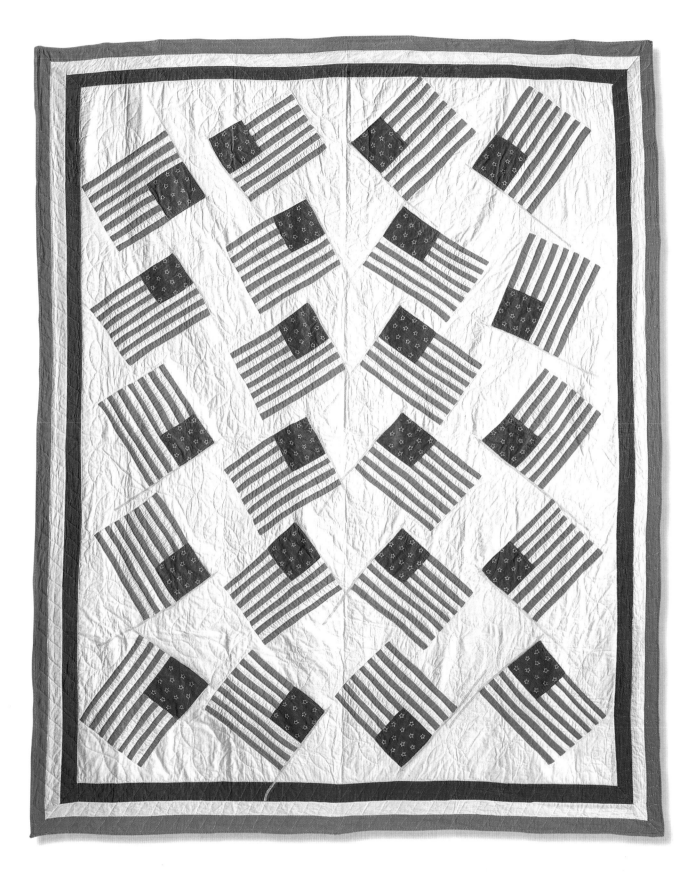

ABOVE: Patriotic red, white, and blue flags flutter at angles, like a parade marching by, in this quilt made in Ohio in about 1915. Note that the flag at the top of the second row on the left is missing its top red stripe.

Flowerpot, consists of a basket with four large diamond-shaped pieces sticking out of the top. Carolina Lily, which is also known as North Carolina Lily, is a more complicated block, which is turned on its point with three pieced lilies on stems appearing out of the basket. Grape Basket and Pieced Baskets are traditional designs in which each motif is set diagonally in the block.

There are almost as many variations of the House block as there are of Baskets. Piecing can be tricky since, to create a realistic effect, it may be necessary to join acute angles, but the effect is charming, and the House remains a popular motif.

ABOVE: This Midwestern quilt was made in about 1940. Its unusual motif may have alluded to the Democratic Party – or perhaps its maker just liked donkeys. The borders have white and brown nine-patch blocks at the corners.

Houses appear facing front, at an angle like a child's drawing, as little red schoolhouses, and those of many other colors, with steeples to become churches, with belfrys to become town halls. Many nineteenth-century quilts have public buildings, many of them very imposing and ornate, as part of their design. Interestingly, the House is one of the two representational blocks popular with quiltmakers from the Amish tradition – the other is Baskets, especially Fruit Baskets.

Almost any subject can, with clever use of a grid, be adapted into a representational block. Flowers are among the most popular subjects, with lilies, tulips, peonies, and roses widely used. Meadow Lily and Tiger Lily are variations of Carolina Lily that have no

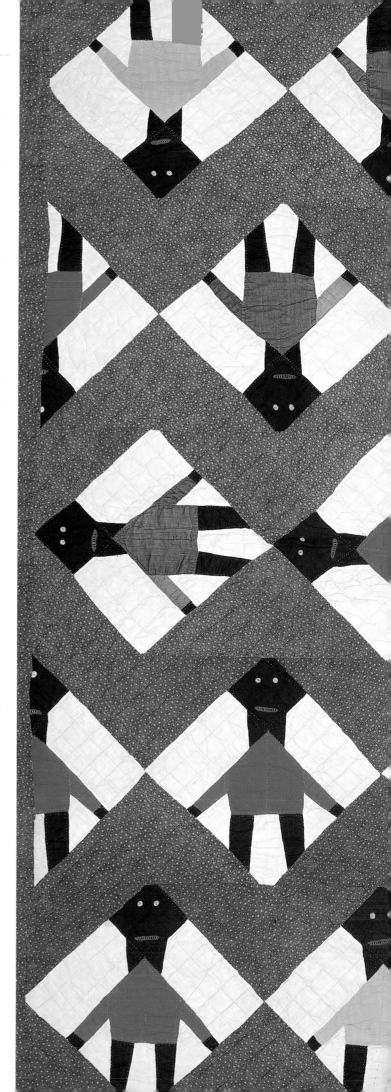

RIGHT AND ABOVE: Hidden in this quilt's design is a Streak of Lightning pattern, but what makes it so unusual, and so charming, are the blocks of highly stylized, but instantly recognizable black-skinned boys. Made in southern Missouri in about 1900.

baskets. In addition, there are many realistic leaf patterns such as Maple Leaf, Tea Leaf, Autumn Leaf, and Sweet Gum Leaf, as well as trees like Pine Tree, Tree of Paradise, Tree of Life, and the charmingly named Little Beech Tree.

Animals from bats, birds, butterflies, and other insects to frogs, donkeys, and elephants can be devised; and boats and ships, as well as airplanes, trucks, and trains make interesting designs. Human figures and patterns based on useful items like teapots or cups and saucers are also possible, and they can make very effective blocks. Designs created from flags and other patriotic motifs are quite popular themes on quilts, and occur quite often, particularly in examples made in the late nineteenth and early twentieth centuries.

RIGHT, LEFT, AND BELOW: The blocks in this deservedly famous 'story' quilt, made in New Jersey in 1854 by Sarah Ann Wilson, are appliquéd, but pieced together with sashing strips of red print fabric. The motifs could be adapted and worked as pieced blocks.

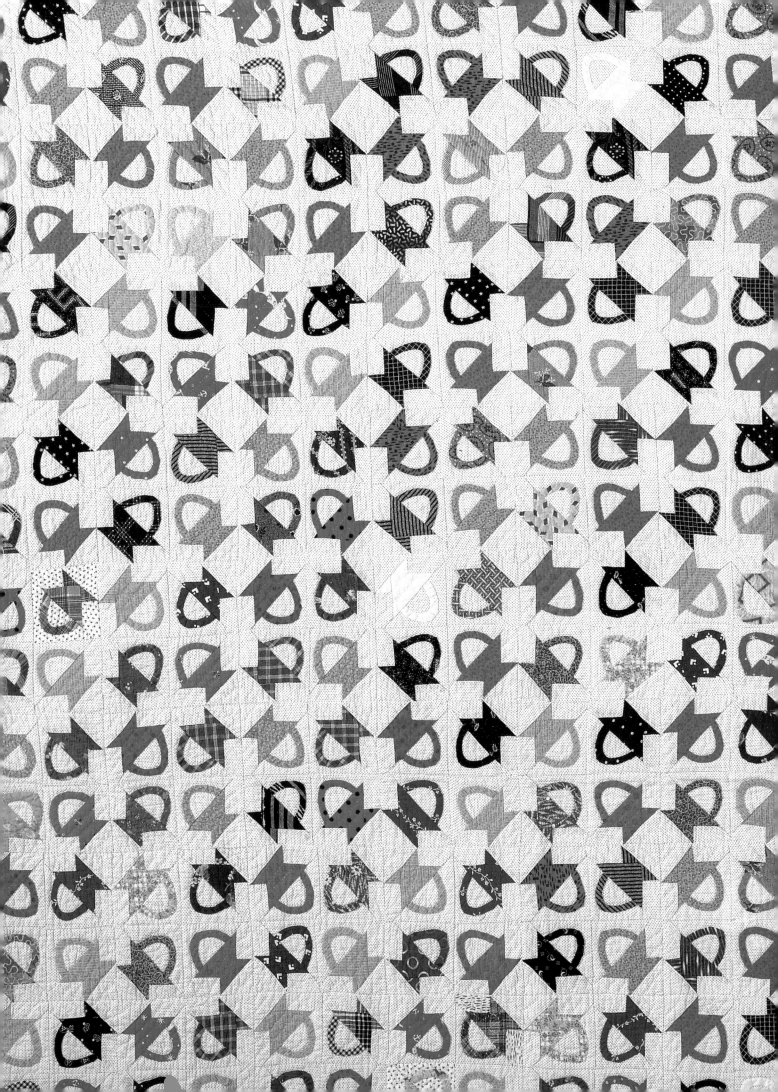

1,000-piece Geometrics

Mosaic patterns made from myriad small pieces create intricate and intriguing designs, many of which have a strong three-dimensional effect. Most are geometric, like Roman and Greek designs of old, and make patterns that are endlessly fascinating.

This quilt consists of 525 tiny baskets arranged to create square-shaped blocks and a strong diagonal line. Noce the occasional blank in the pattern.

1,000-piece Geometrics

LIKE MANY ASPECTS of design, quilts based on a vast number of small, even tiny, pieces tend to rely for their overall effect on the way color is used in their creation. The geometric quality of such designs is enhanced through the careful arrangement of color values to balance areas of light and dark within the piece.

Quilt patterns that are created from hundreds, perhaps thousands, of small geometric shapes such as squares, diamonds, hexagons, triangles, or octagons are sometimes referred to as 'mosaic' patterns. Many of the designs are based on ancient patterns found on floors, walls, ceilings, pavements, and even tiles, especially those from the empires of Rome and Byzantium, when mosaic-making reached its height of popularity. When these patterns are

LEFT AND ABOVE: *This is a fantastic example of a thousand-piece quilt. The pattern is Birds in the Air, made from several thousand tiny right-angle triangles, fashioned into squares that create a feast for the eyes. Two inner sawtooth borders, one blue, the other red, frame areas of light, medium, and dark. The quilt (c.1885–95) is signed: 'Made by Lucretia Sleeper (Northhaven, Mass.) on a voyage on the bark (ship) Addie E. Sleeper.'*

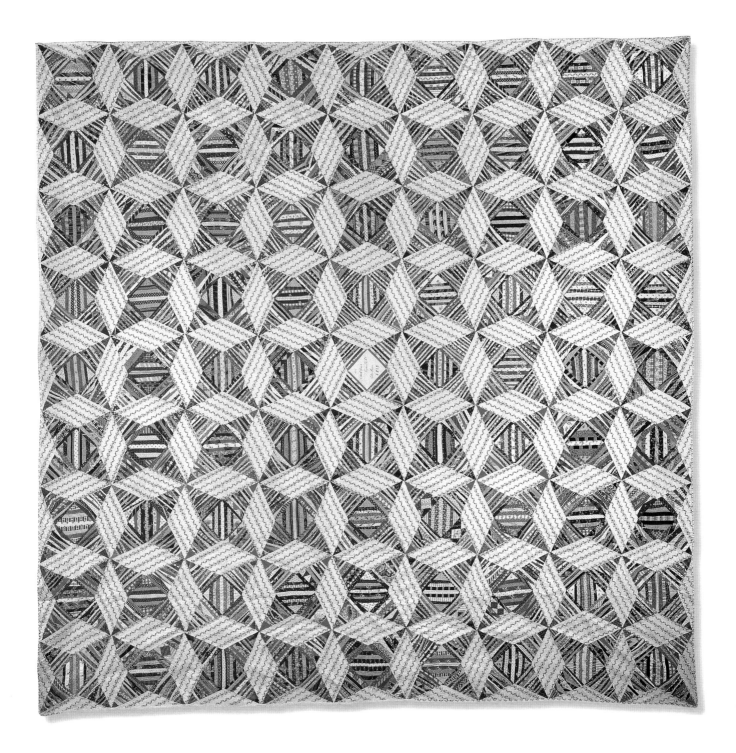

adapted to quilt-making, the geometric possibilities are endless.

Perhaps the best-known of all mosaic patterns is Grandmother's Flower Garden, which uses hexagons to create six-sided rosettes around a central hexagon. The resulting piece can be a stunning example of a scrap quilt, in which fabrics of all sorts are combined and held together visually by a plain background made also from hexagons. There are numerous variations of this pattern, including hexagonal stars, pictorial scenes, and even a hexagonal Trip Around the World. Because no one has yet found a way of strip-piecing hexagons, it is usual to piece them using the so-called English method of basting

ABOVE: This World Without End quilt is made from 5,814 pieces of striped cotton fabric. Signed 'Mrs. P. Harris, Eaglesville, Conn. 1880,' it has a dynamic movement that truly feels like a heavenly body spinning endlessly through time and space.

RIGHT AND ABOVE: The optical illusion created by this kaleidescopic red and white quilt is truly stunning. Pieced in concentric circles composed of alternating squares in ever-decreasing size, this work of art was made in New Jersey in about 1910, long before the era of the Pop artists. The red butterfly-esque shapes in the corners are appliqué work.

each shape over a backing paper to stablize it. Perhaps partly because it is sewn by hand, the design is now used less often than it has been in the past, but many quilters have embarked on such a quilt at some time.

The Tumbling Blocks pattern, based on diamonds and usually worked, like hexagons, over papers, is a popular mosaic design that uses the same repeated shape to create a vibrant three-dimensional effect.

Tiny squares and triangles can all be used to make intricate geometric quilts in patterns with names like Postage Stamp and Thousand Pyramids. These shapes also occur in Birds in the Air, Ocean Wave, and Trip Around the World – indeed, many familiar patterns can be made by using smaller pieces than usual to create mosaic-type patterns.

Some mosaics portray a scene or have a pictorial image in the center with geometric borders positioned around the edge. These effects can be imitated on medallion quilts, on which the central square is surrounded by several borders of varying widths, each different in color and design. Using small or large pieces, geometric patterns can be created that have just the right feel to complement mosaic work.

OPPOSITE: This fabulous version of Ocean Waves contains thousands of tiny dark blue and white triangles. The red pinwheels that occur at each intersection give this quilt, made in Pennsylvania in about 1890, its unique quality. The use of plain red and then a blue and white sawtooth for the inner borders creates a frame to enclose a piece that has the feeling of a calm sea.

LEFT: The Tumbling Blocks pattern is one of the classic mosaic-type designs. Here the blocks are arranged, not in straight rows as is so often seen, but in a pyramid shape. Made in about 1925–35 in the Midwest, it uses soft pastel colors to great effect, leading the eye up its seemingly never-ending steps.

ABOVE: Mrs. Yost Miller, an Amish quiltmaker in Wisconsin, made this 'Flock of Birds' quilt, using a huge number of tiny multicolored triangular pieces, in about 1930. The corner blocks in the black sashing repeat the Flock of Birds pattern and enhance the strong feeling of movement in the piece.

LEFT: The Ocean Waves pattern provides another way of using small triangular scraps to make an effective mosaic pattern. The colors used here are associated more with the Amish of Lancaster County, Pennsylvania, than with Holmes County, Ohio, where it was made.

Curved Patterns

CURVED PATTERNS are somewhat more tricky to piece than those with straight seams, so they tend to be seen less often. But the beautiful lines of many of these patterns make them well worth the effort.

The pastel colors of this lovely Cushion, or Pincushion, quilt, made c.1930, have been arranged to create a diagonal cross in the center of the piece.

Curved Patterns

WHILE THE VARIETY OF CURVES used in patchwork is less than in appliqué work, many beautiful patterns are available to quiltmakers who prefer to piece their blocks. Curving lines give a sense of movement that cannot be achieved by any other design, and many of the traditional patterns consist of only two different shapes.

Of course, curves can be produced within blocks pieced entirely from straight pieces by employing optical tricks, such as combining thick and thin strips as used in Off-Center, or Asymmetrical, Log Cabin, or by the juxtaposition of small squares of color in the technique called Watercolor work, developed by Deirdre Amsden. However, there is a satisfaction to be found in looking at a curve that really is curved.

LEFT AND ABOVE: The Pinwheel Fans, or Wagon Wheels, separated by the striped central cross, have the look of a giant tic-tac-toe board. Made in Ohio in solid colors, it dates from about 1935. The bright pastel hues shimmer on the white background and combine with the lively shapes to bring a vibrant optical movement to this interesting piece.

Identical fans in pale pastels are set on a white background in this Diagonal Wave quilt made in Ohio/Pennsylvania in about 1925.

Although curved patterns have traditionally been joined by hand, many can be pieced by machine, and some blocks or elements of blocks can be chain-pieced to speed up the process. Care must, of course, be taken in joining any curved seams, since they are highly vulnerable to stretching. Accurate marking is essential, and it can be very useful to add notches along the seam for matching.

One of the best known of all curved patterns is Double Wedding Ring. Although quilts have been made from the

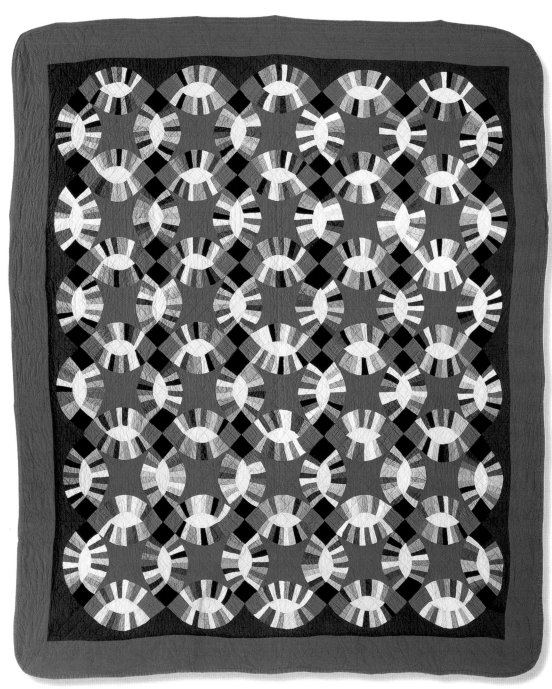

earliest times to commemorate a marriage or as a gift for a bride and groom, there is no evidence to show that the Double Wedding Ring design was used before the end of the nineteenth century. It became popular in the 1920s and 1930s, in spite of its complex construction, after numerous patterns were published in magazines and newspapers, and it probably owes at least some of its fame to the fact that, for many people hit hard by the Great Depression, it proved to be an excellent way of using up scraps of fabric. Today it remains a favorite challenge for the more experienced quilter and is still very popular among the quilters from the Amish community, who generally make the background dark, and then use bright-colored rings to dramatic effect.

ABOVE: The Double Wedding Ring is favored by the Amish for the small size and variety of its many pieces, which lend themselves – as in this 1910–1920 example from Ohio – to this pattern. The black inner border creates a strong outline for the multicolored rings.

ABOVE: *This Midwestern Amish Double Wedding Ring from about 1925 is pieced from multicolored scraps. Setting the rings on a black background would have been dramatic enough, but the quiltmaker has outdone herself by adding a vibrant bright blue piping to bind the edges.*

ABOVE AND LEFT: *Compass quilts come in many variations, but few of them are dated as clearly as this 1856 example. Made in Ohio, it has nine curved Compass blocks that are far from standard Mariner's Compass (see pages 74–77) and a wide, elaborately appliquéd border, both on a pink calico background. The narrow green borders and gold binding echo colors in the motifs.*

ABOVE AND RIGHT: *This Pennsylvania Mennonite quilt of stylized russet and gold flowers has oodles of curves, some pieced and some appliquéd. Each flower shape has four blue and pink buds; they radiate out to the corners of the blocks, which are set on point with the two background colors – pink and russet – alternated. The same pink and gold fabrics are used to make the borders and binding.*

Fans appear in quilts in a vast variety, from a Grandmother's Fan in the corner of each block to Pinwheel Fan, in which four fans are joined into a circle, or Wagon Wheel, with its four fans divided by a crossed strip of narrow sashing. Grandmother's Fan is usually joined with the fans in the corner and all pointing the same way, but if the blocks are turned on point, the fans appear upright. If they are alternated side by side, long diagonal curved lines move across the quilt in a design called Snake in the Hollow. The fan shapes can be joined with the points touching to create a very realistic and effective butterfly. Dresden Plate is a variation of the Fan pattern, with the tapering blades mounted around a full

ABOVE: Fan blocks set on point, so that the fan is upright, have a completely different effect from those set square. Made in the eastern states in about 1900, this cotton example shows an outstanding sense of color.

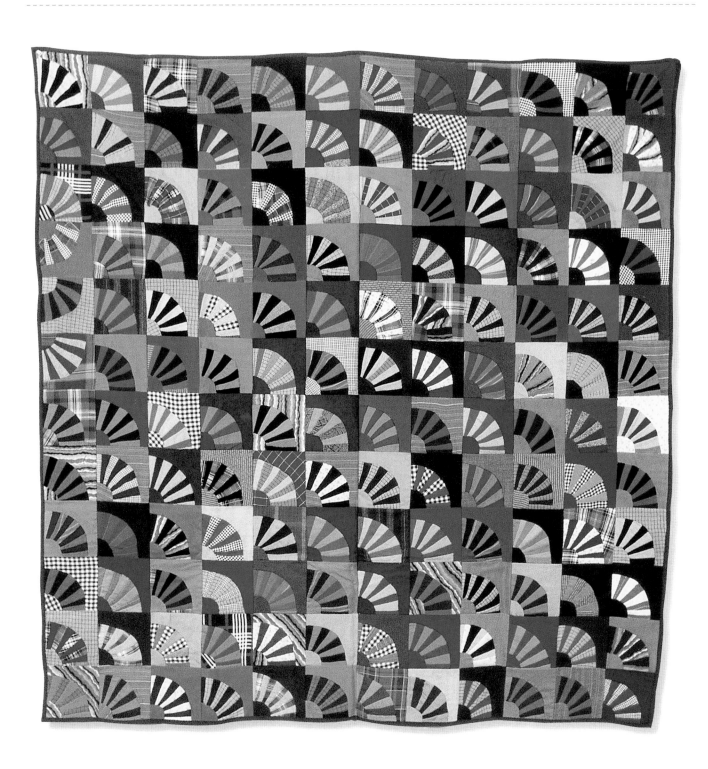

ABOVE: This exuberant American quilt from about 1890 is a true scrap quilt. The blades of each fan tend to be made from only two different cotton fabrics, and backgrounds are both solid colors and checks or plaids, perhaps old shirts.

circle instead of a quarter-circle. The ends of the blades for all of these patterns vary enormously, from flat to rounded to pointed, and sometimes they alternate between two or more of these options. They all offer an excellent way to make use of a scrap basket.

Another favorite curved pattern is Drunkard's Path and its numerous

variations. Highly effective blocks can be made using only two fabrics, and the design, which was used in the nineteenth century to make 'cause' quilts became associated, especially when it was made in blue and white, with support of the temperance movement of the day. It creates jagged crisscrossing diagonal lines through the quilt, supposedly reminiscent

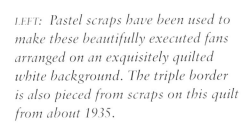

LEFT: Pastel scraps have been used to make these beautifully executed fans arranged on an exquisitely quilted white background. The triple border is also pieced from scraps on this quilt from about 1935.

BELOW: The velvets, silks, and cotton sateen and decorative stitching in this Wagon Wheel quilt made in upstate New York in about 1885 belie its Amish origins, but the plain dramatic colors and use of black do not.

of an inebriate staggering home after a rowdy night out. It has another name – Old Maid's Puzzle – used by the Amish whose strict religious code forbids drunkeness, but the pattern is the same. In this pattern, the squares look as though a bite has been taken out of them. The standard traditional version is usually made with half the blocks using one configuration of the two fabrics and the other half using a different configuration. There are, however, any number of ways to set the blocks to give a different effect.

Among the many other curved designs are patterns with evocative names. Orange Peel is an ellipse inside a square of contrasting color, while Robbing Peter to Pay

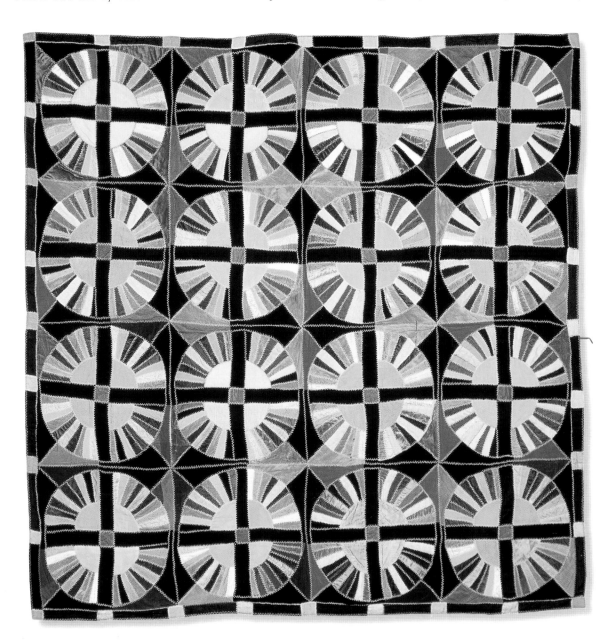

Paul uses a basic Drunkard's Path patch in alternating sequence with the 'bites' in the corners pointed toward each other to create a quartered circle. Cathedral Window is a layered block in which the edges of the backing are turned over onto a square of contrasting fabric and sewn in place. The rolled-over edges create a slight curve that makes a highly decorative quilt that needs no batting or quilting. Alabama Star Beauty, Josephine's Knot, Crown of Thorns, and Clamshell are all curved designs that can be made into wonderful quilt patterns, and which provide an exciting challenge for the quilter.

RIGHT: *The effectiveness of using just two contrasting colors is beautifully illustrated by this Midwestern Drunkard's Path quilt with its large-scale Sawtooth border made in about 1935.*

BELOW AND LEFT: *This Dresden Plate quilt from about 1935 was made in Ohio or Pennsylvania using a large number of multicolored scraps on a white background. The giant red dots add charm and humor.*

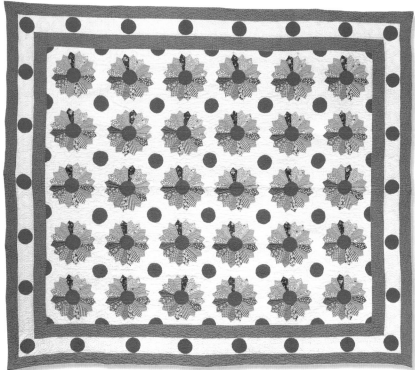

Crazy Patchwork

THE VICTORIAN ERA was certainly the heyday of crazy patchwork, when scraps of fine dressmaking fabrics like silk and velvet were made into throws and table covers galore. However, the roots of this type of piecing go back much further.

This Contained Crazy quilt made from silk and velvet in New York in about 1865–75 is full of charming embroidered motifs of animals, flowers, and even in a woman and a dog in a bathtub!

Crazy Patchwork

THE HIGGLEDY-PIGGLEDY density of crazy patchwork appealed to needlewomen on both sides of the Atlantic in the latter half of the nineteenth century. It allowed them to show off not only their piecing skills, but their adroitness with an embroidery needle and thread, as well as the collections of fine fabrics from which their elaborate dresses were made.

However, crazy patchwork really began much earlier, probably in colonial North America with the earliest settlers. Although spinning wheels and looms were found in homes and used to spin and weave fabric for the family, the setting up of equipment for producing textiles of all kinds on a commercial basis was actively discouraged by the British government. In fact, at certain times before the Revolutionary War, it was deemed illegal to produce any textiles in the colonies, which meant of course that all fabric had to be imported – at

LEFT AND ABOVE: This wool crazy quilt has its date – 1898 – emblazoned across the bottom right-hand corner, and we know it was made by a Leila Butts from upper New York State. It is a veritable encyclopedia of nineteenth-century fashion, with a well-dressed woman or man worked on a panel in each of its blocks.

vast expense – from industrialized textile centers such as Manchester and Liverpool in Britain, which were thereby protected and subsidized, and were, effectively, monopolies.

So, every scrap of fabric, of whatever type and however small, was valuable enough to be saved and reused. The earliest forms of crazy patchwork – perhaps of North American patchwork in general – were therefore almost certainly pieced fabrics made from these little pieces that were sewn together until an adequately sized length of material had evolved. Few of these early fabrics remain in existence, but the technique would have been handed down and refined by subsequent generations.

Once the local industry had gathered pace and a choice of fabrics was available and affordable, the block system of construction developed, and American patchwork came of age. Meanwhile the idea and basic method of constructing crazy patchwork traveled east across the Atlantic to Britain, where Queen

ABOVE: Silks and velvets were crazy-pieced into blocks or strips and joined by Carrie Scott in about 1901. Most of the blocks have a fan motif worked into the design, and the entire piece has been elaborately and beautifully embroidered with a myriad of interesting motifs.

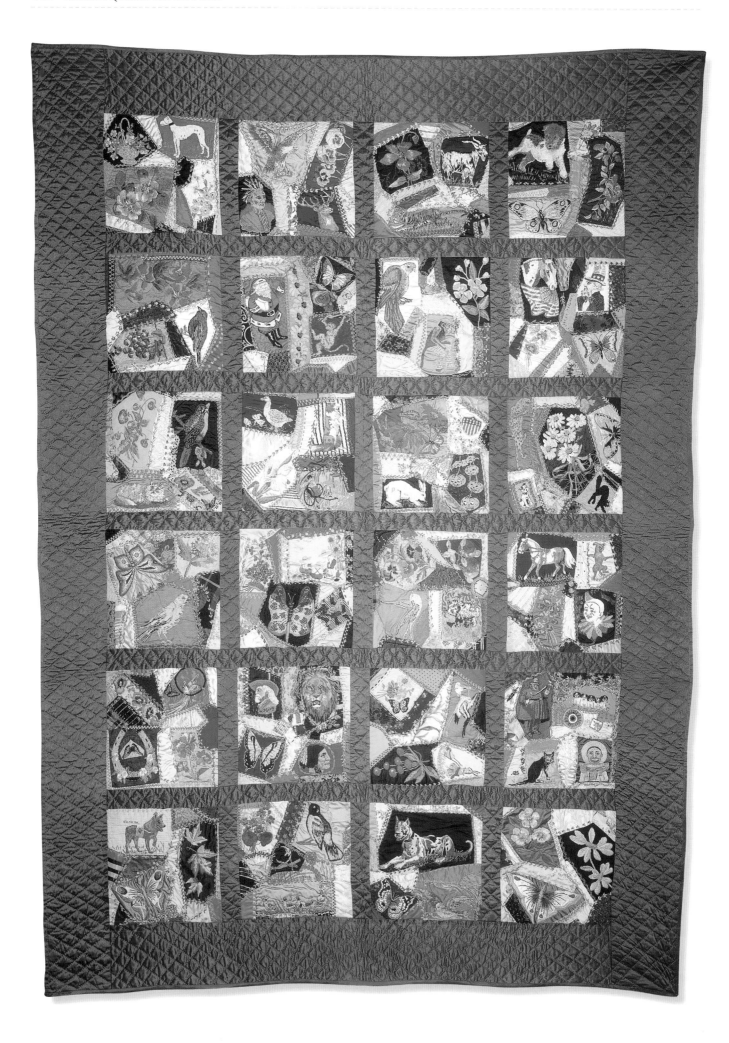

OPPOSITE: Jennie Mackley, an actress who toured in theatrical productions in Europe and the United States in the late 1880s, made this Contained Crazy quilt in about 1900. By then, she had retired to her hometown of Columbus, Ohio, presumably taking with her the collection of remnants that she had bought from dressmakers who were responsible for creating the wardrobes of various European royal personages. The charming motifs include many animals, especially dogs, and at least two Native Americans.

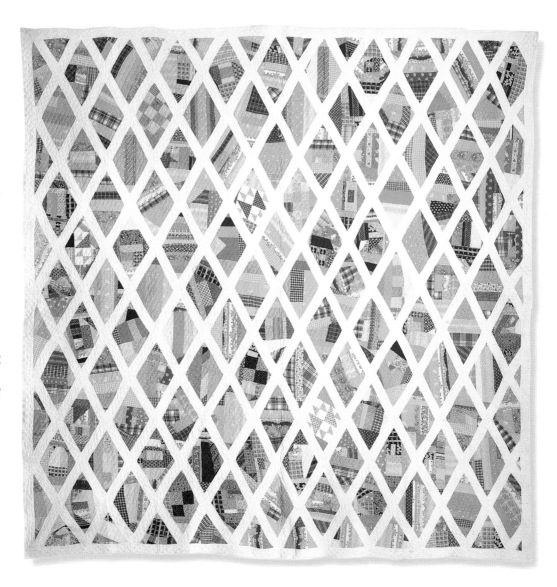

Victoria's subjects embraced it with characteristic enthusiasm. In North America, too, the style was popular.

There are subtle but interesting differences in the crazy patchwork pieces from each side of the ocean. A vast number have survived in spite of being made from fairly fragile fabrics, partly because they were often mounted on a foundation of muslin, which helped to stabilize them.

In addition, they were usually display pieces and rarely subjected to heavy use. Most were made as top bedcovers not intended to be slept under, throws or lap quilts, and table covers, designed to advertise their maker's skill with a needle. British crazy quilts are usually made of silk, taffeta, velvet, and even ribbon. American versions do use these fine fabrics, but can also be found made from wool, cotton, and linen. The scraps are usually applied to a muslin backing, and the raw edges decorated with elaborate embroidery. Quite a few American examples are cut as blocks and put together with sashing, a technique known as 'contained crazy,' whereas British makers were more likely to create a solid piece of crazy patchwork.

ABOVE: This Contained cotton quilt is made of crazy-patchwork diamonds that are contained by white diagonal sashing strips. Made in Pennsylvania between 1845 and 1865, it is worked in muted colors and edged by a strip the same color and width as the sashing.

CLASSIC QUILTS:
Appliqué and Quilting

THE ARTISTIC FREEDOM granted to the quiltmaker is best seen in quilts made in appliqué and in the quilting that gives a piece the texture and pattern associated with work of this kind. Lines can be more flowing than with patchwork, and the choices of subject and design are infinite.

This green and red North Carolina Lily with a selection of stars, made in Pennsylvania in about 1860, is a stunning example of the quiltmaker's art.

Traditional Appliqué

APPLIQUE HAS BEEN USED to decorate fabric in many civiliza-tions. For the past 200 or 300 years, appliqué in Europe and North America has been traditionally associated with the technique now referred to as American appliqué, in which designs are cut out and stitched onto a background fabric.

This elegant appliqué quilt, made in Pennsylvania in about 1850, features white eagles with shields and oval floral motifs on a dark blue background.

BELOW: These appliquéd pots of flowers are set diagonally in red-bordered blocks that are sashed with white, and ornamented with soft blue six- and eight-point stars.

Appliqué is the name given to the decorative technique of applying a shape, design, or motif of one fabric onto a background made of a different fabric. It is sometimes classified as embroidery and is very much a part of the quiltmaking tradition. The method has been used throughout the world, and documented examples exist almost as far back as the history of textiles. There are many variations, each of which gives a different effect to provide variety and interest.

Perhaps the idea for appliqué came first from patching holes in worn

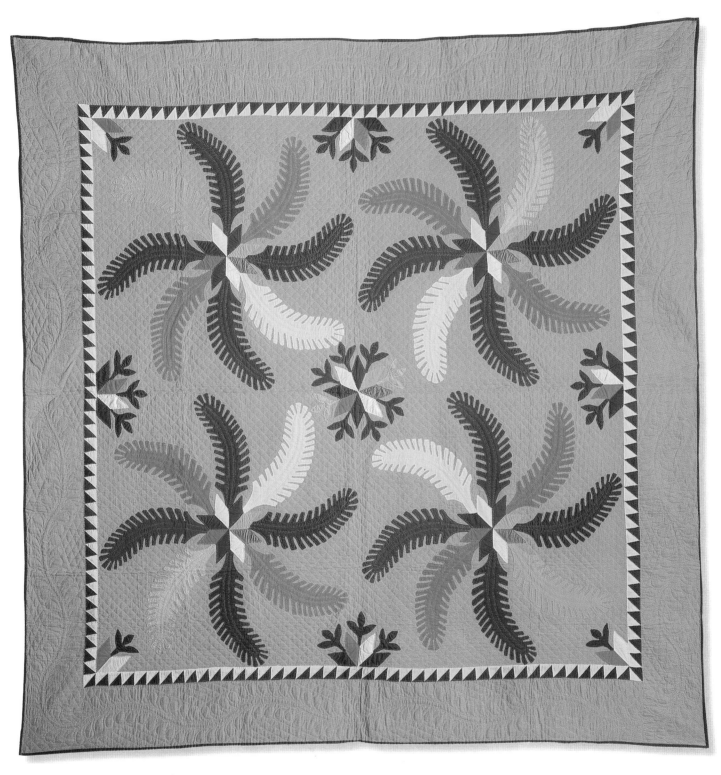

garments and domestic textiles. Mary Queen of Scots is the most famous practitioner of appliqué from Tudor times, but certainly not the only one. By the seventeenth and eighteenth centuries, the technique was well established in Europe as a prudent way of preserving and making the most of

the popular – and expensive – printed cotton fabrics being produced in India and subjected to import controls in Britain because of the threat they posed to the British textile industry. Motifs were cut from increasingly scarce Indian fabrics and applied, usually with decorative stitching, to less expensive,

ABOVE: This traditional appliqué pattern dances across the bold pink background of a Mennonite quilt dating from about 1890. Made in Pennsylvania, the design includes multicolored Variable Stars and a pieced Sawtooth border.

plain background fabric to make bedcovers and other household linen. Individual printed motifs were cut out and sewn to the background to create new patterns in a method that became known as broderie perse. A similar method – chintz scrap appliqué, in which scraps of patterned fabric were cut into shapes unrelated to the printed motif – provided an even more frugal way of preserving fabric. The passion for these types of appliqué spread to other parts of the British Empire, and many fine examples survive.

By the nineteenth century, needlework of all types was widely practiced in Europe and the Americas, and the making of pictures in fabric using appliqué methods was widespread. Among the most prized of all appliqué pieces are the Baltimore album quilts made in and around that city in the mid-1800s. The beautiful and elaborate designs based mainly on flowers, baskets, birds, and patriotic emblems required great skill, and many are true works of art. In other places, realistic shapes became highly

ABOVE AND RIGHT: This Crazy patchwork quilt of silk and velvet pieces of appliqué was made by Florence Elizabeth Marvin in Brooklyn Heights, New York, in 1886. It features animals of all kinds, from birds and insects to exotic wildlife, farmyard friends, and pets. The gloved hand shown above, and many of the animals have also been made three-dimensional with padding, and many are embellished with embroidery as well. The flowers, single and in bunches, are both applied and embroidered, including the stunning multicolored garland of wild flowers on the black border.

intricate pieces that looked like marquetry, and pictorial designs showed trees, buildings, ships, and animals. At the end of the century, the Arts and Crafts movement made beautiful use of appliqué, and the Glasgow School of Art in Scotland became a mecca for the technique. During the twentieth century,

appliqué has been in and out of fashion, but its exponents have remained true to its appealing way of allowing them to express themselves creatively while using up scraps of fabric in the time-honored way.

In other parts of the world, from Hawaii to Panama to the mountains of

ABOVE: This quilt was made in New England in about 1865. Note the fountain with drinking birds, the floral wreaths, the rare eight-point Sawtooth stars, the urns of flowers (different on each side), and the weeping willows.

Southeast Asia, traditions of appliqué have been devised and adapted to local needs and culture to make beautiful household linen.

The quilts shown on these pages have survived the ravages of time and the elements. They are all interesting, and in many cases extremely fine, examples of the appliqué tradition. Luckily, most were looked after with care and treated as heirlooms to be passed down from generation to generation.

BELOW: This traditional North Carolina quilt made in New York, 1845–55, has a border of folk-art trees and leaves, and an edging of Sawtooth "grass".

Natural Forms

THE TRADITIONAL APPLIQUE found on quilts over the past two centuries has concentrated to a large extent on forms found in nature, especially flowers, some realistic, others highly stylized. Trees and leaves are used widely, and fruit and even vegetables are also found.

Many well-known appliqué designs are based on flowers, with roses, lilies, tulips, and daisies among the ones encountered most frequently. Indeed, there are several patterns of roses, including three or four different traditional versions of the Rose of Sharon. Carnations, peonies, poppies, irises, hollyhocks, morning glories, lotus flowers, columbines, and water lilies exist in numerous guises.

ABOVE AND LEFT: This Rose of Sharon variation was made in Ohio, and there is no doubting the date, which is emblazoned across the top of the quilt. The nine blocks are dramatic, with a large center rose surrounded by smaller roses, and the diagonal stems pointing out to the corners and ending in buds. The yellow and orange Sawtooth inner border is pieced, and the outer border strips contain a twining vine with flowers similar to the smaller roses that surround the central one in each block.

Early American quiltmakers took with them ideas and designs, as well as quilts themselves, that had been passed down and altered through several centuries. Motifs from Tudor and Jacobean embroideries and bed hangings were adapted by quiltmakers in the seventeenth and eighteenth centuries, and were transferred to quilts as they became popular as bedcovers. Beautiful examples of appliqué quilts made in delicate colors and patterns still exist from the late 1700s; many of these are medallion quilts with intricate centers framed by several appliquéd borders.

The flowers, leaves, vines, and fruit designs used in these pieces were swapped by quiltmakers and needleworkers on

ABOVE: Made in about 1860 in Ohio, this quilt consists of four blocks. A central flower is surrounded by delicate stems and leaves, and is spaced to create a cross-shaped "path" between the blocks. A leaf-and-flower vine border frames the piece.

both sides of the Atlantic. Commerce and traffic between Europe, particularly Britain, and North America that had begun with the earliest settlers increased during the seventeenth and eighteenth centuries. The exchange of ideas, patterns, fabrics, and quilts continued, with interruptions caused by hostilities between 1776 and 1778, and again in 1812, almost unabated.

In the nineteenth century, as American quiltmakers began to work more and more using the block method of construction, appliqué patterns were devised that could fit onto a square of background fabric, be completed, and be stored away until the maker had finished enough blocks to be able to assemble them into a full quilt.

Wreath shapes fitted neatly into the square format, and flowers and leaves were often added to make a block. Many patterns were designed across the diagonal of a square block, with one flower in each corner and stems and leaves joining them.

In other cases, the flower is placed in the center of the block, and it is combined with stems and leaves projecting into

ABOVE AND LEFT: *These Windblown Tulip blocks, in red and yellow with green leaves and stems, were worked in Ohio in about 1860 and enclosed inside a yellow and red Sawtooth inner border. The outer border is embellished with a magnificent red feathered vine that winds its way around the entire quilt without a visual break to make a truly dramatic piece of work.*

each corner. In addition, blocks could be turned on point.

Flowers are often found held together in bunches, the means of which include bows, vases, bowls, baskets, and cornucopia. Trees occur individually, especially in many intricate and fascinating Tree of Life quilts, in repeating groups, and in groups of individual specimens. Leaves are seen with flowers, on trees, and as design elements in their own right.

There are patterns with oak, hickory, palm, and bay leaves in their names, as well as generic versions, and even clover and shamrocks. The sheer variety of vine patterns and garlands of leaves that are frequently used to make borders is seemingly endless.

While flowers are by far the most often used motifs, other naturalistic forms occur – feathers and shells, fruit and vegetables, acorns and other nuts, and stars and sunbursts. As with flowers and trees, they can all be stylized or realistic, depending on the whim of the maker.

The designs can be simple or incredibly intricate, and the colors inevitably reflect the fashions of the time. The muted soft pastels

RIGHT: Four highly complicated Martha Washington's Wreath blocks, again in red, yellow, and green, the most popular colors for this kind of work in the 1860s when this quilt was made, are bordered by a series of identical vases filled with flowers, leaves, and berries on stems. Almost hidden in the border of this Ohio quilt are five unusually colored miniature cats.

and earthy shades of the early 1800s gave way in the middle of the century to brighter fabrics dyed with the then-new aniline dyes; in particular, red, green, and yellow occur over and over again.

Because the work of creating them is complex and time-consuming, many appliqué quilts were made for "best" and were looked after carefully, so plenty of fine examples have survived to the present day. Most of these are full-size bed quilts that were made presumably for the marriage bed or the spare room. Crib quilts of the period tended to be patchwork, or were quilted as wholecloth pieces.

The Ohio Valley especially was a hotbed of appliqué work, with many beautiful appliquéd pieces from the area surviving in collections around the world. The exception was in the Amish community, where appliqué was considered too "fancy," but a few pieces of appliqué worked by quilters from the Mennonite community are still in existence.

Forms taken from nature – flowers, leaves, trees, and animals – abound on the so-called album quilts made around Baltimore, Maryland, in the middle of the nineteenth century. These exquisite, beautifully appliquéd and quilted pieces are true works of art.

The natural forms found on appliqué quilts vary quite dramatically, from those that are so stylized as to be almost abstract, to the opposite end, where they create a hyper-realistic effect. Trees can be shown as balls of green, with multicolored balls of fruit or flowers atop a plain

LEFT: These bold, highly stylized blocks are set head to head, creating an unusual secondary pattern in this c. 1860 quilt from Ohio. The zigzag inner border contrasts with the flowing outer one.

RIGHT: Made in New York State between 1850 and 1860, this quilt alternates ball-shaped green trees with stylized flower motifs. The colors of the "fruit" on the trees are echoed in the eccentric wide vine border with its small leaves and flowers.

LEFT: *This medallion was made between 1775 and 1795 by John Hewson of Philadelphia. An octagon frame is banded by an intertwined chain, itself outlined by a white and blue Sawtooth border scattered with leaves and butterflies.*

RIGHT: *The delicate leaf vine is framed by a dramatic indigo outer border that features swags, flowers, and bows.*

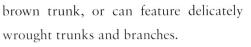

brown trunk, or can feature delicately wrought trunks and branches.

Flowers can be finely detailed, and the species represented can be recognizable. Alternatively, the representations of flowers may be stylized amalgamations of petals, stems, leaves, and colors that have little or no resemblance to any flower that has actually ever existed on earth.

While leaves are often created in a realistic fashion, they are more frequently stylized versions of familiar forms (see the templates on pages 404–408). Vines and garlands are almost always created to decorate a border or a specific area, and as a result, they are recognizably based on reality, but seldom look very much like the real thing.

LEFT: *Made in about 1840–1, this quilt has a central motif of a basket (or bowl) of flowers and ferny leaves surrounded by white five-pointed stars. The bright blue swagged vine with its leaves contrasts with the deep-indigo background of wool.*

Folk-art Themes

AS QUILTMAKERS became more adventurous, more and more new design ideas appeared. Many of the classic appliqué motifs that we recognize today started life in folk art, and many appliqué quilts that have survived into the present day display charming naive forms that are borrowed from folk art around the globe.

Many of the naturalistic themes discussed and shown in the previous section occur in folk art. Flowers, trees, and leaves are all popular, and baskets and flower pots appear here, too. All are, however, much more stylized and display a less sophisticated form than before.

Hearts make a strong appearance, as do hands. Birds and butterflies can be found on many folk-art quilts, together with most of the animals you can think of, both wild and domestic. Because the folk-art tradition came from familiar everyday objects and the lines are greatly simplified, the designs were used to make crib quilts as well as larger pieces. People and houses appear, too; many examples have the quality of a child's drawing.

Many folk-art designs have a large number of thin straight or curving lines, that are easier to cut and stitch than intricate rounded shapes. Many of these

ABOVE: In this unusual crib quilt from Pennsylvania, made between 1855 and 1865, the central basket of flowers and flower stems are made from narrow straight strips, and the flowers are red and pale yellow. The wide vine border frames the quilt nicely, but has eccentric proportions.

RIGHT: *The heavily worked quilting would have been necessary to hold the layers together through the numerous washes needed to keep a crib quilt clean.*

ABOVE: *This wonderfully eccentric quilt was made in New York in about 1860. The red and green are typical colors of their time, and the highly stylized motifs include flowers, trees, hearts, birds, and 16 cats.*

lines are made from strips cut on the bias to make turning curves easier. They add immeasurably to the design potential and can be used to outline, to create patterns within patterns, to act as stems and dividing lines, and to form motifs in their own right.

Traditional Amish quilts were pieced rather than appliquéd, but in the mid-1970s a group of Amish quilters in Lancaster County, Pennsylvania, designed a new appliqué pattern, which they called Lancaster Rose, as their contribution to the American Bicentennial celebrations. Rooted firmly in the folk-art tradition, it has become a popular design made in both traditional Amish colors and in patterned fabrics not usually found in Amish work.

ABOVE: The stems that extend out from the circle and enclose the center motif end in hearts, while in the corners the trailing vine assumes the shape of two leaves and a stylized tulip.

RIGHT: This dainty crib quilt was made in about 1870. Elongated flower stems reach upward from a green urn or bowl. Each branch of the stems ends in a red flower with a yellow center, while in the center of the quilt is a stem of stylized tulips. There is no border, but lines of quilting around the edges give the appearance of one.

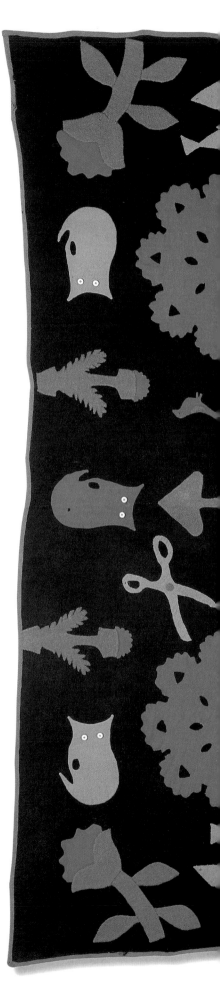

LEFT: *The bright-eyed cats are smaller than the open pair of scissors, each complete with a realistic holding pin. The proportions seen in folk-art quilts are one of the elements that make these pieces so lively to look at.*

ABOVE: *Urns of strange, cactus-like flowers are topped by dove-like birds. The green double-arrow motifs are similar to ones found throughout the world.*

RIGHT: *Made in New York State in about 1840, this quilt shows folk art at its most charming. A regular pattern has been created using the odd proportions and the general naivety of the designs against the black wool background. The four white horses with their tack are the most realistic motif by far. Note the fish swimming happily in a sea of flowers. The motifs in the center top and bottom could be Masonic devices.*

Broderie Perse

THE CUTTING OUT of patterned motifs from a piece of fabric, usually a valuable or scarce one, and then sewing the cutout onto a different background is known as broderie perse. This French term, meaning Persian embroidery, is thought to have originated around the time of the Great Exhibition of 1851, which was held in London at the magnificent Crystal Palace, a vast exhibition hall.

At this time, when the British Empire was at its height, all things Eastern were in vogue, a fashion that traveled quickly from Britain to North America, as did the making of quilts using the technique to apply Middle and Far Eastern motifs, particularly those cut from expensive chintz, onto cheaper plain fabrics.

The method had, in fact, been used for very many years before, with a number of fine examples of broderie perse quilts surviving from the late eighteenth and early nineteenth centuries. Motifs are frequently arranged sparsely, and the background is heavily quilted, frequently with trapunto added. On some specimens the cutouts were arranged to create a central medallion around which several borders were added, some of which might have themselves been made from broderie perse motifs. Most cutouts were applied with a close buttonhole stitch that added a decorative touch.

LEFT AND RIGHT: This magnificent broderie perse "album" quilt, made probably in Maryland, is, thankfully, signed and dated: "Lily Corliss 1842 + Lydia Corliss 1843." Beige printed strips have been laid across the background fabric trellis-fashion, and the motifs, mainly flowers with some pieces of fruit and birds, were applied in the spaces created. Note the cut-off corners at the bottom.

Baltimore Album Quilts

LSO KNOWN AS presentation quilts and autograph quilts, album quilts were originally made as presents to commemorate a festive event such as a wedding, or as presents and remembrances to be given to family and friends who might be moving from one place to another, often far away.

Various people each stitched one appliqué square with a different design on it. These pieces were then joined, usually sashed, and presented to the recipient, who might be going too far away to have much hope of returning for visits with these relatives or neighbors, and the quilt was a reminder of the part of the person's life that was being left behind. Often the designs had particular relevance to the person to whom the quilt was being given, and sometimes the squares were

LEFT AND ABOVE: *Unlike most quilts of the time, many Baltimore album quilts are signed and dated, including this one, that says "Sara Schaefer Baltimore 1850." The colors of this example are absolutely typical of the type, as are the complex motifs, from the municipal building with the flag to the railroad sidecar with its two flags. The elaborate border of swags and individual flower stems is framed by the dark green Sawtooth pattern that acts as a binding.*

signed, hence the form's other name, the autograph quilt. In any case, the intention of the quilt was similar to that of an autograph album, a keepsake from a group of friends.

Quilts of this type were popular in the two decades before the outbreak of the Civil War, from about 1840, and in particular, a large number were made in and around Baltimore. The Baltimore album quilts, as they became known, are highly complex, with intricate designs and in many cases superb workmanship.

Some experts believe that many of the designs were devised by a small number of needlewomen, who then sold them to others to be stitched. The skill displayed on surviving examples of Baltimore album quilts varies from extremely fine, in some cases thought to be done by one

ABOVE: *This Baltimore album quilt, signed "Hannah Foote Baltimore 1850," has a highly personal feel. The red-roofed house in its idyllic country setting, milkmaid with the animals, the man in uniform, the boy with the dog – all create a feeling of involvement.*

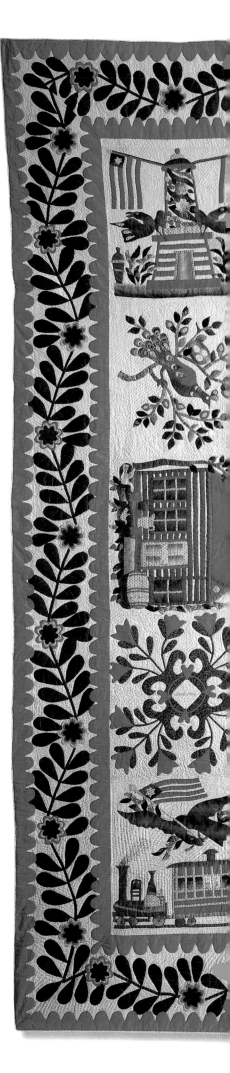

RIGHT: *This elaborate Baltimore album quilt was made in about 1840 by Sarah and Mary J. Pool, who each signed one floral square in cross stitch. The number of buildings and patriotic images is unusually large. The exuberance of the piece is enhanced by the red scalloped frame on each side of the border, which itself has a zigzag vine pattern interspersed with flowers at regular intervals. The sheer variety of baskets, urns, vases, and cornucopia is rivaled by the number of flower forms.*

LEFT: *The motif of a Greek lyre topped by a bird is frequently found on Baltimore album quilts. This one is enclosed by sprays of flowers that are worked in interesting combinations of color.*

BELOW: *The little train has a head of steam, ready to go, and the carriage is very finely worked. A large dark bird hovers overhead, carrying a large flag on a pole. What does the symbolism all mean to present-day viewers?*

individual, to very mixed, clearly made by several people with widely differing sewing talents.

The designs used on typical Baltimore album quilts include highly elaborate flower and leaf patterns, and baskets and cornucopia filled with fruit and floral motifs; trees; seascapes and harbor views; landscapes and idyllic views; churches and other buildings, both well-known landmarks and more personal references; means of transportation, such as trains, ships, and carriages; birds, butterflies, and occasionally other animals; patriotic symbols, such as an eagle carrying a flag

in its beak; and even memorable public events. Another favorite motif was the pineapple – a universal symbol of hospitality – in numerous forms.

Fabrics were usually fine: silk, high-quality cotton, and lightweight wool. Colors on Baltimore album quilts tended to be comprised of bright primaries, especially red, green, blue, and yellow; and the background fabrics were almost always white, allowing the various motifs to stand out.

ABOVE: *Mary Brown's quilt is a superb example of the use of traditional Baltimore album colors.*

LEFT: *This lovely appliquéd quilt, with pieced six-point stars in the first frame surrounding the central section, was made for Israel and Elizabeth Reynolds of East Nottingham (now Calvert), Maryland. It bears the inscription: "Mary Brown/Made in the 75th year of her age 1851." The maker, who was also from East Nottingham, has used floral motifs arranged in a medallion setting to make a most unusual quilt.*

The blocks were usually set square, and when sashing was utilized, it was generally a strong color, to contrast sharply with the white or cream background. Occasionally, quilts are seen without sashing, in which case the areas along the seams are usually quilted heavily instead. Some album blocks are set on point to provide a strong diagonal feel to the quilt.

Luckily for us, because so many of these quilts were made beautifully and from good-quality materials, and because they were almost always regarded as the finest bedcovers in the house, they were well cared for and not used every day. As a result, many have found their way into museums and private collections, where they are looked after and treasured to be passed on to the generations to come.

ABOVE: This Baltimore quilt is unusual in that it is almost entirely floral, with a few birds hiding among the flowers and leaves. Made in about 1850 for Eleanor Gorsuch, whose family then owned much of present-day Baltimore, it is attributed to Mary Simmons.

Pictorial Quilts

ALSO KNOWN AS STORY QUILTS, quilts that are basically pictorial in nature are usually worked in appliqué. This method provides a broader scope for achieving a sense of realism – however stylized – than quilts that are pieced together as patchwork, which tend to assume a more geometric and angular form.

Although much of the inspiration for patchwork and appliqué design comes from naturalistic forms, attempts to create pictures in fabric that carry a high degree of realism are a relatively new aspect in the history of these forms of textile decoration. In fact, quilts that feature landscapes, sometimes known as scenic quilts, are a twentieth-century innovation that probably date from about the early 1920s. Today, many quilts of this type are worked as combinations of

LEFT AND ABOVE: The center block of this charming quilt, made between 1865 and 1875 in New York, depicts a house with a lawn, flowers, and trees. Surrounding this block are smaller album-type blocks showing realistically styled farmyard animals – horses, cows, dogs, ducks – worked mainly in non-realistic colors. Each block is bordered in pink and separated by white sashing with pink strips at each junction, forming a series of Xs in the quilt.

ABOVE: *This delightful crib quilt is known as "Scenes from Childhood," depicting three beautifully drawn and executed images of family life. A cat, two dogs, and a cow vie with a stylized cornucopia of flowers.*

patchwork and appliqué, and can be found made from strips, or small squares that give the piece a mosaic effect, as well as using traditional applied techniques.

Because pictorial and story quilts are, by their very nature, highly personalized representations, it can be difficult to generalize about them. Each piece is truly unique.

In the early 1800s quilts were sometimes made with realistic representations of things like eagles and other patriotic images, ships, and

*LEFT: The quite small size –
38 × 38in (95 × 95cm) – and
highly pictorial content of
this unfinished quilt top from
about 1885 in New York
State makes it impossible to
know whether it was meant
to be a crib quilt or the
center of a larger medallion
quilt. However, its charm
and originality mean that
such quibbles are immaterial.
The choice of fabrics is
superb, from the ticking
house to the wavy-furrowed
fields to the ribbon-printed
trees with the birds on top.*

forms from nature like flowers and birds, instead of from repeated geometric or abstract patterns.

By the middle of the nineteenth century, Baltimore album quilts from Maryland and other parts of the country depicted fairly accurate scenes of buildings and modes of transportation mixed in with the floral and patriotic blocks that are prevalent on these pieces.

After the Civil War, blocks featuring real-looking animals, houses, and people, as well as the ubiquitous trees, vines, flowers, and fruit found in all quilt design, were made and sashed together; and occasionally the figures were simply applied to a plain full-size quilt top. Most examples that have survived are worked in appliqué.

One rare and beautiful group of story quilts, most of which were made by African-American quiltmakers, tells stories from the Bible. There are a number of fascinating examples of story quilts in collections across the United States.

In the twentieth century, as the fashion for home decoration, particularly wallhangings, developed, the scenic quilt has come into its own, with landscapes created by string piecing, and everything from seascapes to portraits fashioned from small squares like mosaic work being made. In addition, many group projects have been created, often by having individuals make blocks depicting local or relevant scenes and then joining the squares to make a large work for a church or local not-for-profit group. Hundreds of projects marking the Millennium have been worked, for example, by members of quilt groups, and as school and civic projects.

*LEFT AND RIGHT: This delightful crib quilt is
a veritable sampler of birds and butterflies
executed in realistic form. Made in
Pennsylvania, it is dated 1874 and emphatically
signed or dedicated "Flora." Several shades of
blue have been used to make the sashing and
matching border, and the color of the binding
is different from the pink used elsewhere.*

LEFT: *As in much pictorial work, the scale of the various elements is somewhat skewed. The small birds could make a whole meal of any of the fruit on this charming tree.*

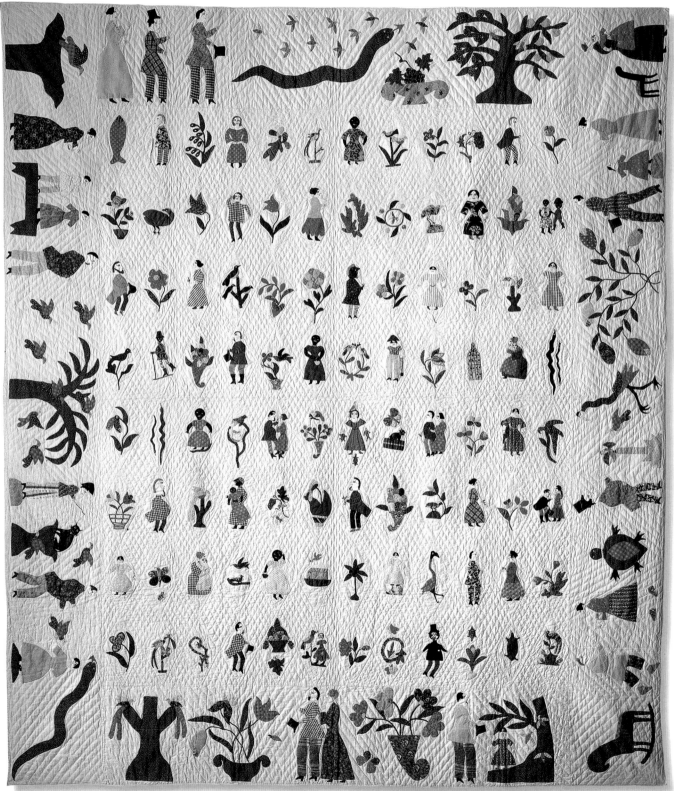

LEFT: *Mysterious figures populate the entire quilt, none more so than a boy waving a stick at a jolly-looking cat that sits in wait for one of the birds to land on the birdbath.*

LEFT: *Known as "The Asylum Quilt," this enigmatic piece was, according to tradition, made in about 1850 by an inmate at Spring Grove State Hospital, the third oldest mental institution in the United States. We know that it was raffled to raise money for the hospital and that it was won by Dr. John Smith of Boonsboro, Maryland. Because medical records are confidential, no one has been able, even today, to do proper research, and the quilt maker remains anonymous, but she was supposedly a young woman who was pregnant when she came to the hospital and who later died there.*

Spring Grove hospital is in Catonsville, now part of greater Baltimore, and the traditional area influence can be clearly seen in the appliqué work, with its parade of interesting characters and the fascinating natural forms. Who all the people are and what it whole quilt means still remain unknown.

ABOVE: *The blocks in this album quilt from about 1930 depict a series of twenty-five different flowers in pots in a fairly realistic fashion. The soft moss-green color of the sashing and side borders complements the brighter colors used for most of the flowers. The multicolored shapes in the border are the most stylized element.*

Bible Quilts

TALES FROM THE BIBLE and other religious writings have provided ideas for all manner of works of art for many hundreds of years, and by the nineteenth century, when quiltmakers began to create quilts that incorporated a narrative thread, the biblical stories, proverbs, and parables they knew so well proved to be a particularly rich source of inspiration.

Quilts based on biblical themes – those with a religious or moral story to tell – were particularly popular in the nineteenth century, especially among African-American quiltmakers, many of whom were former slaves, and few of whom had been taught to read and write. For many of them, the stories with which they were most familiar were the ones that were read at church on Sunday and at home during the rest of the week, and there are a number of surviving quilts on a biblical theme made by nineteenth-century African-American quilters.

BELOW: Noah and his family prepare to enter the Ark after the animals, in traditional two-by-two formation, have climbed the gangplank. The sons are bearded, and their wives are dressed in typical clothes worked in fabrics from the period.

RIGHT: This magnificent Noah's Ark quilt has a printed (or possibly painted) background on which the plants, animals, and people are appliquéd. The work is very fine and highly realistic. It is signed in the center bottom: "Mrs. L.Converse/1853/ Woodville Jefferson Co. N.Y."

Like other story quilts shown in the previous pages, of which most Bible quilts are a form, these religious quilts tend to be appliqué work, and most have a naive quality, frequently with wide discrepancies of scale and a lack of obvious planning that generally add to their many charms.

Other styles of religious quilts exist in addition to the pictorial ones, especially those that incorporate Bible quotations or moral or religious verses worked into their design. These quilts would often include blocks of patchwork patterns inspired by, and named for, biblical and religious themes.

LEFT: *Eve holds the forbidden apple while Adam and the Serpent look on. The fruit tree and the oak would have been familiar to the quilt-maker, but most of the animals were probably known only from pictures in books. Perhaps she traced them and simply used them in the sizes in which they appeared in the original source material.*

ABOVE: *The palm trees might have been exotic specimens to Abby Ross, but most of the insects that occupy the "tropical" islands would certainly have been part of daily life, at least in the warm months.*

ABOVE: *The life forms crowded into the small watery space at the bottom of the quilt include fish, amphibians, and reptiles. The animals above include a bird bigger than an elephant, and a very playful lion.*

ABOVE: The Tree of Life, in which a tree appliquéd to overflowing with animals (especially birds), leaves, and flowers constituted the main motif, became popular in the early nineteenth century. In the earliest examples, the pattern was frequently worked in broderie perse, but it soon had become a standard theme for appliqué work. Before long, it had been transported into the Garden of Eden as a feature in Bible quilts.

In this beautiful quilt, made by Abby F. Bell Ross from Irvington, New Jersey, in about 1874, the big tree and the sky are occupied almost exclusively by birds, with the quadrupeds – who are seen in an amazing variety of sizes – anchored very firmly on terra firma. The overall sense of movement throughout the quilt is quite spectacular.

Alphabet Quilts

ALPHABETS HAVE BEEN used as learning devices on needlework samplers for hundreds of years, and in addition, lettering occasionally appeared on quilts before pictorial (story) quilts and Bible quilts became popular (see pages 152–59). But the use of the alphabet as a design feature in its own right on quilts is a twentieth-century innovation.

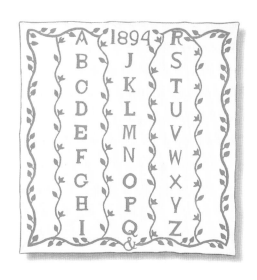

A few alphabet quilts appeared just at the end of the nineteenth century, but the fashion for quilts, and later wallhangings, featuring all the letters in order really took off during the 1920s. Numerous patterns for letters and numbers in different type styles appeared in magazines and newspapers, and were marketed by the many

ABOVE: *This elegant red and white piece, made in Pennsylvania – without a doubt in 1894 – uses the letters in three vertical strips separated and bordered by appliquéd vines.*

LEFT: *By adding the date, 1912, at the bottom, the maker of this Pennsylvania quilt has created 30 squares that can be arranged symmetrically. The large chunky letters are red appliquéd to a white block, and the sashing, in the same yellow that has been used on the border, is broken at each intersection by a four-leaved appliqué motif.*

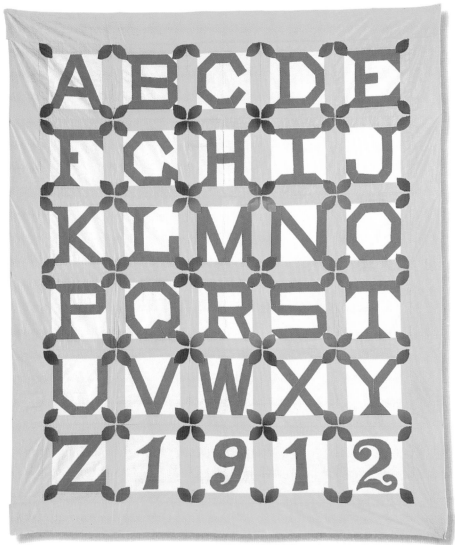

companies that sold needlework patterns, not just for patchwork and appliqué, but for quilting and embroidery as well.

Some of the surviving quilts from those early days of mass marketing combine sequential blocks of the applied letters with patchwork, while others show the letters arranged to create monograms and initials, and to spell words and to write verses and quotations, many of which have a religious theme; these were particularly popular in rural areas.

ABOVE: *The Lord's Prayer is reproduced on this quilt from Pennsylvania made in about 1895. Its simple colors add to its overall effectiveness.*

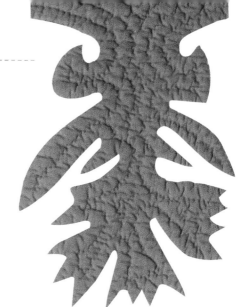

Hawaiian Appliqué

THE TERM "HAWAIIAN APPLIQUE" refers to both a quilt pattern and a stitching technique. The complicated curving shapes that are used in Hawaiian appliqué designs are usually turned under and sewn in a particular method that, although it is used in other ways, is called Hawaiian appliqué.

Hawaii was an ancient country long before it became an American state. Originally occupied by Polynesian explorers who ventured from farther south and west in the Pacific, it was colonized by European settlers in the late 1700s. By the mid-1800s, the colonists included missionaries who taught the local women to sew, a skill they had not needed before, since clothing in the balmy climate was minimal and was fashioned from full widths of local material.

LEFT AND ABOVE: This wonderful mulberry-colored Hawaiian quilt is a variation of the "Kukui O Kahuku" pattern. A Hawaiian appliqué quilt was traditionally given its name by its maker, and many, such as this one, were based on plant forms and given the name of the flower that inspired the design – here the kukui. Made in about 1880, this example was owned by a family by the name of Wilcox from Kahuku on Oahu Island, hence the name means "kukui of Kahuku." The echo quilting is spectacular.

ABOVE: This splendidly intricate quilt is red on white, making it a highly traditional piece of work, since these colors are the ones most often used. Called "Breadfruit," it was made between 1915 and 1925.

Sewing technique was quickly learned, but the traditional patchwork and appliqué block patterns that the missionaries taught were discarded for the designs that now carry the name of Hawaiian appliqué. Based on the universally known papercut with four folds in the square, these patterns, with their intricate flowing curves, are cut from a single piece of fabric and evoke the islanders' passion for natural forms to create a unique type of quilt. The echo quilting, which follows the shape of the pattern with parallel rows of stitching, represents the waves of the ocean lapping against the shores.

RIGHT: The colors used to make this beautiful Hawaiian appliqué quilt may not be traditional, but the design most assuredly is. This quilt was made in about 1988 by Mealii Kalama of Honolulu, who named it, in keeping with her traditional right, "Flower Garden." The pale-colored streak across the center is probably the result of the quilt's having been folded and exposed to the light. The stitching of the design is superb, especially the petaled terminal shapes, and the fabulous echo quilting has been executed with great sensitivity and precision.

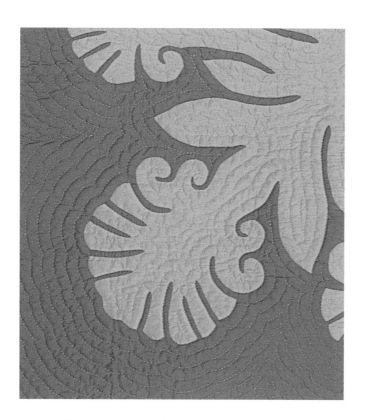

ABOVE: Each element in the design – the points of the leaves, the curves of the flowers, and the bottoms of the indentations – has been sewn in place beautifully, and the quilting within in the pink areas enhances the shapes extremely well.

Reverse Appliqué

REVERSE APPLIQUÉ is, in a sense, a quilting technique that is worked backward. Two, or many more, layers of fabric are basted together and a design is cut out of the top layer to reveal the fabric underneath, and it is then stitched in place.

The two most famous types of reverse appliqué occurred, presumably independently, on opposite sides of the world. The Kuna, or Cuna, tribe who live in the San Blas province and islands off the Atlantic coast of Panama developed the characteristic "mola," while the Hmong, a tribe found in the mountains of Laos, Vietnam, and Thailand, have a tradition of needlework called "pa ndau," literally "flower cloth," which includes their version of reverse appliqué.

While the technique used by both groups is similar, and the colors are almost always bright and highly contrasted, the designs, and the traditional uses to which the finished products are put, are very different. The Kuna molas are generally parts of garments, especially women's blouses,

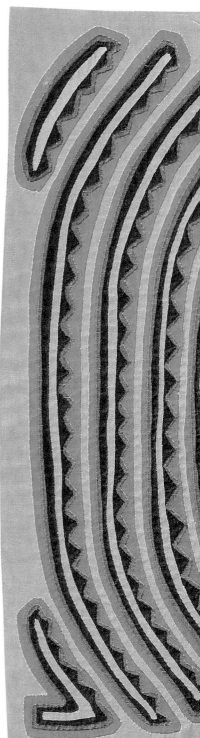

LEFT: *Made in about 1960, this mola is one of a pair used to make a traditional blouse of the type worn by the women of the San Blas Islands.*

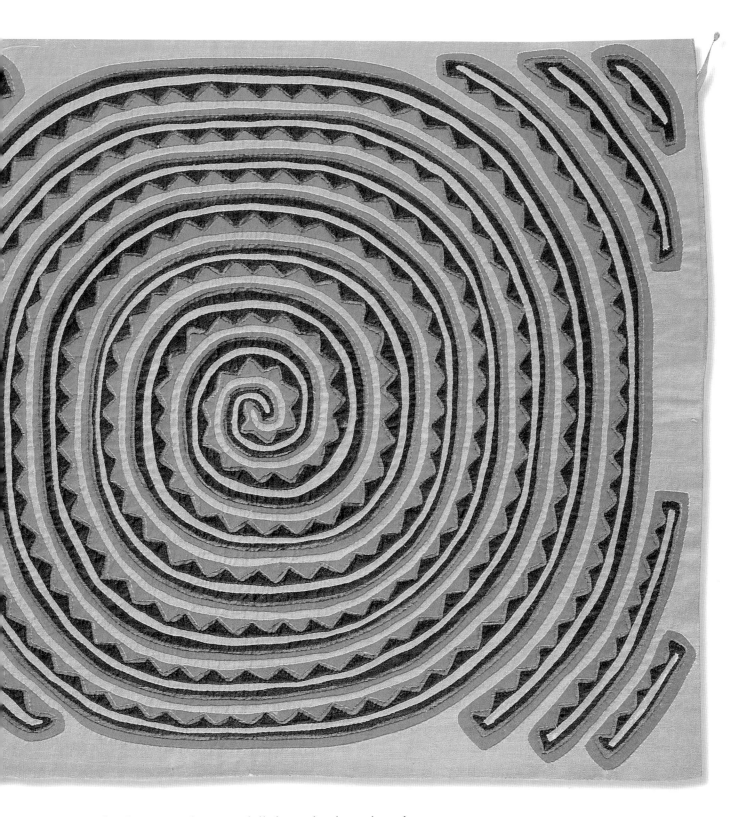

ABOVE: *The elegance and artistic skill shown by the maker of this mola, also from the San Blas province and dated about 1960, is equaled by her superb stitching technique, from the smoothness of the curves to the sharpness of the points. Abstract in design, it is nevertheless wholly traditional in its effect. Like many of its contemporaries and successors, this quilt was probably made for the tourist trade.*

RIGHT AND BELOW: *The "Angel de la Guardo,"
or Guardian Angel, on this mola was worked in
cotton in about 1960. The Kuna needlewoman
who made it must have wanted to make sure there
was no mistake about what was depicted – she
worked the title twice, top and bottom, in
wonderfully intricate, multicolored letters. The
chains of flowers along each wing and on the
angel's bodice (see details below) are chain-stitch
embroidery. The straight lines of the "feathers" on
the bottom edges of the wings are unusually
narrow and tricky to work. The moon and stars
(or is the right-hand one a comet with its tail?) are
golden yellow, while the background is a riot of
color. Note her fairy's wand on the right-hand side.*

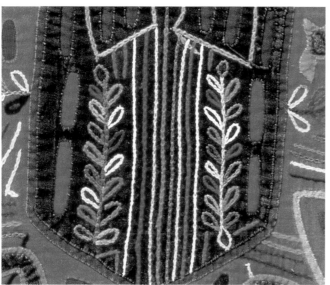

ABOVE: *The fanciful figures on this mola, dating probably from the 1930s, are probably taken from known animals. Perhaps the central figure is a mythological creature or an ancient god. The figures in the top corners have flat tails a bit like beavers, and the winged beast on the right might be an insect or a bird. The underlying fabrics have been laid down as scraps and have not been sewn together, so raw edges can be seen in places where they overlap. Embroidery, mostly chain stitch, embellishes the detail areas on all the figures.*

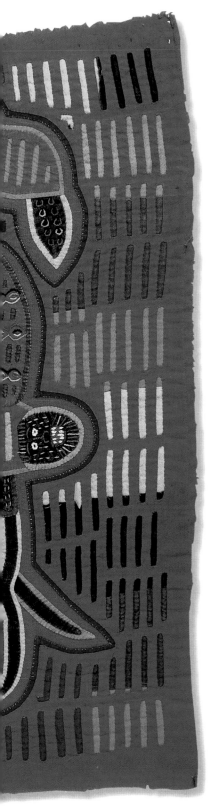

while pa ndau textiles, which include embroidered pieces as well as appliqué, are used in bedcovers and tablecloths as well as to decorate accessories such as belts and hats.

Large pa ndau pieces, such as bedspreads, have a backing, but are not quilted and have no batting. Any example of reverse appliqué will, of course, be fairly thick because of the multiple layers of fabric that are used to create the design.

The designs of both traditions are often taken from nature. Pa ndau work is generally highly geometric and abstract, while molas feature vast numbers of fanciful forms including people, fish, animals (both real and imaginary), and plant life. There are plenty of examples of purely geometric work in molas, too. Traditional designs are wonderfully intricate and multicolored, with molas showing many shades of primary colors.

BELOW AND RIGHT: This upside-down flying lizard is a later piece, and is much more finely finished than the one opposite. Each cutout strip, except for the lifelike eyes, is backed by a single color, and it appears that black was used for both the top and the bottom layers of fabric. The zigzag white teeth look almost like rickrack.

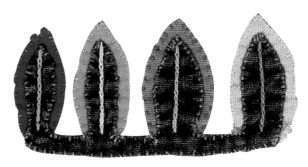

Traditional Quilting

QUILTING – THE STITCHES that hold the layers of a quilt together – makes the quilt. Each stitch can be large or small, even or uneven, placed at random, or carefully planned and executed. They enhance a piece of fabric, plain or pieced, in a unique way.

This vibrant Mennonite Joseph's Coat quilt, with its diagonal border and exquisitely worked stripes, was made in Pennsylvania in about 1890.

Quilting has probably been used on fabric since humans began to clothe themselves. Many ancient civilizations have yielded evidence of quilted garments, and fragments of quilted cloth from the Middle Ages still exist. The word was used in various forms before the thirteenth century, and could describe quilted bedcovers as well as clothing. Quilted armor was worn by medieval soldiers under their chain mail for comfort and protection; and women in many areas of Europe wore quilted petticoats, which were taken by the first settlers to North America, where they were worn until the eighteenth century.

ABOVE: *The double nine-patch blocks are quilted, like the rest of the piece, with straight lines that form a grid. Because the blocks are on point, the stitching is worked through the diagonal of each square.*

LEFT: *The maker of this floral strippy quilt is unknown, but it comes from Haydon Bridge, Northumberland, in the Northeast of England. Made in about 1870, it consists of nine strips of printed cotton, five dark and four light. The quilting, which follows the strips in traditional fashion, is especially fine, particularly the beautifully planned and executed running feather.*

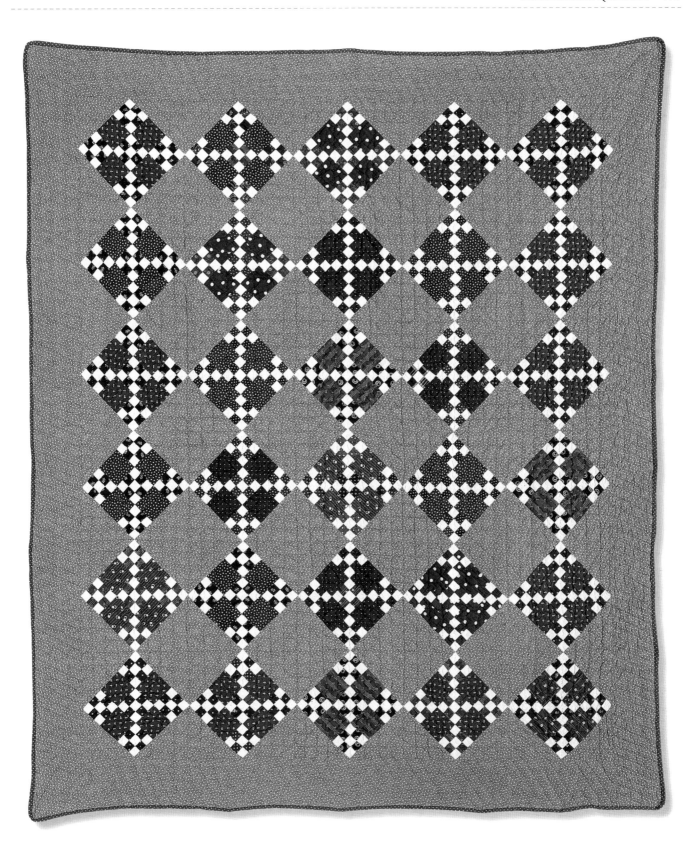

Fine quilted clothing was extremely fashionable in seventeenth- and eighteenth-century Europe, and the skills needed to produce it were widely known and practiced. The techniques went with the early colonists to North America, and the garments and covers that were produced no doubt helped many people to survive the harsh extremes of climate.

By the nineteenth century, the skills involved in quilting were being used particularly to create bedcovers, many of

ABOVE: Navy print and white double nine-patch blocks are set on point and spaced and bordered with sharp green in this quilt from about 1885.

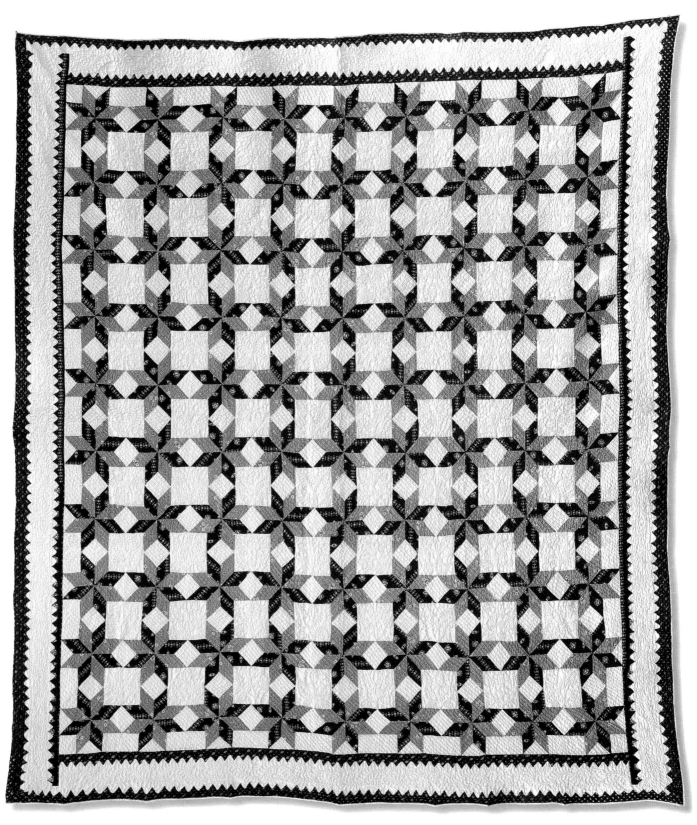

ABOVE: *The LeMoyne Stars on this fabulous quilt from Ohio, made in about 1860, are pieced from red and blue calico prints, spaced with white squares, and finished with a Sawtooth border. The exquisite quilting in the white spacer squares and border consists of floral motifs, while the rest of the quilt is stitched with simple crosshatching.*

RIGHT: *It is hard to beat navy and white for dramatic impact, and this Feathered Star quilt, made in about 1860, certainly has it. Each feathered star has at its center a simple navy-blue LeMoyne star surrounded by white, and the large stars, also navy, are spaced with big white squares. The triple border, quilted in simple crosshatching, frames the piece beautifully.*

BELOW: *Each of the large white spacer blocks is beautifully quilted with a feathered wreath, and crosshatching is used to fill in the blank areas.*

them highly decorative, on both sides of the Atlantic. During this time, three of the most-admired quilting traditions that we know today reached their height – the quilts, mainly wholecloth and strippy, from the Northeast of England, the geometric woolen quilts from Wales, and the wealth of quilts made by the Amish people, mainly in Pennsylvania and then in the Midwest.

The quilt as we know it consists of layers of fabric – usually two with a layer of batting between – held together by decorative stitching that creates a pattern. The top layer can be a single piece of cloth, known as a wholecloth quilt; or it can be pieced, either as patchwork or appliqué patterns or from long strips of cloth (a strippy). The middle layer of padding was originally made from natural fibers like wool fleece or combed

cotton, or from old blankets. Nowadays, the most widely known batting is made from polyester, although wool and cotton, or a blend of polyester and cotton, are all used. The bottom layer, called the backing, is generally made from a single piece of plain fabric in a color that coordinates with the top, but prints are often used, and some quilts have a pieced patchwork backing that creates effective reversible bedcovers.

ABOVE AND LEFT: This Mennonite piece, made in Pennsylvania in about 1865–75, is unique. The large, abstract floral motifs are appliquéd, and they and the bright yellow background are beautifully quilted.

A wealth of patterns has been handed down. Designs include cables and ropes, feathers, wreaths, baskets, and floral motifs such as leaves, vines, and flowers. Modern abstract motifs can be found, together with stipple and meander quilting; and simple shapes can be adapted for trapunto or stuffed-work quilting, as well as Italian, or corded, quilting. Quilting traditions from other cultures abound, most notably the echo quilting found in Hawaiian appliqué quilts and Japanese sashiko.

ABOVE AND BELOW: Made in about 1855–60 in Ohio or Maryland, this exquisite appliqué quilt, with its latticework baskets, pinwheel flowers, and vine border, is quilting at its best. The flower blocks are cross-hatched, and the blocks are separated by running feather "sashing."

Strippy Quilts

L ONG A FAVORITE of quilt collectors and interior decorators, the strippy quilt, which has been around for well over a hundred years since it was first made on the borders of England and Scotland, has a clean, modern look that goes with most types of decor, from loft minimalist to subdued country.

RIGHT AND OPPOSITE ABOVE: **This strippy quilt is unusual in that all 13 of its strips are made from calico prints in cream, brown, mustard, and pink. The quilting style is traditional, following the strips in patterns such as twist, zigzag, and diamonds. Made in Dinnington, Northumberland, it dates from about 1830.**

OPPOSITE: *Neither the maker of this quilt, nor the place where it was made are known, but its form, and the quilting patterns used, make it fairly certain that it is a Northeast strippy. Made in about 1900, it has five strips of yellow and four of gold faded almost to cream. The beautiful quilting follows the strips in traditional fashion, showing from each edge running diamond, plait, rectangle, fan, and swag. The intricate rectangle pattern is not as well known as the others.*

The strippy quilt, as well as its descriptively quaint name, seems to have originated in northern England, particularly in the northeastern counties of Durham and Northumberland, and the Scottish Borders. In these areas from the early 1800s until the end of the century, when machine-made bedcovers became more popular, both men and women were engaged in quilting as a livelihood. They participated in a cottage industry – literally, as most of them lived and worked in the small cottages that were standard housing for the large numbers of working miners in the area – that kept the skills of quilting alive until the late twentieth century, when the importance and artistic value of quilts were generally recognized again.

Strippies, as they are affectionately known, probably provided a way to stretch more expensive fabrics into a size large enough for a bedcover. Cotton fabrics in the past were almost always

RIGHT AND BELOW: This heavily quilted mustard and cream strippy quilt was made in 1899 by Mrs. Isabella Calvert, of Thornley, County Durham, as a wedding present for her sister Barbara. The Roman sateen fabric was very popular, both for its sheen and for its texture when it was quilted. The running diamond, fan, and rose patterns follow the strips, while the feathered cable, crosshatching, and diamond infill patterns overlap the seams in places. The back of the quilt is also made of sateen, in dark pink.

woven only a yard wide, which was only half the width needed for a bed. By cutting a costly length of fabric into strips the right length for the bed and alternating them with strips of less expensive, usually unpatterned, material, an attractive and useful quilt could be created.

Most strippies are arranged with an even number of plain – often white or cream – strips alternated with an odd number of solid-color or printed ones, which means that the colored strips are generally placed on the outside edges and in the center of the quilt. The quilting generally follows the strips, although there are beautiful examples in which the pattern strays over the seam to give the feel of a wholecloth quilt. Even the simplest border-type patterns and grids on most strippies were finely worked, and they give a beautiful texture to the finished article.

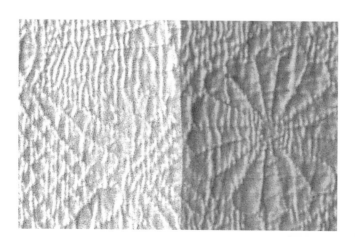

ABOVE: *The maker of this Turkey red and white strippy quilt was Miss Nixon, of Slaley near Hexham, Northumberland, who had a quilt club that she ran with her sister. The quilt was made between 1870 and 1880, and was given to another Nixon as a wedding present. This is an unusual quilt in that it has six strips of each color. The quilting alternates from strip to strip between running feather and diamond.*

RIGHT: Made by Mrs. Harriet Walton in Frosterley, County Durham, in about 1933, this lovely pastel strippy quilt is known by its present owner, the Beamish Collection in England, as the Weardale Chain Strip Quilt, named for the Weardale Chain pattern used to quilt some of the blue strips. The other beautifully worked patterns include running feather, leaf and feather, feather twist, and rose.

All manner of rope, braid, twist, and cable patterns can be found on old strippies, as well as vines and flower border patterns. Running diamond border designs, and fans in various sizes and shapes occur frequently. In addition, crosshatching is a widely used technique, usually on alternate strips. Sometimes individual strips were marked and quilted before they were joined together – the reason for this presumably being that this method took up less space both to work and to store them.

Most English strippies have no border, and they are often bound by turning the raw edges into the middle all around and sewing them in place, usually with a double line of stitching, to enclose the batting. North American strippies from the nineteenth century frequently have a decorative, often pieced, border, and they may or may not be bound. The backing fabric is usually plain, but printed fabrics were sometimes used, and occasionally the quilt is "reversible," with another pieced quilt on other side.

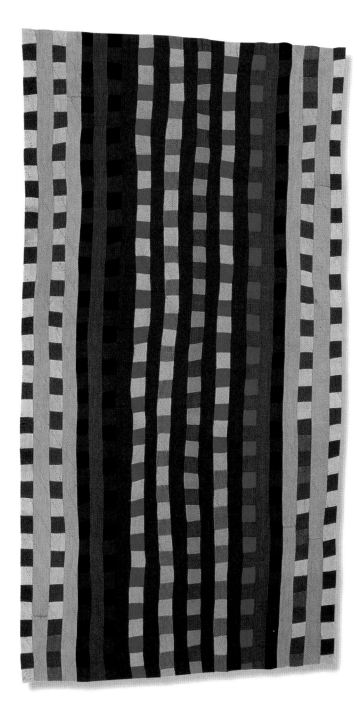

ABOVE: *This narrow cotton quilt is Midwestern Amish and dates from about 1940. It was probably made for a single bed, perhaps a child's. The strips are thin and alternate between pieced Chinese coins and plain strips of either black or brown. The somewhat rough-and-ready quilting consists of simple diagonal lines, fairly widely spaced for such a utilitarian piece.*

RIGHT: *The unusual strippy quilt was discovered in a thrift shop in Consett, County Durham, and like so many beautiful old quilts, almost nothing is known of its history. However, we do, somewhat unusually, know its date and the name of its maker: it is signed and dated "J. Foster, 1877." Blue and white four-patch blocks are turned on point and set with red triangles to make five strips, which are alternated with four strips of gray lengthwise stripes and two of a yellow-gold print fabric. It is beautifully made and finely quilted along the strips in twist and running diamond patterns, and unlike many of its contemporaries, it has a piped edge. The back of the quilt is made of white cotton.*

Many experts believe that the inspiration for the Amish Bars pattern came from the Northeast strippy. Neighbors of the early Amish settlers, some of whom would have come originally from the Northeast of England, would have used the strippy pattern, and the idea could easily be adapted to make use of large scraps or strips left over from other sewing projects by adding the typical wide borders to make the piece large enough to be used as a full-size quilt.

The strippy still flourishes today. On old quilts, the strips are usually cut to the same width. While many modern examples follow this pattern, there is now a great deal more flexibility in the size of the strips, and there are some lovely quilts with wide variation in the width of their strips.

Wholecloth and Medallion Quilts

THE FIRST QUILTS that were used to cover beds were probably created from whole cloth – simple pieces of material with batting and backing held together with rudimentary quilting. Medallion quilts, incorporating a series of borders surrounding a central motif, followed, and both have remained popular throughout many centuries.

A wholecloth, or plain, quilt is made from a single piece of fabric – or so it appears. In fact, several lengths of the same cloth – usually three – are almost always joined to make a piece wide enough for a quilt; to avoid having a seam down the center, one piece of fabric is usually cut in half lengthwise and sewn to each side of a full-width section. The fabric can be solid-colored or printed, but the textured design that is such a characteristic feature of wholecloth quilts comes entirely from the quilting.

Wholecloth quilts feature widely in the quilting traditions of the British Isles. Almost all early Irish, and many Welsh examples are wholecloth. Most are made from wool and are filled with fine wool batting, hence the closely worked quilting, which would have been necessary to keep the padding from shifting as the quilt was used and cleaned.

In the North of England likewise, particularly in the two neighboring counties of Durham and Northumberland, which are also well-known for

RIGHT: This Amish Open Square design is a medallion pattern. Made in Lancaster County, Pennsylvania, and dated "1914," it is typical of the way in which Amish quiltmakers took existing patterns and made them their own.

LEFT: Made in about 1900 in County Durham, this beautifully stitched Roman sateen wholecloth quilt lacks the filling patterns typical of the area's quilting. The corner fans in graduated sizes are particularly attractive.

LEFT AND RIGHT: *Elizabeth Sanderson, the best known of the "Allenheads stampers," often used this patchwork star pattern, and this particular quilt was probably put together and marked either by her or one of her apprentices in about 1900. In places, the marking is still visible. The intricate pattern in the stars is balanced by the simple crosshatched background of the center square.*

the strippy quilts discussed in the previous section, the wholecloth quilt was widely made, first from wool and later from finer, closely woven fabrics such as cottons like muslin, poplin, and sateen, and silk.

Many of the beautiful wholecloth quilts from the nineteenth century come from these northeastern areas. In the recently industrialized cities and urban conglomerations in other parts of Britain, people were being paid more and were spending more. They were buying home furnishings and textiles more cheaply than ever before, in the process abandoning the needlework skills, including quilting, at which many people had been highly proficient for several

RIGHT: *This quilt of Roman sateen was made by Mrs. M.E. Shepherd of Amble, Northumberland, for her son when he married. He never wed, so the quilt was never used. After Mrs. Shepherd's husband was injured in a mining accident, she ran quilting clubs to earn money.*

generations. However, in the isolated and sometimes inaccessible northern areas, where a large percentage of the population's breadwinners depended, often precariously, on mining for their livelihood, quilting remained an economical way to create warm bedcovers for family use and eventually became a method by which many people, both men and women, earned money.

Some of the Northeastern quilters were itinerant workers who traveled from place to place, living with a family for whom they marked and stitched one or more quilts before moving on to another job. A few became famous through their work. One, Joseph Hedley, known as Joe the Quilter, was in great demand as a quilter during his working life. After he retired, he went to live alone in a small thatched cottage in Homer's Lane near Warden, Northumberland, and there, sometime between 3 and 7 January 1826, he was brutally murdered. No one was

ABOVE: This quilt was made in about 1910 by Mrs. Stewart, a widow from Bowburn, County Durham. She ran a quilting club, which allowed purchasers to pay over a period of time – in this case, one shilling for 20 weeks – to give the buyer time to earn the money while the quilt was being made – an early layaway plan.

BELOW: *The maker of this sateen wholecloth quilt was Mrs. Lowe of Spennymoor, County Durham, whose family used its design for generations. Made in about 1940, the large whorl in the center finishes with a feathered circle. Crosshatching fills the background area, and the border is double running feather with corner swirls and fans.*

ever charged with his killing, but the shocking circumstances of his death lead to much publicity, and his celebrity grew. Only a few quilts can be verified as his work, but his fame lives on.

Many quilts of all kinds – wholecloth, strippies, and pieced work, both appliqué and patchwork – were made by quilting clubs that operated on the layaway plan. Those who wanted to have a quilt made, but could not afford to pay the high costs of materials and labor all at once, paid a

local quilter by the week. For the quilter, having a number of clients paying a certain amount each week meant that she – for most were women, either widows or those whose husbands had been injured in mining accidents – could afford the materials needed to make a quilt.

When North America was settled, quilting skills and patterns were carried from all parts of Britain to the New World, and the wholecloth tradition went, too. Fabrics were imported, and

the Early American designs that survive bear striking similarity to their British ancestors. Early quilts were usually wool and the quilting patterns were adapted from the familiar ones from Europe; but as the new nation expanded and developed, the wholecloth tradition was replaced by other forms of quiltmaking.

Medallion quilts were also widely made in Britain, especially in Wales and to a lesser extent in the Northeast, and by the end of the eighteenth century, the format had become part of the North American tradition. A medallion quilt has a clearly defined, almost always square center surrounded by at least one (but usually more) borders. The central area can be quilted, patterned, pieced, or appliquéd. In the nineteenth century, numerous quilts were made on both sides of the Atlantic, using as the central medallion cotton handkerchiefs printed with patriotic and historical motifs.

Welsh medallion quilts are recognized as being among the finest examples of the art. The quilting patterns used are generally geometric and, like Irish designs, they are based on traditional Celtic forms. The stitching in the best quilts is so beautifully worked on both

RIGHT: *This lovely rectangular medallion quilt is made using only three fabrics – two calico prints and solid blue – and piecing has been kept to a minimum. The center rectangle is an hourglass block, and four of the borders, which increase in size toward the outside, have triangle squares in the corners. Good contrast is achieved by the judicious use of curved quilting patterns, among them wave, fan, cable,*

RIGHT: This spectacular medallion quilt was probably made in the 1830s, possibly in Kentucky or Maryland. The main techniques used are highly intricate broderie perse and some extremely fine stuffed work, much of which is based on forms found in the chintz pattern, especially in the second quilted section from the center motif. Even the narrow outer border of tiny steps is appliquéd and the edge is corded. Quilts such as this, representing many months of work, usually made judicious use of expensive chintz fabric, but were rarely this elaborate.

LEFT: The Running Feather border flows fairly freely around the quilt, turning corners according to the quiltmaker's fancy. Each petal is stuffed separately, as are the grapes in the area surrounding the center motif. Occasionally a leaf or flower from the broderie-perse borders on either side is taken over into the stitching and stuffing.

RIGHT: Where the cream background areas are not covered with appliqué or stuffed, they are background-quilted. The wide outer section between the narrow stepped border and the biggest broderie-perse one is quilted with a closely space diamond grid, while all the other background areas are very finely stipple-quilted.

sides that they are effectively reversible, with the medallion design on one side and a wholecloth quilt on the other.

While the overall effect of a finished wholecloth quilt is completely different from that of a medallion quilt, the approach to designing and executing the quilting has much in common. In most cases, attention focuses on the central area, and many wholecloth quilts have a

quilted square in the middle that functions as a medallion around which the rest of the stitching is worked.

On medallion quilts the quilting in the borders usually follows the piecing, while the quilting patterns on wholecloth quilts tend to be worked in linear bands around the center to create the look of a series of borders, usually graduated in size and often with separate corners.

Amish and Mennonite Quilts

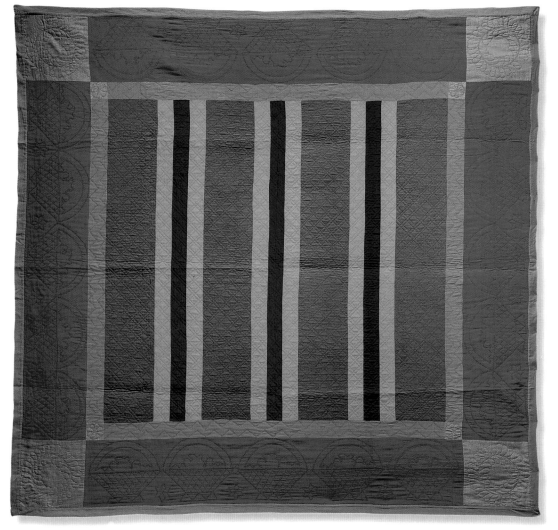

THE STITCHING OF QUILTS by Amish makers represents the best-known major tradition in American quilting. Amish quilts made before the 1970s and 1980s are highly collectible, and most have found their way into museum collections around the world. Those made in the previous generation are also popular and highly sought.

The Amish, the so-called Plain People, settled in self-sufficient communities in Pennsylvania in the eighteenth century, where they fled from their homes in Germany and Switzerland to escape religious persecution. During the nineteenth century numerous migrations took breakaway groups of Amish and a separate, less strict religious sect, the Mennonites, to New York State, Ontario, and the American Midwest, including Ohio, Indiana, Kentucky, and Oklahoma.

LEFT: *One quintessentially Amish design is Center Diamond; the other is Bars, where strips of different colors, and sometimes of varying widths, alternate within a series of borders to make a splendidly simple quilt with universal and timeless appeal. This version, made in Lancaster County in about 1925, is a prime example of how well this pattern can work. The colors do not blend, nor do they jar. Each element looks exactly right, from the bright blue corner square to the wide olive strips, and the quilting is superb.*

The Plain People came to the New World after two centuries of division and persecution in a number of European countries. By the late 1600s, two distinct groups had formed from a group of nonviolent Protestants known as Anabaptists: the Mennonites, named for their Dutch leader, Menno Simons, and a new group, the Amish, named for their Swiss leader, Jacob Ammann. Both groups had suffered greatly from persecution and a famine that was then raging through Europe.

When William Penn, an English Quaker who had been granted land in North America, decided to use his tract

ABOVE AND OPPOSITE ABOVE: This Lancaster County quilt from about 1920 is called Sunshine and Shadow, depicting light and shade in the fields. The borders are "floating" because they have no corner squares to anchor the center section.

ABOVE: *This Lancaster County Split Bars quilt, made in about 1920, shows signs of being an extremely well-designed scrap quilt, with its use of two different fabrics for the outer blocks and spacer strips between the corners and the borders.*

for what was at the time a particularly audacious plan, in which people of different religious faiths would attempt to live side by side in harmony, he contacted the Amish and the Mennonites with an invitation to become part of his "great experiment." His offer was accepted by boh groups, and by the middle of the eighteenth century nearly a hundred

families had arrived in Pennsylvania to begin new lives in their new home.

It was, and still is, the practice of the Amish to use and re-use that which was regarded as essential, and to eschew anything that they considered unnecessary. They still live simple lives in close-knit communities much as their ancestors did. They do not use electricity

or natural gas from municipal supplies. Their fields – for most Amish families are farmers and live on the land – are plowed by horses and planted and weeded by hand. Transportation for getting to town, to church, and to visit neighbors is provided by horse and buggy. Amish children are educated in one-room schoolhouses by Amish teachers, and religious meetings are attended regularly by the entire community.

The strict moral and religious code by which they live leaves little time for frivolity in any aspect of their lives, from the unadorned clothes they wear to their refusal to use cars or tractors. It has long been part of the Amish tradition to use fabric left over from dressmaking, done

ABOVE: Made in Pennsylvania between 1890 and 1900, this beautifully quilted Mennonite Diamond in the Square has Sawtooth edges, which are used fairly often for this pattern, and a very unusual tulip appliqué in the central square.

LEFT: *The center diamond in this Lancaster County quilt from about 1925 is made from nine-patch blocks and alternating plain blue spacer blocks quilted with the same flower that appears in each of the baskets in the outer border. The single clamshell quilting along the edges of the pink square is an unusual feature.*

ABOVE: *Each of the 13 multicolored Nine-Patch blocks has been quilted with a simple crosshatch worked across the diagonal of each square in both directions.*

by the women of the household, to make the quilts needed to cover all the members of the family during the bitterly cold winters, and while creating highly decorated work was not even considered, pride in their work and innate creativity could not be stifled.

A number of patterns, many probably adapted from those used by their non-Amish neighbors (all of whom are referred to as "English," which indeed most of them were in the days after the arrival of the earliest settlers), were gradually adopted and became generally associated with, and considered characteristic of, Amish work. Amish

quilts are almost never wholecloth, for buying a large piece of fabric for quiltmaking would certainly be thought wasteful when so many scraps were always available.

Some of the designs associated with Amish work, such as Bars and Diamond in the Square, or Center Diamond, are made from large scraps of fabric. These patterns often lend themselves to being heavily quilted; indeed, they require it to add interest to what would otherwise be an unbroken expanse of solid color. Other patterns, such Nine-Patch and Sunshine and Shadow, make use of the tiniest pieces of leftover fabric that every thrifty Amish housewife keeps in her scrap basket, and many of them have so many seams that the quilting patterns chosen are usually relatively straight-forward to stitch, but even they generally have a wide, plain border that can be heavily embellished.

The clothes worn by the Amish are always made of unpatterned fabric. Men wear black pants and jackets, and women's skirts and aprons are also dark-colored. All clothes are made at home, so black, dark brown, and navy always appear in scrap baskets. However, contrary to popular belief, not all Amish clothing is dark – blouses, shirts, and children's clothes all occur in bright, solid colors, from green, burgundy, and purple to magenta and turquoise, so a huge range of shades from pastel to rich can be found among a quiltmaker's selection and put to ingenious and striking use.

People who are unfamiliar with the Amish quilting tradition are often

ABOVE AND BELOW: The Double Nine-Patch blocks vie for attention with the Diamond Chain border of this wool Lancaster County quilt from 1890–1910, just as the Running Feather competes with the sashing.

ABOVE: The dramatic colors lift this Lancaster County quilt of about 1920–25 out of the ordinary. The center Diamond in a Square, made from small blocks of Sunshine and Shadow, has superb stitching around it.

surprised by the vibrancy of the colors they use: the combinations are often so unexpected and flamboyant that they seem to sizzle with verve and energy – particularly when set against a dark background, as is so often the case.

On the whole, members of the Mennonite sect are not as strictly proscribed as the Amish. They do wear patterned fabrics, so pretty, bright-colored prints – usually calico – are found on Mennonite quilts, combined with solid colors and the dark contrast shades. The reds, yellws, and oranges that were once forbidden to the Amish are a feature of Midwestern Mennonite pieces.

Mennonite patchwork and appliqué patterns were similar to the ones used by their Amish cousins, and many of the same quilting patterns are also seen. Simple single or double crosshatch is a widely used technique, and borders frequently have running diamond, sometimes with pumpkin seed, or plain or feathered cable. Flowers, particularly in the forms of stylized roses, feathered wreaths, and baskets – a very standard, utilitarian image – are also typical, popular motifs.

The stitching on most Amish and Mennonite quilts is finely worked, making them, for all their simplicity,

ABOVE: *This beautiful example of a 1920s Sunshine and Shadow quilt from Lancaster County has one unusual feature – the outside row of squares is, at second glance, a pieced inner border in the Chinese Coins pattern.*

objects of great beauty. Quilting patterns are traditional, and a number of them are similar to many of the ones that were used by the Durham quiltmakers (see pages 182–89).

Patterns were no doubt exchanged between friends and relatives across the ocean, and among neighbors, Amish and "English." The metal and wooden templates used to mark patterns were used over and over again, and many became treasured family heirlooms that were passed down from one generation to the next.

Appliqué is associated with "fancy" work in the Amish tradition and is much

RIGHT: This wool crib quilt in the Color Wheel design is Mennonite, made in Pennsylvania in about 1875. The wheels are pieced from scraps, including prints and plaids, and combined with a tan background and brown border to make a vibrantly earthy piece. The outline quilting and diagonal lines on the border are strictly utilitarian.

BELOW: This simple Center Diamond, made in Pennsylvania in 1920–25, displays a typical Lancaster County flair for dramatic color. The quilting, including the unusual flower pattern seen on the inner border, is of an extremely high standard.

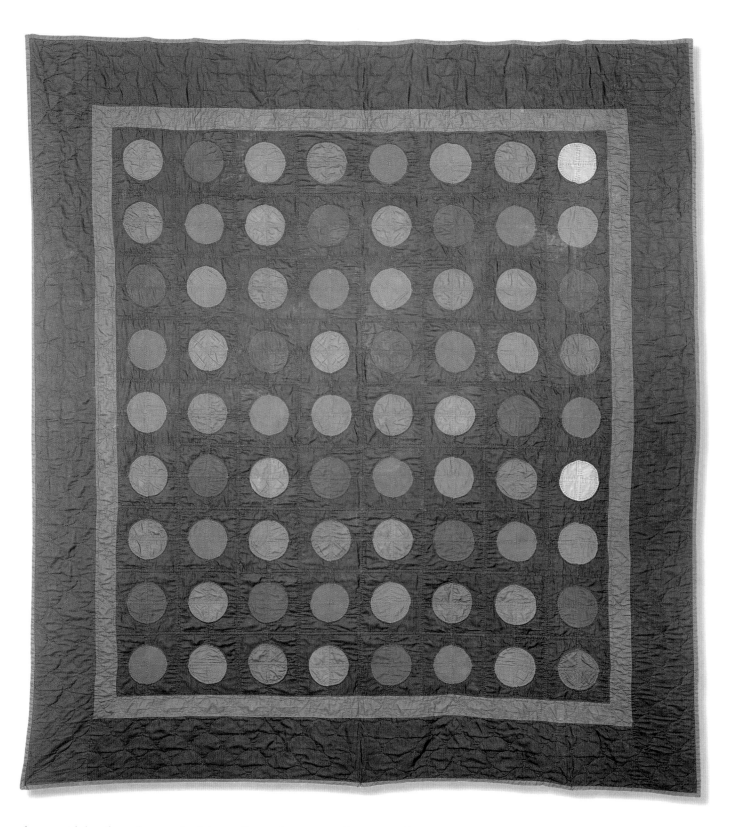

less widely found on Amish quilts, although some Mennonite quilts have applied work as part of their design. One exception is the Lancaster Rose, a simple but effective appliqué pattern that was originally devised by a group of Lancaster County quilters in 1976. Based on a traditional Tudor rose, the design was the women's contribution to the American Bicentennial celebrations and has become a very popular design. It is a pattern made for the highly developed

ABOVE: The bright, rich colors of the Circle pieces and the inner border look scintillating against the black background of this Ohio Amish quilt made between 1930 and 1940.

ABOVE: This Amish crib quilt, made in about 1890, is clearly a labor of love. The black-bordered square blocks alternate with bright blue plain squares quilted with a leaf. The quilting in the inner border is a simple double cable, while the outer border is an even simpler crosshatch grid.

cottage industry in quilts that has grown up in Pennsylvania in the past generation and, in a somewhat radical departure from traditional Amish custom, is often seen worked in patterned fabrics.

Amish quilts dating from the nineteenth and early twentieth centuries are sought by collectors around the world, but the tradition of making simple, beautiful quilts continues, especially in Lancaster County, Pennsylvania – long the heartland of the Amish people in America. Here, quilting is these days a thriving industry, and a wide selection of beautiful quilts made in the time-honored way by Amish quilters, utilizing the patterns and techniques that their mothers, grandmothers, and great-grandmothers used before them, can be found for sale.

Quilted Appliqué

WHEN MOST PEOPLE think of quilts, they have in mind thick bedcovers with a pieced or appliquéd top, a layer of batting in the middle, and a backing, in which the three layers are held together with decorative stitched designs. The permutations and variations are endless, and every quilt is unique.

There are two main approaches to quilting appliqué and patchwork. One is to follow the lines of the pieced design, either with simple outlining or more elaborate echo quilting. This method generally works well with appliquéd pieces, which are generally more intricate, and certainly less geometric, than patchwork patterns. Hawaiian appliqué is almost always quilted this way, for example, but simple quilting, like stippling or crosshatching, worked in the

LEFT AND ABOVE: *This unusual appliqué quilt is the work of a Pennsylvania Mennonite quiltmaker in about 1895. Each of the rather amazing, almost abstract eagles holds what looks like a lit cigarette in its beak. The vibrant colors, complementary red and orange offset by purple, are embellished with simple quilting that gives cohesion to the piece.*

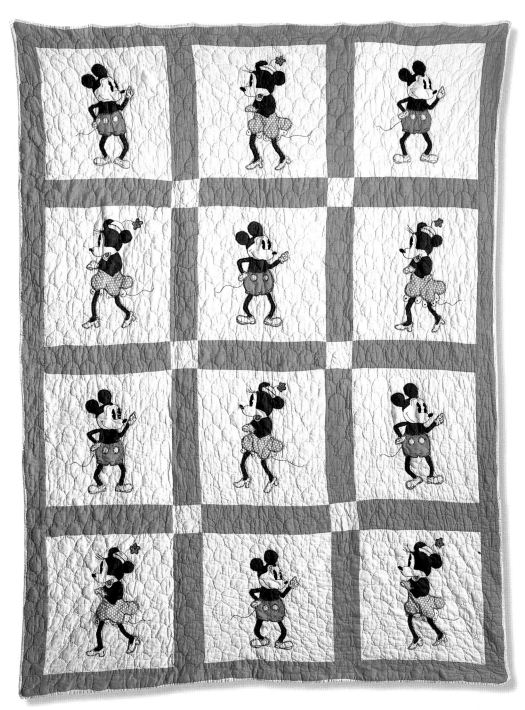

LEFT AND BELOW: This charming, naive piece has been dated at about 1935–40, which makes it a very early interpretation of Mickey and Minnie Mouse. It was almost certainly a child's quilt, with its repeating cartoon motifs and the bright red sashing. The quilting is an all-over clamshell pattern, which has been executed somewhat inexpertly.

background areas around appliquéd designs, generally makes the applied pieces stand out.

The second approach, which is better applied to patchwork, is simply to ignore the design created by the pieced work and to overlay it therefore with something completely different. Curved quilting on strip-pieced patchwork can provide a quilt with an entirely new effect, for example, as can straight lines worked on curved patterns. Quilting elaborate designs on to patterned fabric is usually wasted effort, because the fabric design will generally hide the stitching pattern. It is nearly always better to stick to simple background patterns on large printed areas.

The secret is to get the balance right and to use motifs of the proper size and

RIGHT: *This lovely, lively North Carolina Lily quilt was made in Ohio in about 1855–65. The pieced blocks are set on point with plain white spacer blocks, so the flower sprays are not slanted in the most usual setting for this pattern. The Double Running Feather quilting, worked in vertical and horizontal rows between each flower, creates the effect of sashing and blends the seams into the background, while the closely spaced parallel lines make each flower stand out from the white ground. The triple-banded border is quilted in a zigzag pattern that changes direction when the color changes.*

BELOW: *The red, mustard, and green flowers are pieced, and the stems and leaves have been applied to the white background.*

style. Well-known British quilter and teacher Barbara Chainey suggests looking for the "cues and clues" in the finished quilt – for instance, when making spacer blocks, you could use a quilted motif that echoes the patchwork or appliqué design.

If the pieced pattern is intricate or elaborate, it may be best to stick to simple quilting designs, but on quilts with a simple pattern, the quilting can be highly decorative, as on the best wholecloth quilts and strippies from Northumberland and Durham in Northeastern England.

As a contrast, although the Amish quilters normally tend to avoid fancy patterns, on many traditional Amish quilts the quilting is often complex, offering a stark contrast to the simplicity of the piecing.

Quilting in borders and sashing presents additional challenges. Narrow inner borders and sashing are usually improved by the addition of a simple quilting design, while wide outer borders, especially those that incorporate solid colors, offer a golden opportunity to enhance and lift any quilt out of the ordinary. Border patterns that match up in the center and at the corners look most professional, and can be achieved by careful measuring and marking.

RIGHT: *The shape and setting of the central flowerpot give this piece, made in Pennsylvania in about 1865, the feel of a medallion quilt. The quilting around the medallion is a flower-and-leaf design worked with tiny stitches; beyond this, the background is simple crosshatching stitched across the paired leaves as well. The appliqué motifs are quilted individually. Note that the corner leaf is missing in the top left-hand corner.*

LEFT: *The appliquéd flowers echo the colors of the pieced Sawtooth border in this quilt made by Mrs. Phoebe Watson, a widow from Low Burn Farm, Ireshopeburn, County Durham, in about 1840. She made this closely quilted piece by candlelight, and it was taken in lieu of rent by her landlord.*

Utility Quilting

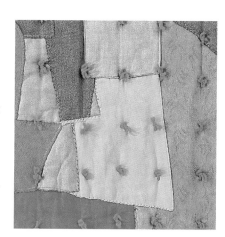

U TILITY QUILTING, also called big-stitch quilting, is a far cry from the tiny, neat, evenly spaced stitches of fine quilting, but it is still very much a part of the quiltmaking tradition. Types of utility quilting, humble in origin, are found in most cultures, used to secure layers of fabric and batting together to provide warmth.

The best-known type of utility quilting is almost certainly tying, in which threads are taken through the layers of a quilt from the top, brought back up close by, and tied in a secure knot before being trimmed and repeated at intervals all over the quilt. This is a quick and easy way to hold layers together, particularly if the batting is fairly firm. It is widely used on Log Cabin quilts, which have so many

LEFT: This scrap quilt was made in Pennsylvania in about 1920. Attributed to an unknown African–American maker, it is a wonderfully abstract version of the medallion form, quilted by tying at regular intervals with bright green thread that contrasts startlingly with the dark, somewhat somber colors used for the quilt.

ABOVE AND OPPOSITE ABOVE: *Made probably between 1920 and 1930, this lovely quilt is also attributed to an African–American quilter. Made of an eclectic assortment of oddly shaped scraps, it has at its center a rather squashed heart shape. It is tied at regular intervals with red thread in a way that has the effect of uniting all the elements into a whole.*

LEFT: This sashiko sampler was stitched in 1999, to be made into a bag later. The four designs are all traditional geometric forms that have evolved over hundreds of years.

seams that they can be quite difficult to quilt normally, and tying in various forms is a strong part of the African–American quilting tradition.

Japanese in origin and design, sashiko is an ancient and complex form of utility quilting that has become popular worldwide in recent years as a decorative technique. Worked traditionally on dark blue fabric using white thread, it was originally used to hold several layers of worn fabric and interlining together to make warm garments, and many examples of antique sashiko are so densely stitched that the thread not only creates the pattern but actually appears to be the fabric itself.

Another utility quilting tradition, kantha work, originated in the part of the Indian subcontinent that is now Bangladesh. Originally used to hold several layers of badly worn cloth together, it can now be seen on textiles of all kinds.

Most of the traditional "big" stitches are based on embroidery stitches, including cross stitch, French knot, half buttonhole, Mennonite tack, Methodist knot, and crow's foot. They generally have a rough-and-ready look that works well with many traditional patchwork patterns, and have the added advantage of being quick to stitch. Most of them can be worked in embroidery thread and even narrow ribbon, as well as quilting thread.

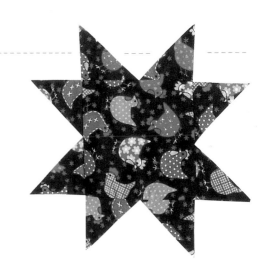

BELOW AND RIGHT: *This cheerful child's quilt was made by Sally Brown of Kingston upon Thames, England, in 1997 for her grandson, and is his favorite quilt. She has deliberately made the outline quilting stitches large, and the border is quilted in a meandering pattern of what she calls "chicken feet," based on the traditional crow's-foot stitch. The regular eight-point stars are pieced together from squares and triangles.*

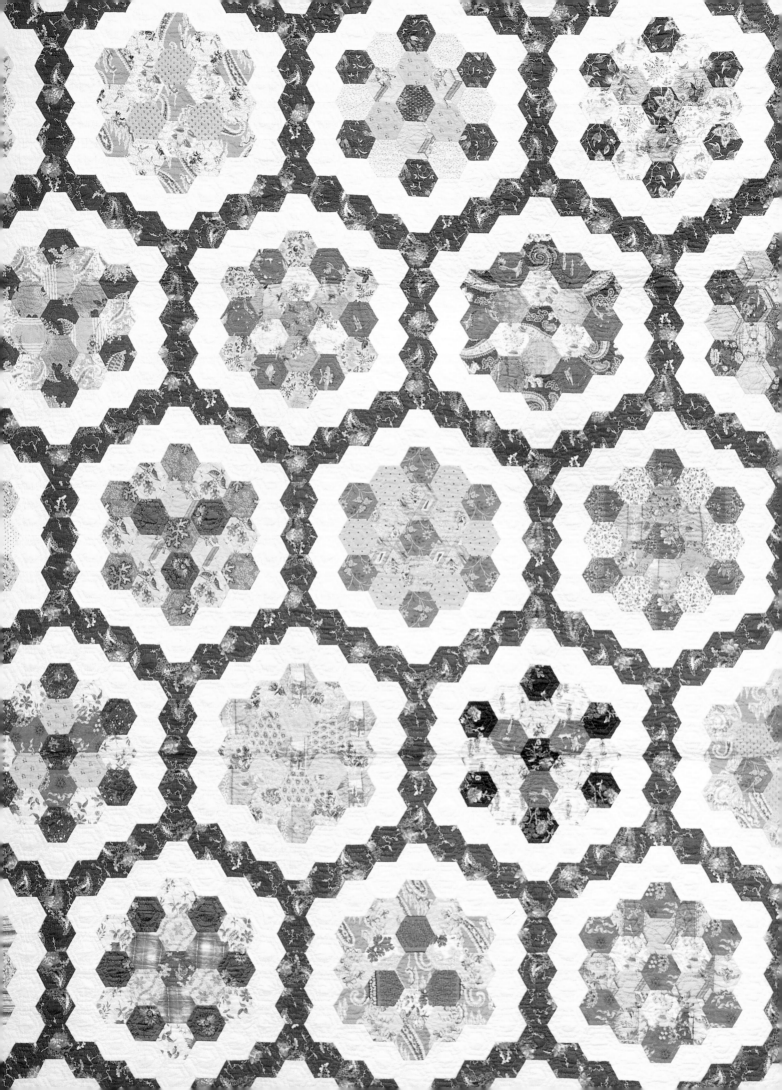

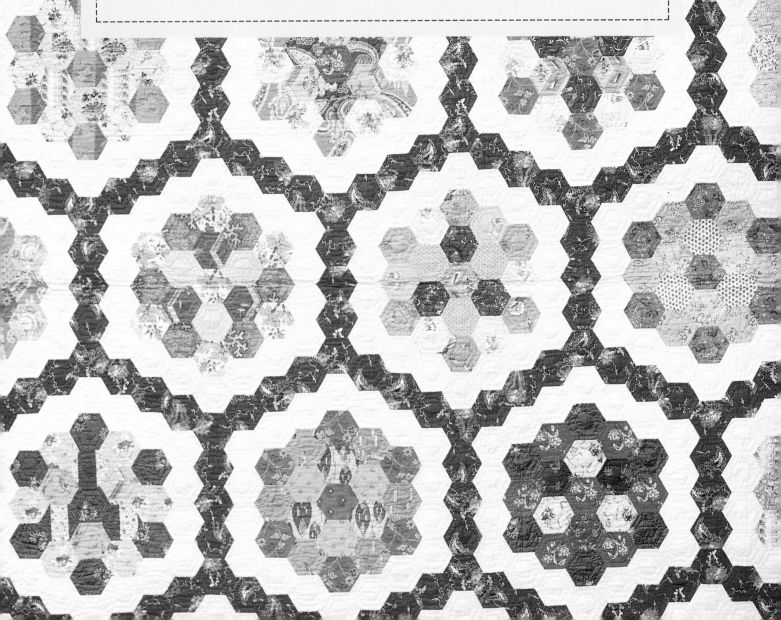

Patchwork

THE PLEASURE OF PATCHWORK comes from both the tactile feel of working with textiles, and the visual fun of mixing and matching colors to create interesting patterns.

The fabrics in this Honeycomb Hexagon quilt from about 1835 have been chosen and organized to make a fascinating piece of work from one of the quintessential patchwork designs.

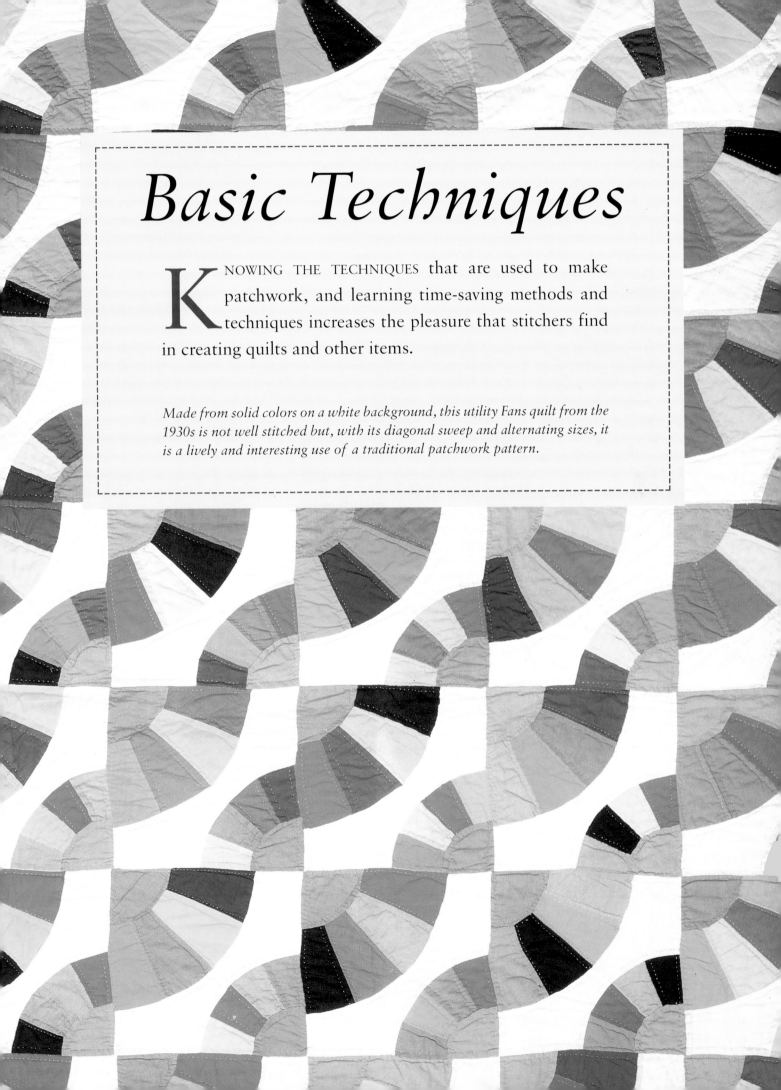

Basic Techniques

KNOWING THE TECHNIQUES that are used to make patchwork, and learning time-saving methods and techniques increases the pleasure that stitchers find in creating quilts and other items.

Made from solid colors on a white background, this utility Fans quilt from the 1930s is not well stitched but, with its diagonal sweep and alternating sizes, it is a lively and interesting use of a traditional patchwork pattern.

Tools and Equipment

TRADITIONALLY, STITCHERS throughout the world have made their quilted and patchwork pieces without the need for specialized equipment. But today there are dozens of labor-saving devices on the market to make the process of measuring, cutting, marking, and stitching easier and less laborious than it has ever been before.

Marking and Measuring Equipment

Patchwork is about accuracy, and accuracy is about careful marking and measuring. Most of the measuring tools you need can be found in a desk or sewing box, but some specialized marking tools, such as water-soluble pens and quilter's pencils, whose marks are much easier to remove than lead-pencil ones, are worth investing in.

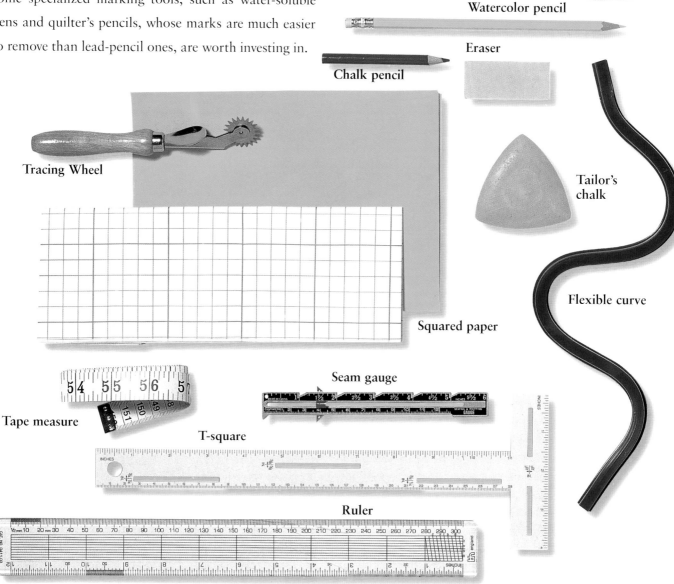

Water-soluble pen

Watercolor pencil

Eraser

Chalk pencil

Tracing Wheel

Tailor's chalk

Flexible curve

Squared paper

Seam gauge

Tape measure

T-square

Ruler

Templates and Stencils

Ready-made metal or plastic templates come in an array of styles and sizes, and although they can be expensive, they are also highly accurate and long-lasting. The "window" sets have a solid inner piece with a separate see-through outer panel. Others are multisized, with ¼ in (5mm) variations. A sharp craft knife and self-healing cutting mat are essential when cutting templates by hand. There are two choices of template material: plastic and cardboard. While cardboard is useful for single templates, template plastic is better for multiple cutting since it holds its shape better and doesn't drag or tear at the sides.

Quilting stencils are usually made of translucent plastic, which allows you to see through to the underside for matching patterns. If you prefer to make your own templates, there are useful aids for cutting and measuring accurately. The quilter's quarter and quarter-inch wheel are used for adding a ¼ in (5mm) seam allowance to straight and curved seams.

Sewing Equipment

The patchworker needs basic equipment for stitching, including needles, thread, both straight and safety pins – the latter can be used for "basting" the layers together ready for quilting – and thimbles.

Two types of needles are considered standard for quilters: "sharps" (ordinary sewing needles) for piecing and "betweens" (shorter needles) for quilting. For piecing, use ordinary sewing thread to match the fabric: cotton thread for pure cotton, polyester for cotton blends. Most people stitch in white or cream unless the fabric is very dark. Quilting is best carried out with special quilting thread, which is heavier than ordinary thread and pre-waxed. Many people don't like wearing thimbles, but you will probably find it useful to wear one when you are quilting large areas of fabric by hand.

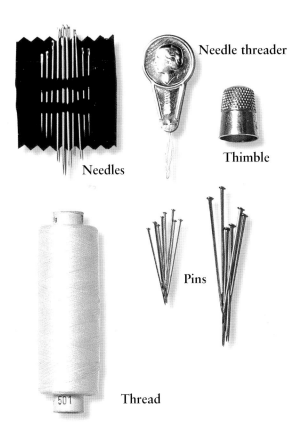

Needle threader

Thimble

Needles

Pins

Thread

Cutting Equipment

The rotary cutter, ruler, and self-healing cutting mat have changed the face of patchwork in the past 20 years, and most of us would be lost without them. They speed up the tedious process of cutting out by giving us unparalleled accuracy and allowing us to cut several layers at once, and the strips that we cut with them can be stitched speedily and chain-pieced. But scissors are still essential for cutting curves and templates, and for trimming and snipping threads. Keep three pairs handy: sharp fabric scissors for use with fabric only; paper scissors, which can also be used for cutting synthetic batting and templates, and small thread scissors. A seam ripper is vital for unpicking mistakes quickly.

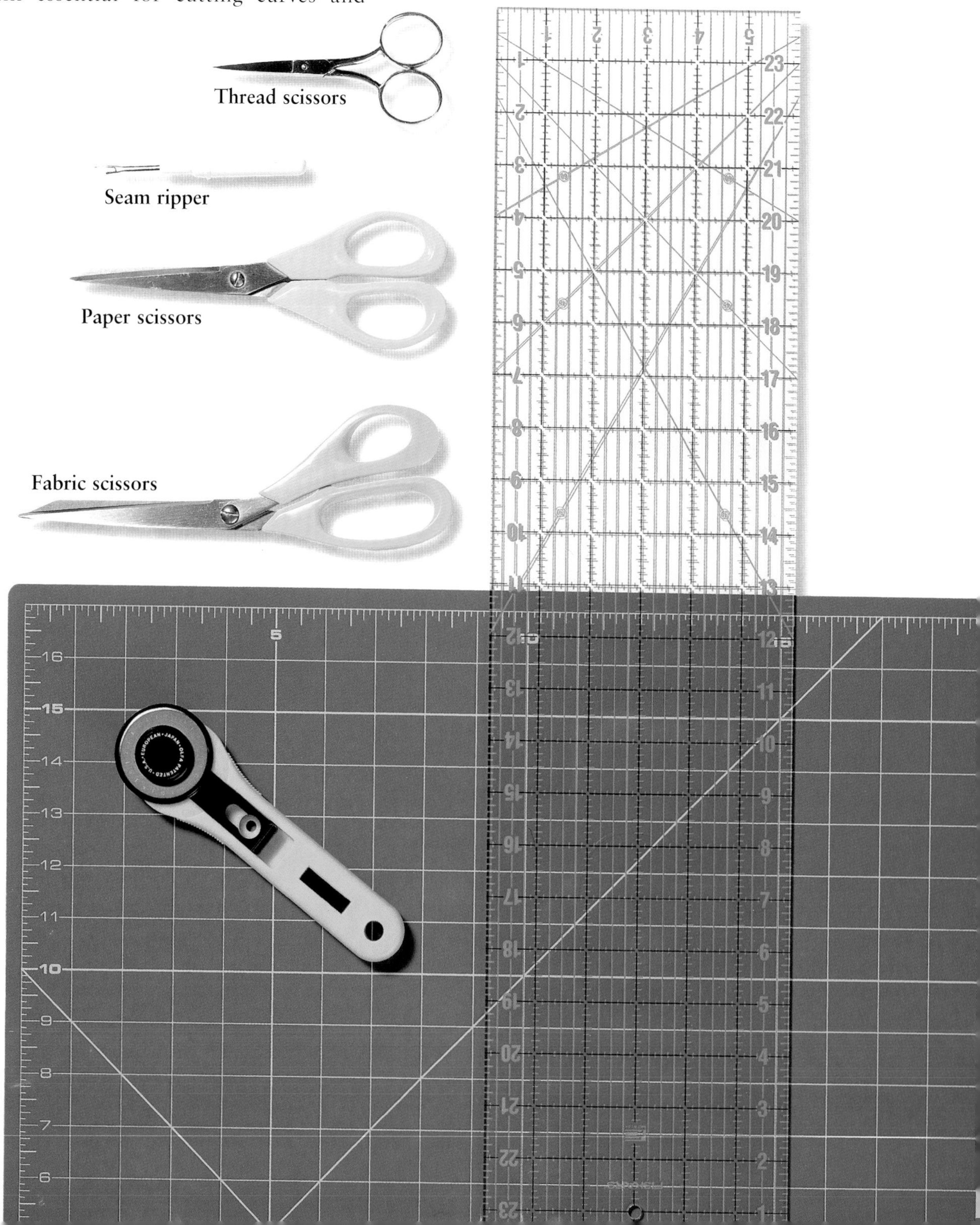

Thread scissors

Seam ripper

Paper scissors

Fabric scissors

Rotary ruler

Self-healing cutting mat

Rotary cutter

Sewing Machines

While all sewing machines have certain features in common, every machine is slightly different. The best way to become familiar with the way your sewing machine works is to experiment with the various functions and try out different thicknesses of fabric and batting. Always test before you begin work, especially when you are quilting by machine.

One of the most useful machine accessories for quilters is the ¼ in (5mm) foot, which measures the seam standard in most patchwork today. All sewing machines take up the fabric layers being stitched at a slightly different speed, and a walking foot is designed to compensate by drawing the top and bottom layers along at the same pace. A circular foot with an open presser is another useful tool.

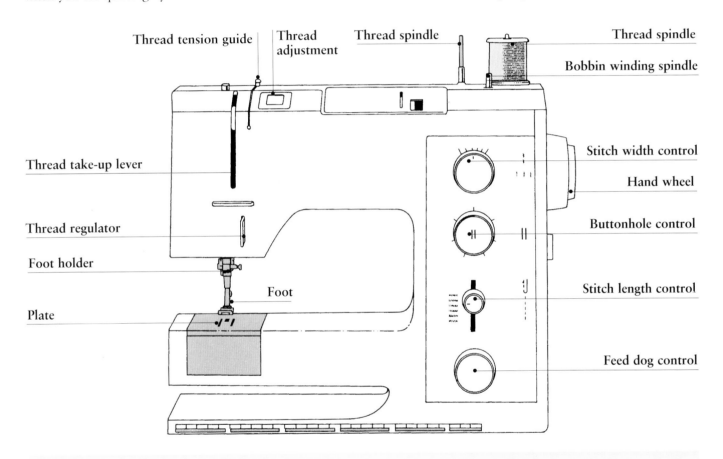

Thread tension guide   Thread adjustment   Thread spindle   Thread spindle

Bobbin winding spindle

Thread take-up lever

Stitch width control

Hand wheel

Thread regulator

Buttonhole control

Foot holder

Foot

Stitch length control

Plate

Feed dog control

Pressing

Pressing is a fundamental part of quiltmaking, and you will probably find that your ironing board is permanently set up when you are piecing a quilt. Never hurry or take short cuts – it is advisable to press seams after every step. Seams are normally pressed to one side – usually toward the darker fabric to prevent them from showing through on the right side – but occasionally they are pressed open. As a general rule, always press on the wrong side of the fabric to prevent shine. If you are using textured fabrics or those with special finishes, it is advisable to use a pressing cloth. Heavily creased cotton can be pressed with a steam iron.

Color for Quilters

COLOR CAN BE said to make the quilt, and certainly the choice of color is a crucial part of designing a piece of work. Color is a complicated subject upon which many words – and complete books – have been written, but there are a few areas with which patchworkers and quilters need to familiarize themselves. Color theory starts with the three primary colors.

Analogous Colors

Colors that occur side by side on the color wheel are known as analogous colors. Here three yellows – the primary, the red secondary, and the red tertiary – from the color wheel are shown as a possible color combination from which to begin planning a color scheme for a quilt.

The Color Wheel

BELOW: *Colors and their relationship to one another can be easily seen when they are combined in a circle known as a color wheel. Here versions of the three primary colors – red, blue, and yellow – are positioned in the center with secondary colors, made from mixing two primary colors in equal amounts, and tertiary – also called intermediate – colors, made by mixing a primary color with a secondary one, around the outer edge.*

Complementary Colors

Colors that appear opposite one another on the color wheel – often one primary and one secondary – are frequently combined. This juxtaposition of so-called complementary colors is a device used in many areas of design to give a lively feel – just think of red and green, the quintessential Christmas combination.

Combining Colors and Patterns

Choosing fabric for a quilt can be a difficult task since it is usually very hard to visualize with accuracy how swatches or bolts of material will look once they have been cut into pieces and stitched back together again. Experience is usually a good teacher, but if you begin by following a few rules, you can then learn how to break them successfully to create quilts that have exciting and unique colors and paterns. Perhaps the most important aspect of color for quilters is value – the lightness or darkness of a fabric – for the most successful quilts tend to be those that have adequate contrast between the lights and the darks.

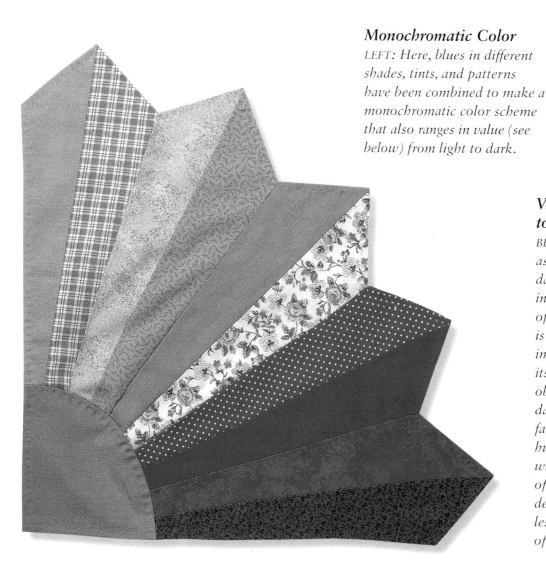

Monochromatic Color

LEFT: *Here, blues in different shades, tints, and patterns have been combined to make a monochromatic color scheme that also ranges in value (see below) from light to dark.*

Value from Light to Dark

BELOW: *Value is defined as the lightness or darkness of a color, and in many quilts the value of a particular fabric is sometimes more important than the color itself. Some colors are obviously light and others dark, but when you sort fabrics you will find a huge middle area in which the perceived value of a piece of fabric depends to a greater or lesser extent on the color of the fabric next to it.*

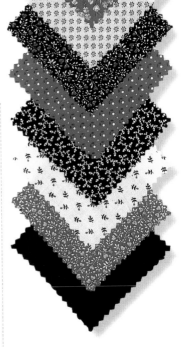

Patterned and Plain Fabrics

ABOVE: *Patterned fabric used wisely has a visual texture that enhances any piece of work, and combining patterns with solid-colored fabrics provides a contrast that is highly desirable in creating patchwork and appliqué quilts. Take account not just of the colors but also of their values when you are choosing.*

Scale

LEFT: *When you combine a number of patterned fabrics in the same piece, it is wise to bear in mind not only the color and the value of each one, but to consider the scale of the pattern as well. Here eleven red, white, and navy blue prints have been selected in a range of values from light through dark. Their common thread is the small-scale pattern used in each case.*

Two-color Combinations

Combining two highly contrasted colors gives a visual richness that cannot be achieved in any other way. Black or navy blue and white (as here), and red and white are perhaps the most popular combinations, but any two colors can be used. A white background will make a spot of bright primary color stand out vividly, while black will make it positively glow, and equal amounts of each color fool the eye and create optical illusions. Pale pastel hues do not generally show enough contrast to make successful two-color designs. However, two differerent shades of the same color, or two colors from the same family but with different values, do work well in combinations.

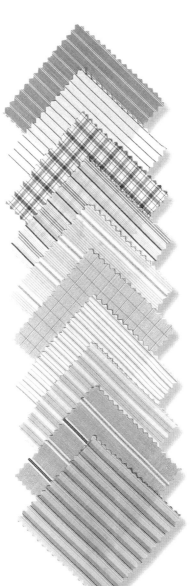

Geometric Patterns

RIGHT: *A selection of geometric patterns – checks, stripes, or plaids – can be put together effectively as shown here, and they can be combined with other types of pattern and solids to create wonderfully textured work. "Country" style uses a great many geometric patterns.*

Fabrics for Quilters

FABRIC IS THE MEDIUM by which the quiltmaker creates. The choices available are vast and can be confusing. Selecting appropriate fabrics is one of the basic steps in making quilts.

On the whole, natural fabrics are best for patchwork and quilting. They are comfortable to handle and easy to stitch, whether you work by hand or machine. Many synthetic fabrics and blends of natural and synthetic fibers can be used, but they are usually harder to fold and press, and quilting them by hand is not as easy or as tactile as working on fabrics made from natural fibers.

Cotton is by far the most popular fabric for patchwork. It is woven from the fibers of the cotton

Fabric Grain

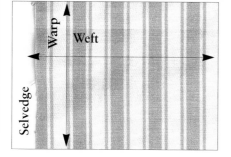

All fabric has three "grains" or directions of woven threads. The lengthwise threads, the "warp," are strung on the loom, with the "weft" threads crossing them horizontally in and out, under and over. The rigid edges on each side of a length of fabric are called the "selvages." The diagonal grain is the "bias." The warp and weft threads remain fairly stationary under tension, but the bias stretches easily and must therefore be handled with care.

Wool and Linen

RIGHT: Most wool and linen fabric is solid in color. Although both can be patterned, their main interest comes from their texture.

plant and comes in a myriad of weights – from fine cotton lawn and gingham to heavyweight denim and duckcloth – and weaves, from closely woven or knitted to open-weave like cheesecloth. It can be dyed any color of the rainbow, woven into such patterns as plaids, or stamped with a design after weaving. It feels good to handle, launders well, and is easy to press. Like all fibers, cotton is prone to shrinkage so it is advisable to launder fabric before piecing.

Quilts have been made from wool for centuries, and for warmth and a traditional look, it cannot be bettered. Wool was easier to come by in the cold climates where quiltmaking was widely practiced, and it was used not just as woven fabric but also as batting.

The other natural fibers, silk and linen, are also used for quiltmaking. Both are more expensive than cotton and need careful handling. They fray easily and are harder to clean, but both can be turned into quilts of great beauty and texture.

Cottons

BELOW: *The vast choice of cotton fabric can be overwhelming, but the number of patterns and weaves available means that with careful selection, quiltmakers can almost always find just the piece to make a quilt look right.*

Unusual Fabrics for Quilts

Most quilts today may be made from cotton, but there are plenty of other options. Silk is also used, and while its tendency to ravel can cause problems for inexperienced quilt makers, it creates special effects that cannot be duplicated by any other material. In many ways, silk is the ultimate quilting material. It is strong and can be woven into an enormous variety of weights and weaves, from gossamer sheers to heavy slubbed close weaves. It is easy to cut and to press, but it tends to fray easily and must be handled with care. When pieces are cut and turned in different directions, the play of light on the surface makes them seem another color altogether, and their sheen is visually rewarding. A beautifully stitched silk wholecloth quilt is without a doubt the finest bedcover in the world, and working by hand on silk is a pleasurable experience for anyone who loves fabrics. Wool quilts are warm and cozy, but it can be difficult to work with anything but a lightweight version. Suit-weight wool can be used effectively, but heavier weaves are best made into comforters or used sparingly in appliqué. Linen is the other natural fiber that is sometimes found in quilts, but its relative coarseness and reluctance to shed wrinkles and creases makes it more useful when it is used sparingly. Quilters are generally advised to use fabrics of uniform type and weight in patchwork, but by combining different fabrics, especially novelties like velvet, satin, taffeta, organdy, and brocade, you can come up with wonderfully creative visual and textural effects. Think of the crazy quilts of the late nineteenth century.

Making Templates

THE FIRST STAGE in making patchwork is to make the patches. There are two basic methods: making templates so you can outline the shape to be cut out on the fabric, and rotary cutting. Making templates is the traditional way and is widely used for working irregular-shaped pieces, while the straight edges that can be cut quickly with a rotary cutter are easy to stitch into strips that speed up the process.

Making Templates

The first step in the construction of a patchwork is to design and cut the templates. If you are making one of the projects in this book, some of them have templates you can simply trace from the back of the book, which include seam allowances of 1/4 in (5mm), and transfer them straight onto template plastic ready for cutting out. However, if you are designing a quilt from scratch, you must first draw your patchwork unit to finished size on graph paper. You then need to trace the individual elements before you cut out the templates. The first step is to cut a template the exact size of each finished patch (see below). Then you must cut one with seam allowances added, known as a window template (see opposite), that can be used to cut backing papers.

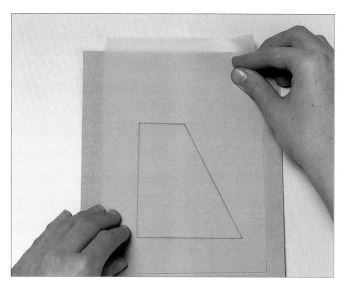

1 If you are designing a quilt from scratch, or making one that is composed of awkwardly shaped pieces, draw out each shape to the required finished size on graph paper and then carefully trace around the outline. Glue each tracing to a separate piece of board, taking care not to crease or crumple it.

2 Cut out the cardboard shape precisely, using a sharp craft knife and a straightedge or metal ruler. (It is best not to use plastic rulers, as it is very easy to accidentally cut into the ruler itself.) You will need to cut one template for every shape in your design.

3 Lay the cardboard template on a sheet of template plastic and draw around the shape, adding a ¹/₄ in (5mm) seam allowance on all sides. Use a quilter's quarter for accuracy.

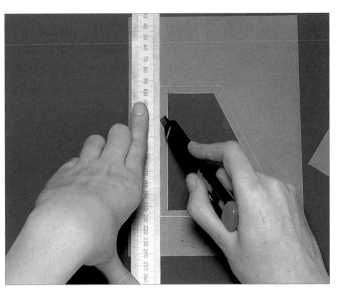

4 Using a craft knife and metal ruler, carefully cut out the inner "window" and then the extended template around the outside edge. Draw around the outer section to mark out fabric patches the correct size plus seam allowance. Mark around the inner "window" to indicate the stitching line as well as any support papers.

Making Patches from Templates

In the "English" method of patchwork, fabric patches are mounted on backing paper for support during stitching. This is because many of the patches used for this method have bias-cut seams, which would stretch during the assembly process if they were not supported. Backing papers are cut to the finished size of each patch; fabric patches are cut along the outer edge of the window template to include seam allowances.

1 Draw the shape onto backing paper, following the inner line of the window template. Cut a paper for every fabric patch.

2 Place the window template on the wrong side of the fabric; align the grain if possible. Draw around the template inside and out. Do not drag the marker or you may stretch the fabric. Cut out the fabric along the outer line. Pin a paper to the wrong side of every patch.

Cutting Out

CUTTING PATCHES accurately for patchwork is crucial to the finished look of the piece. There is a plethora of modern equipment used for cutting that enhances precision and speeds up the process. The rotary cutter and its self-healing mat and choice of rulers have made strip-piecing far and away the most popular approach to patchwork.

Hand Cutting

Cutting patches by hand is the time-honored way of making quilts, and while using the rotary method (see right) is quick and accurate, it is not alway the best way to cut. Many shapes cannot be cut in straight lines, and those with bias seams can be pulled out of true if a rotary cutter is used. If you do not have access to rotary equipment, scissors will do the job nicely, whether you are cutting small curved shapes, larger squares, or strips.

Scissors come in a huge choice of sizes, types, and formats, from small scissors for cutting thread and clipping seam allowances to dressmaking shears. The blades on scissors used to cut paper, template plastic and polyester batting will become dull quickly, and you should keep a separate pair of scissors for these tasks. Fabric scissors should be kept very sharp and treated with great respect.

Cutting Multiples

1 *It is easier to cut some pieces using a paper pattern like a dressmaker's pattern. Pin the pattern to the fabric, aligning the edges of the pattern with the fabric grain. You do not need to cut out the paper pattern before you cut the fabric pieces – in fact, with awkward shapes it is sometimes better if you do not, as it is easier to follow the line marked on the pattern than to cut around an imprecise cut edge.*

2 *Unless you are using very thick fabric, it is possible to cut two or more layers at once – but make sure that you always use sharp dressmaker's shears. This way, the excess paper will simply fall away with the cut-off fabric. If possible, use thin tissue-weight paper, since thick paper can dull the blades of the scissors.*

Rotary Cutting

Rotary cutting is a method based on twentieth-century technology and the modern liking for speed in all things. You can use a rotary cutter for cutting fabric into strips for strip-piecing and for cutting individual patches with straight sides. When working with a rotary ruler and cutting mat, remember to align and measure the fabric with either the ruler or the mat – never both. There are many different versions of mats, rulers, and cutters available. If possible, experiment with them in classes or workshops before you buy.

Safety

Rotary cutters have very sharp blades, so remember to replace the safety guard after every use. Always cut away from you, using a self-healing cutting mat to protect your work surface.

Cutting Strips

1 *Fold the fabric along the straight grain to fit on the cutting mat. Place the ruler over the "good" fabric to avoid cutting into it, and hold it steady with one hand. Trim away the uneven edge, cutting away from yourself.*

2 *Turn the fabric so the ruler covers the area of fabric that you want to end up with. Using either the marked ruler or the mat to align and measure the fabric, cut strips of the desired width along the grain.*

Cutting Pieced Strips

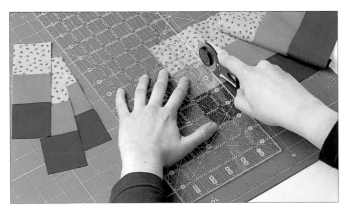

1 *After stitching the strips of fabric together, press the seams to one side. Lay the pieced strip on the cutting mat, align the ruler across it and cut into strips of the desired width.*

2 *You can either cut at right angles to the seams (see step 1) or diagonally at various angles, as here, to create short lengths for Seminole patchwork.*

Hand Piecing

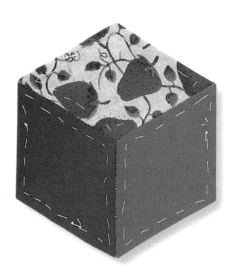

WHILE MANY PATTERNS lend themselves to the ease and security of machine stitching, others are easier and more accurately worked by hand. There are a few traditional designs, especially among the curved patterns, which are difficult to stitch on the machine and are almost always hand sewn.

English Patchwork

The technique known as "English" patchwork involves basting fabric shapes to backing papers to achieve the correct shape, and joining them by hand. This method is suitable for assembling patches with sharp angles or bias-cut seams, the advantage being that the papers support the fabric and prevent the seams from stretching.

Although the "English" technique is time-consuming compared with rotary cutting and machine assembly, it is the only way to assemble many of the traditional designs including Grandmother's Flower Garden , which

is formed from hexagonal patches, and Tumbling Blocks, which is cut from diamond patches (see below). There are also a number of curved motifs that are cut and assembled using the "English" method, including Clamshell and Double Axhead.

The first step is to make and cut templates and to mark the cutting lines on the wrong side of the fabric. Window templates give you a consistently sized seam allowance. You then need to cut a backing paper for every patch to the exact size of the finished patch.

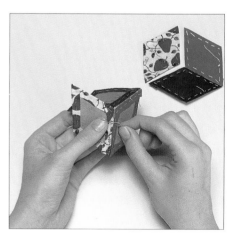

1 Pin a backing paper to the wrong side of every fabric patch, matching the edges of the paper to the stitching line. Fold the seam allowance over the paper and baste it in place. (Begin basting by pushing the needle through from the right side of the fabric so that the knot is on the right side for easy removal later.)

2 Place two patches right sides together and line up carefully to make sure that the corners are level. Whipstitch the edges of the two pieces together, taking care not to stitch through the backing papers. You will need to leave the backing papers in place until all the blocks have been joined together.

3 Take a third patch and match the inside point. Working from the center out, whipstitch or slipstitch one side and then the other to complete the block. It is much easier to align each corner if you work from the center out.

Straight Seams

Some small patches with straight seams are fiddly to stitch by machine and these are often better stitched by hand. Patches can be joined with running stitch or backstitch. Pin your work carefully before you sew. Do not stitch into the seam allowances in case you need to trim them later.

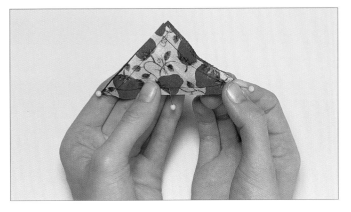

1 *With right sides together, pin the patches along the straight seam, matching the corners on each piece. We have added a pin at the center; you may need more.*

2 *Sew along the marked seam, making sure you begin and end precisely at the corners. Handle all bias seams with care to avoid stretching the fabric.*

Four-piece Seams

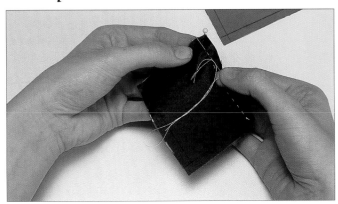

1 *Join two contrasting patches along the marked stitching line. Repeat and press the seams.*

2 *Pin the two units right sides together, first pushing a pin through the center seam to mark it precisely.*

3 *Working from the center out, use running stitch or backstitch to join the two units first on one side, then on the other.*

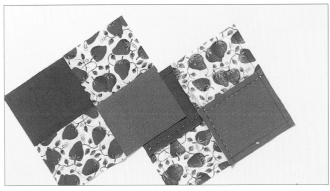

4 *Seen from the right side (left), the units have been turned into a block in which the corners meet exactly in the middle.*

Machine Piecing

Q UILTMAKERS HAVE used sewing machines since early home models were introduced in the 1830s and 1840s. Hand-turned and treadle machines are still widely used, while electric versions have been computerized to carry out a wide variety of sewing tasks.

Patchwork is all about accuracy and accuracy is all about careful measuring. This is especially important when you are stitching by machine, since if you make an error in estimating the size of seam allowance that you need this can result in blocks of differing sizes that do not join together. Most machines can be fitted with a special foot that measures a precise ¼-in (5-mm) seam, but if you do not have one, you can mark the needle plate with a piece of masking tape positioned the correct distance from the needle and use this as a visual guide when stitching.

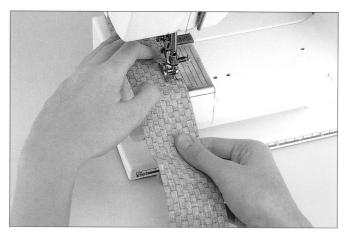

1 *Here, two strips are being joined right sides together on the machine. There is no need to pin or mark stitching lines, but it is vital that your seam allowances are even and that your stitching line is straight.*

Joining Pieced Units

Pieced units are formed by joining several strips together along their length and then cutting them into short units. Here, two pieced units are being joined together with colors alternating. To reduce bulk, it is important to press the seams of each unit in opposite directions before joining units together.

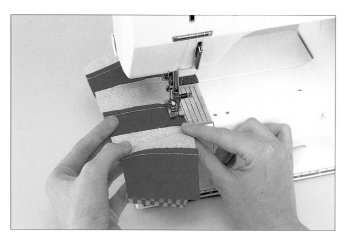

1 *Press the seams of each unit to one side. Place two units right sides together so the pressed seams face in opposite directions; align seams and stitch carefully ¼ in (5mm) from the raw edge.*

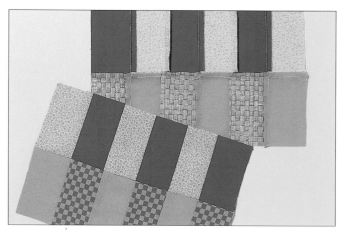

2 *The joined unit, shown here from both front and back, has evenly matched rows with squared-up corners at each meeting point.*

Chain-piecing

This is a quick way of stitching, since it allows you to sew in a continuous line, feeding prepared patches through the machine one after another without breaking the thread. If the technique is repeated at each stage in making a block, the piecing process is speeded up. Here, four sets of two-patch blocks are being joined together to create a chain of units. The chain is held together by short threads, which are cut apart once all the elements have been pieced together.

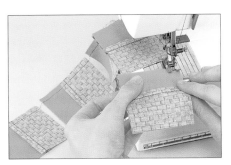

1 *Place piles of units within reach and feed through the machine one after the other, without lifting the foot or breaking the thread.*

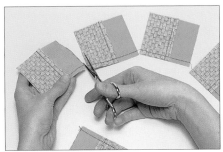

2 *Cut the threads that hold the chain of units together once they have all been pieced.*

Curves

Careful preparation and pinning is essential when stitching curved patches together by machine. The process is made more tricky by the bias-cut seams, which require careful handling. It is a good idea to mark the stitching line on the wrong side of the fabric before you begin.

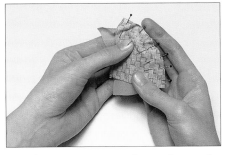

1 *Placing pins at right angles to the curved edge, pin the patches right sides together, first in the center, then at each end, then in between.*

2 *Stitch along the marked line, removing pins as you go.*

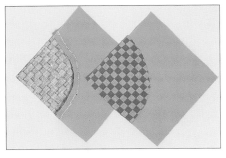

3 *Press the seam toward the concave edges so that it lies flat.*

Unpicking Seams

Sometimes you may need to unpick a stitched seam, either because you made a mistake or because the construction method involves sewing a series of seams that are then manipulated before one or more of them are opened up again. To avoid damage to the fabric, always use a seam ripper for the purpose. Clean away all bits of thread before restitching.

Ripping One Side

1 *Holding the seam taut, insert the point of the seam ripper into every third or fourth stitch and break the thread.*

2 *Hold bottom layer and pull layer to separate stitches.*

Ripping Down the Middle

Holding the seam open, insert the ripper between the layers and break the thread. Gently pull the seam apart and repeat.

Setting Blocks

SETTING BLOCKS refers to the way in which the elements of a quilt are positioned for assembly. The set of a quilt is sometimes called "sets and sashes". There are a few basic ways to set a quilt, but as usual in quiltmaking, the variations that can be created are practically endless.

The most basic way to set a quilt is known as a block-on-block, or edge-to-edge, straight setting, in which finished blocks of the same size are set side by side and joined with the corners matching. This setting can be used for a vast number of patterns and almost always creates secondary patterns that only become apparent when the blocks are joined. Blocks can also be set in straight lines with vertical and horizontal sashing, or the sashing can have corner squares. If the blocks are set on point, a diagonal setting is achieved. Again, the blocks can be set edge to edge, or they can be sashed with strips that run diagonally. Many block patterns work best if they are separated by plain spacer blocks the same size as the finished pieced block.

This way of setting, a version of which is shown below, is called a pieced and plain, or alternate, set. Other ways to set a quilt include the medallion or British frame quilt, which has a large square or rectangle in the center surrounded by several borders of varying width, and the strippy composed of strips, which can themselves be pieced, that run the full length of the quilt. Both methods rely on bold design and colorways for maximum impact.

Pieced and Plain (Alternate) Set

1 *Make a pieced block of your choice. (Above, two squares of contrasting fabric are cut diagonally to form triangles, and restitched to form a square the same size as the original piece). Cut a plain square the same size as the finished pieced square to act as a spacer block.*

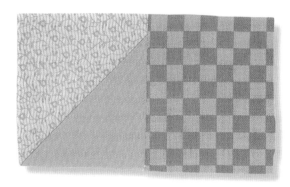

2 *Join the two units together and repeat as necessary until you have the number required by your pattern. Flipping one two-unit block, as shown right, creates a four-unit block with an interesting diagonal pattern. This particular pattern ios known as Pinwheel.*

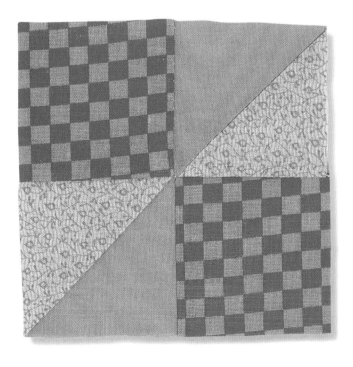

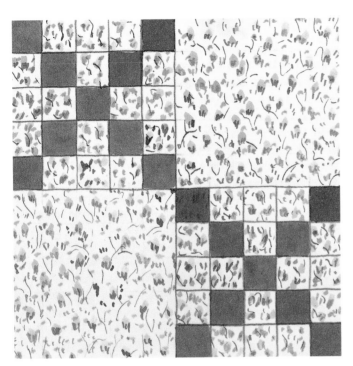

Using Spacer Blocks

LEFT: *With a more elaborately pieced block, such as the pieced square in this Single Irish Chain design, the secondary pattern – a strong diagonal line – is even more obvious. This type of setting, using so-called spacer blocks, is a good method of stretching a few blocks into a quilt, and – particularly effective when a solid fabric is used instead of a printed one for the unpieced blocks – it provides large blank areas that the dedicated quilter can go on to fill with texture.*

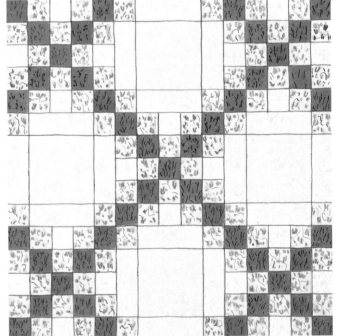

Two-block set

RIGHT: *In this variation, both blocks are pieced – although, since much of the second block is taken up with a large center square, the overall effect is very similar to that of the basic pieced and plain set. This set (Double Irish Chain) produces two secondary patterns in the design – thin lines running diagonally across the quilt in both directions, as in Single Irish Chain, and large squares positioned to give a kind of stepped effect, rather like bricks in a wall.*

Pressing

Unlike seams for dressmaking, those used to join patchwork pieces can be less thoroughly pressed at the early stages, especially when you are working with small pieces. Light pressing of small pieces can be carried out with the fingers, although more intricate pieces with long seams are better pressed with an iron. "Press" means just that – do not drag the iron along the seam or you may stretch it.

Seams are usually pressed to one side, although there are exceptions. To prevent seams from showing through on the right side of the fabric, press toward darker-colored fabrics unless otherwise stated.

Fingerpressing

Press the seam down on the wrong side with a finger or thumb to make it lie flat. Take care not to stretch the fabric.

Pressing with an Iron

With the iron set at the appropriate temperature, press down on the wrong side long enough to make the seam lie flat.

Sashing and Borders

WHEN ALL THE BLOCKS for a quilt are completed, they must be joined together. Some blocks are joined edge to edge, creating secondary patterns, while others need to be separated by narrow strips of fabric called sashing. Borders are usually a narrow inner one combined with a wider outer one.

Straight Borders

The width of the border depends, of course, on the quilt itself. Its overall size and the size and complexity of the blocks will set the tone for choosing borders. Inner borders are usually narrower than outer borders, which can be up to 4in (10cm) wide.

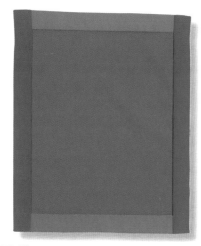

Top and Tail
Straight borders are added to the top and bottom (short) edges first. Side borders are then cut and added to each long edge.

Round and Round
Start on any edge, 3–4in (7.5–10cm) down from the top corner. Apply the first strip, which must overhang the top edge of the quilt by at least the width of the strip. Add the second, third, and fourth strips, working in a clockwise direction. Finish by opening out the first strip and continuing the line of stitching, catching in the end of the fourth strip. Square off the corners if necessary.

Pieced borders

A well-executed pieced border gives a quilt extra pizzazz and flair. From left to right: Seminole chevrons, Flying Geese, squares, two-tone patches, and Prairie Points.

Sashing

Sashing strips are used to separate blocks to emphasize the pattern in the block itself. They can be horizontal and vertical, or they can run diagonally if the blocks are set on point. Sashing is necessary on sampler quilts and on any design where the individual blocks need to be given a separate identity or emphasis.

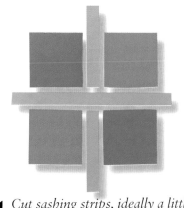

1 *Cut sashing strips, ideally a little longer than the block to be sashed, to the chosen width plus seams.*

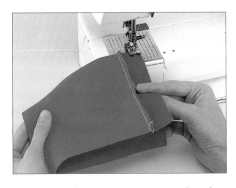

2 *Join a short strip to one side of the block, then join the next block to the other side of the strip.*

3 *Open out the sashed unit and press seams to one side.*

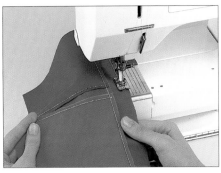

4 *Stitch a long strip to the long side of the sashed unit, then join the remaining unit on the other side.*

5 *Open out and press seams to one side. The sashing strips form a perfect cross in the center.*

Corner Squares

Adding corner squares to borders or sashing will enhance a quilt beyond measure. Careful color planning is vital. Strong colors can be used to jazz up a plain or simple design, while complementary shades are useful for drawing the elements of a complex pattern together.

1 *Cut strips for the borders and squares the same width for the corners. Stitch squares to strips.*

2 *Line up first strip so seam is $^1/4$ in (5mm) from top edge. Insert pin 4in (10cm) from top.*

3 *Working around the sides of the quilt in a clockwise direction, add the remaining strips, pressing seams each time.*

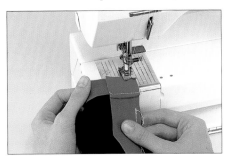

4 *When you get back to the beginning, incorporate the first square, continuing the initial seam.*

5 *Note how the seams meet on the right side. On the wrong side, see how the seams are pressed in the direction dictated by the construction.*

The Four Bs of Quilting

THE FOUR Bs OF quilting – batting, backing, bagging, and basting – are stages between finishing the quilt top and beginning the quilting. Batting is the fabric used for interlining a quilt, backing is the fabric used for the back of the quilt, bagging is a way of finishing the raw edges, and basting is the stitching that holds the layers of the quilt together.

Batting

Batting is the padded material used in the middle of the quilt to provide warmth and softness. Originally consisting of old blankets, remnants of fabric, or combed wool, its modern equivalent is available cut to size or on rolls that can be measured like fabric. Synthetic polyester is the most widely used, with cotton and cotton/ polyester blends also popular. Wool and silk versions are available, usually by special order.

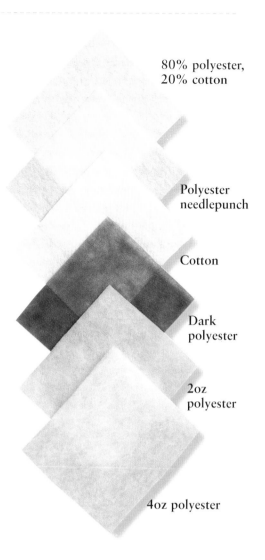

80% polyester, 20% cotton

Polyester needlepunch

Cotton

Dark polyester

2oz polyester

4oz polyester

Basting Spray

Washable spray adhesive formulated for quiltmaking can be used to baste layers together.

1 *Spray batting all over and lay backing on it.*

2 *Repeat with top, wrong side to batting.*

Basting

Basting is used to hold the layers of the quilt together for quilting. It is done vertically and horizontally, and sometimes diagonally, with rows 4in (10cm) apart, and can be stitched or safety pinned. Baste bound quilts before quilting; baste and quilt bagged quilts after quilting.

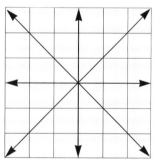

Always baste from the center outward, as shown above.

1 *Sandwich the layers together and smooth out creases. Insert safety pins at 4in (10cm) intervals.*

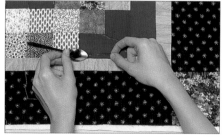

2 *Taking large slanted or running stitches, stitch through all layers. Use a spoon to lift the needle.*

Turning Corners

There are times when you are sewing on a machine that you need to change directions sharply without breaking off the threads – when you reach a corner, for example, or when you are machine-quilting a design that requires a sharp and precise change of direction in the quilting. To keep the thread continuous, you can raise the presser foot without lifting the needle and turn the work to a different angle, as shown below.

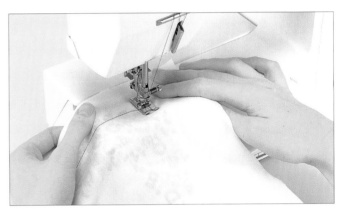

1 *When you reach a corner, stop the machine a seam width from the perpendicular edge, leaving the needle in the fabric. Lift the presser foot and turn the work at a right angle to the seam you have just stitched.*

2 *With the needle still in the fabric, lower the presser foot and continue stitching along the next seamline. This method is the same for all machine sewing.*

Bagging

Although most quilts are quilted and then have their edges finished with a narrow binding, it is possible to join the three layers first by stitching them around all the edges, leaving a gap for turning them right side out. This procedure – bagging – must be carried out before the piece is quilted.

1 *Lay the batting flat and place the quilt on top, right side up. Place the backing fabric right side down on top and smooth the wrinkles. Pin and stitch around the outside edges, leaving a 5–10in (20–25cm) opening for turning.*

2 *Cut away the excess batting and backing fabric, trim the corners to reduce bulk, and turn the quilt right side out through the opening. Turn the raw edges of the opening to the inside and press gently. Pin and slipstitch the opening closed.*

Backing

Backing fabric should match or coordinate with the quilt top, and should be of a weight and weave that are easy to quilt. Most stores sell sheeting in extra-wide widths, which is ideal for backing a quilt. If you cannot find anything suitable, simply join several widths of your chosen fabric together.

To avoid having a seam down the center, place a full width of backing fabric in the middle and a narrow piece on each side.

Binding

BASIC BINDING techniques are Single and Double Binding – applying narrow strips to the edges of all three layers at once; and Edges to Middle, and Back to Front – folding backing over to the front edges and stitching.

Single Binding

This is the most common method used to finish the raw edges of a quilt. You can either buy prefolded binding to complement your quilt or you can make it yourself. To do this, simply cut strips of fabric 1–2in (2.5–5cm) wide and then join them together into long lengths.

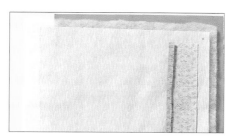

1 Mark a point in each corner ¹/₄in (5mm) in from each side edge. Press a ¹/₄ in (5-mm) seamline along one long edge of the binding strips. Assemble the three layers as shown.

2 Place the binding right side down on the quilt top, aligning the unpressed edge with the raw edge of the quilt. Stitch in place starting and finishing at a marked point.

3 Open out the stitched binding and pin a new strip along the adjacent edge. Stitch between marked points, taking care not to catch the first strip in the stitching line.

4 Turn the binding to the quilt back to cover all raw edges and pin carefully in place.

5 When you reach a corner, fold the cut edge at the end of each strip to the inside and square off the corner. To finish, pin and stipstitch around all edges.

Double Binding

This method makes a version stronger than a single binding because it involves using double-thickness strips of binding. It is ideal for quilts that will be laundered frequently, especially baby quilts.

1 Cut strips twice as wide as the finished binding plus ¹/₂ in (10mm) seam allowances. Fold in half lengthwise, wrong sides together, and press flat.

2 Mark, pin and stitch as for Single Binding, sewing along double thickness raw edges of the binding. Turn the folded edge to the back and slipstitch in place to finish.

Edge to Middle

For this technique, the batting is cut slightly smaller than the backing and quilt top. The raw edges of the backing are folded over the edges of the batting to enclose them, and the edges of the quilt top are folded to the inside. The edges of all three layers can then be stitched down.

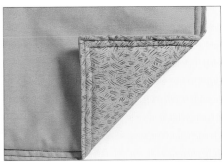

1 *Cut the batting ¹/₄ in (5mm) smaller all around than the backing. Fold the backing edges over the batting and pin. Turn the edges of the quilt top under and pin.*

2 *Secure in place with a double row of top stitching. The first row should be ¹/₄ in (5mm) from the finished edge; the second row should be ¹/₄ in (5mm) in from that.*

Back to Front

Here, the batting is cut the same size as the quilt top, but the backing is cut larger all around. The edges of the backing are folded to the front and make a strong, neat edge.

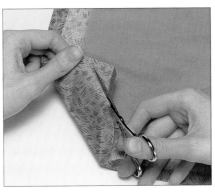

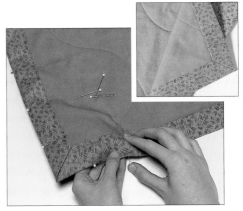

1 *Turn ¹/₄ in (5mm) to the wrong side on all edges of the backing. Center the quilt top and batting on the backing. Fold a miter at each corner and trim the seam allowance.*

2 *Fold the pressed edges of the backing to the front of the quilt and pin in place. Stitch neatly by hand or machine along all sides. Slipstitch the miters to finish.*

Mitering Corners

Mitering is an attractive way of finishing a corner with a 45-degree angle. It is used in quiltmaking most often on borders and binding.

Mitered corners must be neat and precise. Smooth, even mitered corners give a profess-ional finish to the edges of a quilt. Accurate pressing can help you achieve a sharp line along which to work.

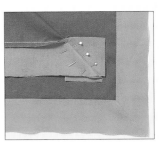

1 *Cut strips longer than the quilt sides, plus twice the width of the border. Mark a point ¹/₄ in (5mm) from the corner of the quilt and apply a strip in each direction, starting at the mark.*

2 *Fold back each strip to a 45-degree angle and press to mark the fold (top). Working from the right side, pin along the fold to hold the seam in place.*

3 *Turn to the wrong side and re-pin at right angles to the fold. Match the two folds precisely and stitch from the inner corner to the edge. Trim the ends.*

Patchwork Patterns and Projects

M AKING PATCHWORK QUILTS is a creative pastime that brings pleasure to millions. The projects and patterns that follow in this chapter will provide plenty of inspiration.

Trip Around the World is a quilt design that is based entirely on squares. This unquilted top, made in 1995, uses several cotton fabrics overprinted with gold to achieve a rich, warm quality.

Four-patch Blocks

THE FOUR-PATCH BLOCK is probably the simplest of all patchwork designs. Constructed from four squares, it is one of the easiest to make, but it provides the basis for a myriad of other patterns.

Four-patch

ABOVE: *The basic pattern of the four-patch block relies for its effectiveness on a strong contrast between light and dark color values. Different shades of a single color, or two solid-colored or two coordinating prints, can be striking, although the use of one plain and one patterned fabric is more usual. It can be constructed as shown below right, or it can be made by simple strip-piecing.*

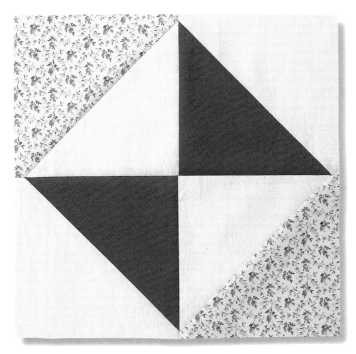

Broken Dishes

LEFT: *The simple design known as Broken Dishes is formed entirely of right-angled triangles. It is traditionally made into units of four blocks and alternated with plain background blocks. If each unit is turned a different way, the broken dishes look is enhanced even more.*

While the basic four-patch is made from four simple squares, there are numerous variations. The basic pattern (shown top right) alternates two contrasting fabrics. Combining two of these four-patch blocks with two plain squares that are the same size as the pieced ones creates a pieced-and-plain block that can be joined to other similar blocks to make strong diagonal patterns that run across a whole quilt in both directions.

Combine four four-patches and you get a setting that is known as a "double four-patch". Double four-patch blocks are generally more interesting if you use two different four-patch blocks (two of each design). Dividing squares into triangles and then restitching triangles of different fabrics into squares opens up an even wider field of possibilities. For ease of construction, most patterns are based on right-angle triangles, made by cutting a square diagonally from corner to corner – as in the Broken Dishes pattern, shown above, which consists entirely of right-angle triangles reassembled into squares, and Pinwheel (also known as Windmill), opposite, which also combines pieced triangle squares.

The orientation of the triangles is critical in patterns such as this: here, the pieced squares are turned so that the points of the triangles meet in the center, thus giving the appearance of the blades of a windmill. Cutting these elements down even more – for example, by cutting

Pinwheel
This popular pattern, also known as Windmill or Flutter Blades, is simple to make and has endless variations.

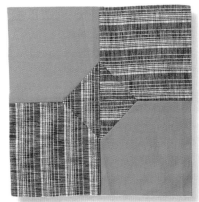

Bow Tie
A basic four-patch block based on large squares, with corner triangles that meet in the center to form the "knot."

some of the triangles in half to form two right-angle triangles and then reassembling them in a recognized pattern – gives an even more intricate block. The pattern known as Double Pinwheel (not shown) is an interesting variation: squares are cut into triangles, as in the basic Pinwheel, but then triangles in contrasting colors are also cut in half, forming right-angle triangles half the size of the first set. When they are pieced, the appearance is of alternating large and small blades.

In addition to right-angle triangle designs, there are a number of patterns based on isosceles triangles. They tend to create shapes that have a slight visual curve, even though the lines are straight. Storm at Sea and certain Spiderweb patterns are examples of this type of optical illusion.

As with all types of patchwork blocks, lay out the elements before you piece them to make sure you've arranged them in the right order. A few of the best-known four-patch blocks are shown here. It is obvious how patterns such as Bow Tie, shown opposite, or Birds in the Air, or Streak of Lightning, got their names. But there are hundreds more patterns, such as Northern Lights, which actually look nothing like their namesakes!

How to Construct a Four-patch Block

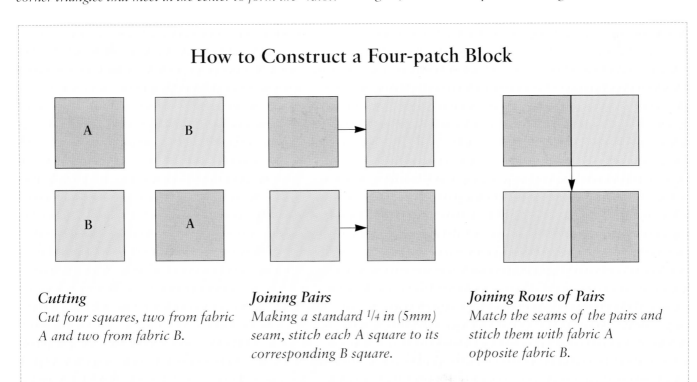

Cutting
Cut four squares, two from fabric A and two from fabric B.

Joining Pairs
Making a standard 1/4 in (5mm) seam, stitch each A square to its corresponding B square.

Joining Rows of Pairs
Match the seams of the pairs and stitch them with fabric A opposite fabric B.

Nine-patch Blocks

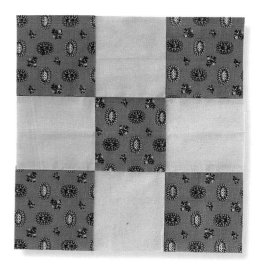

THE BASIC NINE-PATCH block is not much more complicated than the four-patch, and it is even more versatile. There are so many permutations on the design that it is not possible to include them all in any book, but they are such a basic form of patchwork construction that it is fun to look for them in any quilt you encounter.

Like the four-patch, the nine-patch can be made from individual squares or it can be strip-pieced as shown top right. The simplest form of nine-patch is shown above, and consists of three rows of three squares each, alternating in color to make a cross shape.

If five of these blocks are combined with four plain squares, alternating pieced and plain squares, to form a larger – double – nine-patch, diagonal chain patterns can be created.

If only the center square of a double nine-patch is pieced, with all the other squares are made from one of two alternating fabrics, then an impression of the design "exploding" outward from the center is achieved.

A large number of patterns, including the evocatively titled Puss in the Corner, Patience Corner, and Homeward Bound, can be devised using nine-patch blocks fashioned only from squares. As always in patchwork, the placement of the colors is the main factor determining the pattern in these designs. Even something as simple as reversing the light and dark fabrics in a design can have a dramatic impact on the overall effect.

When the squares in nine-patch blocks are divided into right-angle triangles, the number of patterns that can be produced rises dramatically. Some of the best known are shown on these pages; all have a number of widely used variations. Railroad, for example, a variation on Jacob's Ladder, is made almost entirely from unpieced squares apart from a small number of pieced triangles alongside the "track", but it conveys very graphically the feeling of a straight track running across open country.

Some star patterns – always a favorite motif with quilters – are made of nine-patch blocks. In the Friendship Star, triangle patches are arranged into a four-pointed star, giving the block the appearance of tumbling or whirling through the air. This is particularly effective

Rail Fence

The simplest form or Rail Fence consists of three fabrics, which can be strip-pieced and cut into squares. These are alternated between vertical and horizontal placement to create a chevron or zigzag pattern.

How to Construct a Nine-patch Block

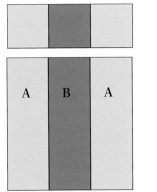
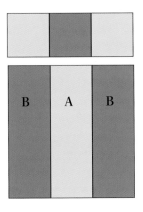
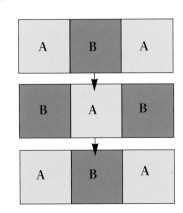

Cutting and Strip-piecing
Cut the fabrics into equal strips and arrange in two sequences, ABA and BAB. Stitch together along their long edges, then cut across the pieced strips in rows.

Joining Rows
Matching seams, stitch three of the pieced rows together into a block, alternating between ABA and BAB settings.

when the "star' is made in a light fabric overprinted with gold or silver and the background is a dark color such as midnight blue. The Ohio Star, too (although no one can say for sure that it actually originated in Ohio), is made

from five plain squares and four pieced triangle squares. Its symmetry and regularity of this design are part of its appeal. All these patterns are relatively simple for beginners to piece, yet still allow scope for creativity.

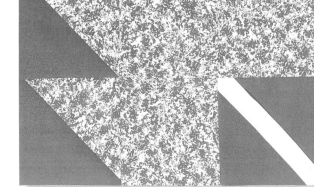

Maple Leaf
This simple nine-patch, which has many variations, looks like its namesake. To emphasize the leaf shape, blocks are usually sashed or alternated with plain squares. The stem can be pieced or applied by hand.

Jacob's Ladder
Several patterns were given biblical names that reflected the religious nature of their makers' daily lives. The pieces in this pattern are small, allowing the maker to be frugal with fabric but still create an intricate design.

Irish Chain Blocks

ECAUSE THE IRISH CHAIN design is so straightforward to make, it is, together with Log Cabin, perhaps the most popular quilt pattern chosen by beginners making their first quilt. However, it has several variations and can be elaborated upon to create traditional bedcovers of wonderful intricacy.

Irish Chain

ABOVE LEFT AND RIGHT: Double Irish Chain, the version shown here, is probably the best-known of this family, in which a block made of small squares alternates with an almost plain one to create a diagonal pattern that runs throughout the quilt. While no evidence has been found to show that the pattern originated in Ireland, it has been widely used in Britain and America since the eighteenth century. All the variations are constructed from two different blocks, one intricately pieced from small squares and the other either a plain square or a pieced block. The blank areas created by the plain squares provide scope for elaborate quilting or appliqué.

Irish Chain in its simplest form is constructed from a simple nine-patch block in two colors that is alternated with a plain square of the same size, made either in a third color or in one of the two colors used in the pieced block. The effect is of a diagonal chain running in both directions over the quilt. As with so many patchwork patterns, it works best if the fabrics in the pieced square contrast strongly with each other – perhaps with one being a solid color and the other one a print, or one dark and one light solid. If more patches are used in the pieced square, a more intricate pattern results.

Double Irish Chain (shown above; see also the construction diagram opposite) is more complicated. Three colors must be used to create the effect, and both blocks are pieced. In one version, the first block consists of five rows of five squares, and the other is made from a large center square and small corner squares with a rectangular strip running along the center of each side.

In Triple Irish Chain, each block is made up of twenty-five squares, with half the blocks made in the same way as the elaborately pieced block for Double Irish Chain shown, and the other using the same fabrics in a different configuration (see diagram, opposite).

There are examples of Irish Chain quilts made using assorted scraps, but for the pattern to be entirely effective, the color values must be carefully chosen. As a result, most Irish Chain designs are made from just two or three fabrics, which can be cotton, wool (as in many of the oldest historical quilts), or silk. I have seen a stunning version of this design in a Double Irish Chain quilt made in the middle of the nineteenth century, which used two shades of brown for the chain set against white. The contrast between what appeared to be a white background fabric, heavily embellished with intricate quilting, and the richness of autumnal-looking chestnut and chocolate browns gave what is essentially a very simple setting a feeling of tremendous sophistication.

Single Irish Chain

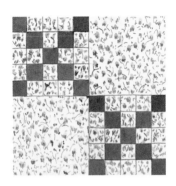

This version is made up of five-by-five square blocks in two colors combined with plain, unpieced blocks. These provide a smooth, unpieced surface for quilting.

Double Irish Chain

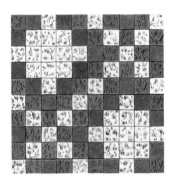

A traditional Double Irish Chain formed from nine of the basic blocks. Each time a set of blocks is added, a longer chain is revealed with more chains developing in the corners.

Triple Irish Chain

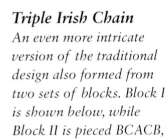

An even more intricate version of the traditional design also formed from two sets of blocks. Block I is shown below, while Block II is pieced BCACB, CAAAC and AAAAA.

How to Construct Double Irish Chain Blocks

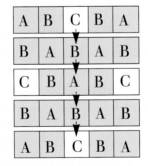

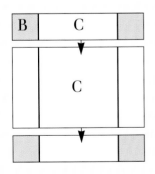

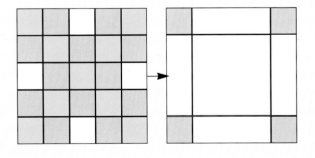

Block I
Cut strips and join into three arrangements: ABCBA, BABAB and CBABC. Cut across the pieced strips in rows and stitch together.

Block II
Cut a center square from C, four corner squares from B and four strips the same width as the corners from C. Join into three rows, then into a block.

Making the Pattern
Taking a standard ¼-in (5-mm) seam allowance, join the two pieced blocks along one edge, matching seams carefully as you work.

Plaid Baby Quilt

THIS HANDSOME BABY'S QUILT is quick and fun to make, and would make a welcome addition in any child's room as a bedspread, a floor cloth, a changing mat, or a play mat. Bear in mind that whatever its use, it will get plenty of wear and tear, and it will probably be washed more times than you care to remember, so finish it carefully, avoiding buttons and loose threads.

Making the Corner Hearts

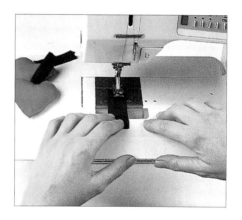

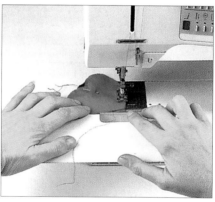

1 *Cut the binding fabric across the bias into 1¹/2 in (3.75cm) strips. You will need four 2in (5cm) lengths. Fold in half lengthwise, right sides together, and stitch ¹/4 in (6mm) from raw edges. Turn right sides out and fold in half to make a loop.*

2 *Cut eight small hearts from solid fabric (templates are on page 406). Pin in pairs with right sides together, inserting a bias loop inside the top of each. Stitch around the edges, leaving a 1in (2.5cm) gap at the base for turning.*

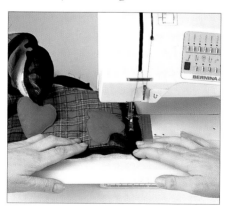

3 *Turn right side out and stuff with pieces of batting. Slipstitch the gap to close. To finish, zigzag or straight stitch around the edge of each heart.*

4 *Stitch the hearts securely in place on the quilt after you have attached the piping (see page 265, step 10).*

YOU WILL NEED

plaid fabrics in your chosen colors for the quilt top (we used three variations)

solid fabric for the backing and hearts

contrasting fabric for the binding

piping cord

batting

thick chenille or wool yarn for outlining the hearts

paper-backed fusible web for attaching the hearts

sewing thread

Heartfelt Happiness
The quilt can be personalized for the child by embroidering his or her name and date of birth in one of the appliqué hearts.

Making the Quilt

1 Cut 35 x 6¹/₂ in (16.5cm) plaid squares for the quilt in your chosen colors (see opposite). Cut five large hearts from solid fabric and five from fusible web (template is on page 406).

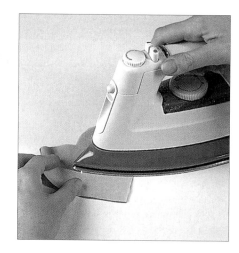

2 Iron a fusible web heart to the wrong side of each solid fabric heart. This should prevent the hearts from puckering when stitched in place on the quilt.

3 Peel the paper backing from each heart, revealing the adhesive surface.

4 Place an adhesive-backed heart on the right side of each of the plaid squares and iron in place.

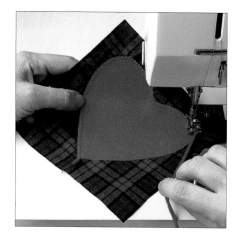

5 Pin a length of chenille yarn around the edge of each heart and zigzag in place for extra definition. You will need about 17in (43cm) of yarn for each.

6 To assemble the quilt, start by stitching seven squares togther to form a row. Press all seams open.

7 Next stitch the pieced rows together to form a block, matching seams as you go. Press all seams open on the wrong side

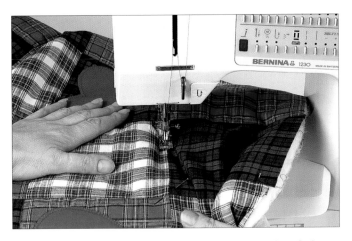

8 *Pin and baste the batting to the wrong side of the finished quilt top. Stitch along all seams through both layers using zigzag or straight stitch.*

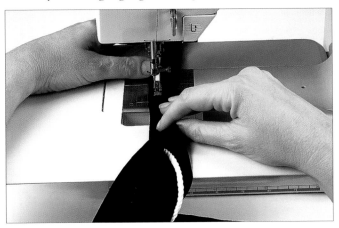

9 *Cut the binding fabric into 2¹/₂ in (6.25cm) bias strips. Join several strips together. Fold the binding around the piping cord, wrong sides togther, and using a zipper foot stitch close to cord.*

Assembling the Quilt Top

The quilt top consists of 35 x 6½ in (16.5cm) squares in three contrasting plaid fabrics, which are arranged in a repeat pattern. You will need to cut 12 from red, 12 from white, and 10 from blue/green plaid. Templates for the hearts, which are cut from solid fabric – as is the backing – are on page 406.

10 *Pin and baste the piping around the edge of the quilt top. Clip into all corners for ease. Stitch in place using a zipper foot, leaving both ends free. Trim the ends of the cord, overlap the edges of the binding neatly, and finish by hand.*

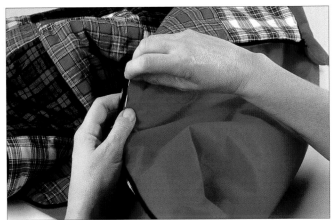

11 *Attach the corner hearts (see step 4 on page 262). Cut the backing to fit the quilt top, allowing extra for seam allowances, and pin in place on the reverse. Slipstitch around all edges to secure.*

Gingham Shirting Quilt

THIS QUILT, WITH all its blocks made from men's old shirts, is a recycler's dream. We have used a combination of stripes and plaids to make the four-patch blocks. The striped fabrics in the spacer blocks have been turned in different directions to give the finished piece a lively feel, while the gingham for the binding has been cut on the bias for extra definition.

This blue and beige quilt has the feel of an old-fashioned utility quilt, reminiscent of those made by the early settlers in North America for whom all fabric was a valuable resource to be used until it simply disintegrated into shreds. The original inspiration for this piece would almost certainly have been made from heavy homepun wool fabric, and the batting would probably have been either carded wool or cotton, or even an old

blanket, to keep out the intense winter cold that lasted many months.

This version is more appropriate to modern centrally heated houses. Although it is made from worn shirts, it is much lighter in weight and padded with synthetic batting. In keeping with its utilitarian origins, it is tied through all three layers at the corners of each block. A heavier quilt could be made from cotton flannel or lightweight wool, or you could recycle old pajamas.

Making the Quilt

1 *Start by removing all the sleeves from the worn shirts using a rotary cutter. Discard if they are worn at the elbow. Otherwise, cut off the seams and press flat.*

2 *Make a template for the large squares from cardboard or plastic. Our template measures 6½ in (16.5cm) square. Cut out 50 large squares in your chosen colors.*

Gingham Check
This quilt is the perfect way to use worn shirts, abandoned because they have frayed-out collars and cuffs.

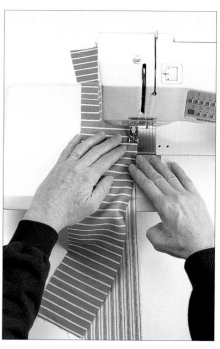

3 *Using a rotary ruler and cutter, cut enough strips of assorted gingham and striped fabric to make 49 4-patch squares. You will need 196 squares in total, each measuring 3¹/₂ in (9cm) square. For interest, cut some strips with the stripes running vertically and others horizontally.*

4 *Place two strips right side together and stitch their long edges. Press seams toward the darker side.*

5 *Using a rotary cutter and ruler, cut across the pieced strips to make pairs (see page 241). Press seams to one side.*

6 *Matching seams, join pairs together into four-patch blocks. Make a total of 49 blocks. Press seams to one side.*

7 Alternating plain squares with four-patch squares, chain-piece them into rows. You will need 11 rows of 9 squares each. Press.

8 Join the rows together to form the quilt top, taking care to align seams. Press seams to one side.

9 Cut the batting and backing to size. Sandwich the three layers of the quilt together: backing right side down, batting on top, and quilt top right side up. Pin carefully. To secure the layers, zigzag around all raw edges before trimming away the excess with a rotary cutter and ruler.

10 To keep the three layers of the quilt together, use crochet cotton to tie double knots at regular intervals across the quilt. Trim the ends to 1$\frac{1}{2}$ in (3.5cm).

11 Cut the binding fabric across the bias into 3in (7.5cm) strips. You will need to join several strips together to form long strips. With right sides together and raw edges even, stitch the binding to the quilt top (see page 252). Turn the binding to the back to cover all raw edges and pin, then slipstitch in place.

Irish Chain Quilt

KNOWN AS IRISH CHAIN in North America and American Chain in Ireland, there is no evidence that this traditional design came from either place. Its origins are lost in the mists of time, but the pattern has been repeated in countless variations for centuries. The version here is Double Irish Chain, by far the most popular of the numerous variations.

Irish Chain is one of the oldest quilt designs, and it is often the first project attempted by a novice. It looks more demanding than it is. It consists of two basic blocks that are pieced individually until you have enough of each to put the whole thing together and watch the bold checkerboard pattern emerge.

This Double Irish Chain consists of chains, pieced by machine, that are three small squares wide, made in two strongly contrasting colors – gray calico print and terracotta orange – against a solid cream background. The binding is made from the same gray print, and the backing is a coordinated floral print.

The solid areas provide scope for simple or elaborate quilting, depending on your level of expertise. Here we have used a grid of parallel lines to set off the checkerboard effect, but you may prefer a more ornate design, such as a traditional feathered cross.

YOU WILL NEED

For the Irish Chain blocks:
1 dark all-over print
1 dark solid fabric
1 light solid fabric

For the borders:
1 dark solid fabric
1 light solid fabric

light all-over print for the backing

batting

water-soluble pen for marking quilting lines

sewing thread

Making the Quilt

1 *Cut the fabric for the checker-board blocks into 2in (5cm) strips. You will need 9 of fabric A (shown as terracotta); 16 of B (gray print); and 4 of C (white).*

2 *Join five strips together along their length, arranging them in three different combinations: ABCBA; BABAB; and CBABC. Press the seams to one side.*

Irish Checkers

This simple patchwork pattern, using nothing more complicated than squares in two sizes, has been assembled with an eye for color to make a stylish quilt.

3 *Using a rotary cutter and ruler, cut across the pieced strips in rows 2in (5cm) wide. To make the checkerboard blocks, you will need 36 rows of ABCBA; 36 rows of BABAB; and 18 rows of CBABC.*

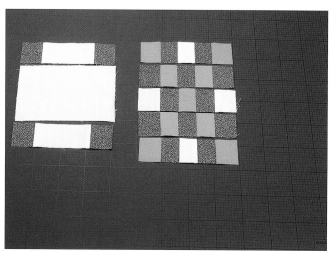

4 *To make the spacer blocks, cut 5in (13cm) strips of fabric C. Join one strip C to two 2in (5cm) strips of fabric B along the longest edges, arranging them BCB. Press the seams to the darker side. Cut the pieced strips in rows (see page 274).*

5 *Cut out 17 pieces of fabric C measuring 5 × 8in (13 × 20.5cm). Arrange the two variations of Irish Chain block as shown. You should have 18 checkerboard blocks and 17 gray-cornered blocks.*

6 *To assemble the checkerboard blocks, stitch five rows together in the correct order, matching corners. Press seams to one side.*

7 *Assemble all the gray-cornered blocks together and press the seams to one side.*

8 *Next, join seven alternating blocks together to form rows. Make five rows.*

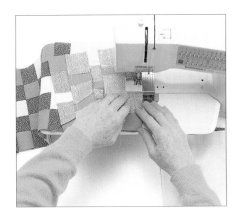

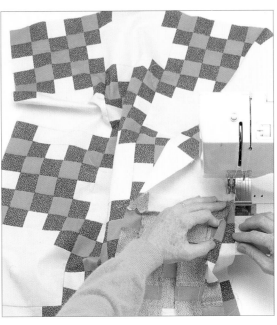

9 *Stitch the rows together to complete the quilt top, taking care to match seams. Press seams to one side.*

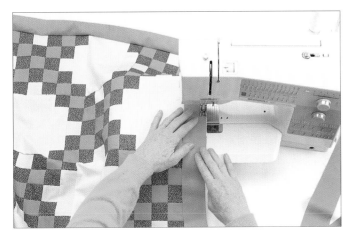

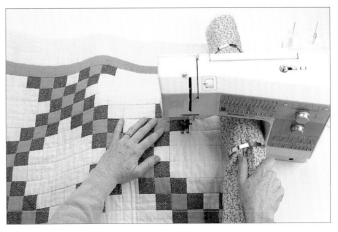

10 *Attach an inner 2in (5cm) border of fabric A around the outside of the quilt, followed by a wider 5in (13cm) border of fabric C.*

11 *Cut the batting and backing to fit. Sandwich the three layers with wrong sides facing the batting and baste. Mark parallel lines 2in (5cm) apart on the plain squares and machine quilt.*

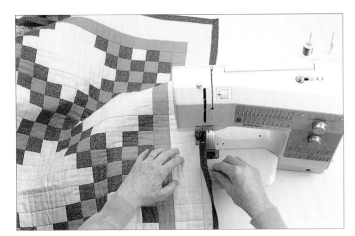

12 *Cut the binding fabric into 3in (7.5cm) strips. Join pieces together as necessary to make long strips. Sew in place around the outside edge, using the back-to-front method.*

Strip-piecing

STRIP-PIECING PROVIDES a way of using up leftover scraps of fabric and of making an item of a particular size or shape. The method has probably been used since the beginning of stitching to join pieces of cloth and leather.

Traditional strip-piecing features in a number of quilting traditions, from the frugal Amish to the impoverished African-American, and was widely used by eighteenth- and nineteenth-century quilters on the American frontier, where new fabric was hard to obtain.

Joining long pieces of fabric with straight seams by hand is, of course, a tedious process, but with the advent of the sewing machine in the mid-nineteenth century, strip-piecing became a time-saving way to assemble a quilt more quickly and more accurately.

However, the modern method of strip-piecing has evolved in the past 20 or 30 years with the invention of rotary cutter and its attendant accessories, the rotary ruler and the self-healing cutting mat. The pieces for a

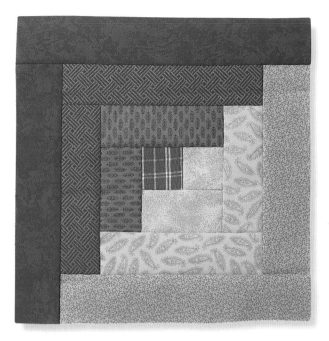

Log Cabin

One of the favorite traditional patterns, Log Cabin is frequently used by beginners, but it is also loved by experienced quilters for its versatility and its variations. The basic block consists of a center square, traditionally red to represent, according to legend, the hearth fire. The "logs" are strips of light and dark values which are stitched around the center square. The farther away from the center you go, the longer the "logs" become. This pattern is equally attractive worked in silk, cotton, or wool, and the strips can be cut from the same fabrics on either side or different fabrics from two color families.

How to Construct a Log Cabin Block

A Log Cabin block may look intricate, but provided you stitch the strips together in the correct sequence and make sure that your seam allowances are accurately measured, it is relatively simple to make.

Cut strips of an equal width from your chosen fabrics, and cut the center square (1) the same width as the strips. Taking a standard 1/4 in (5mm) seam allowance, join the first strip (2) and fingerpress the seam. Add strip 3 in the same color and fingerpress again. Continue adding strips around the center, working in a clockwise direction, until the block is the desired size, fingerpressing each time so that all the seams lie in the same direction.

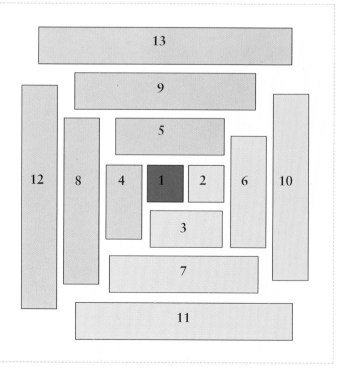

Combining Log Cabin Blocks

One of the fascinations of Log Cabin is its ability to create secondary and subsidiary patterns when it is used in combination with identical blocks. Four of the best known are shown here, but it is worth experimenting by laying finished blocks out and moving them around until you are pleased with their arrangement. Log Cabin blocks, and most of their variations, are pieced side by side without sashing or setting blocks.

Light and Dark
Arranging blocks with four darks side by side creates this traditional setting. The secondary pattern gives square blocks of each color, apparently set on point, throughout the quilt.

Barn Raising
Here, the blocks are organized as concentric bands to make a diamond-shaped pattern that radiates outward from the center of the design. The more blocks you add, the more diamond bands you eventually create.

Straight Furrow
With its name evoking plowed fields and country lanes, this setting creates light and dark alternating stripes that run diagonally across the quilt.

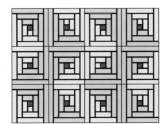

Streak of Lightning
Many traditional quilting patterns derive their names from natural phenomena or the daily lives of the people who made them. The strong zigzag lines of this setting pattern are reminiscent of flashes of jagged lightning.

Log Cabin Chevron
A chevron pattern is formed by adding strips to the small square on two sides only. The colors are usually alternated light/dark or dark/light and added in sequence until the block reaches the desired size.

Chimneys and Cornerstones
This variation creates a diagonal line of squares the same size as the center squares and worked in the same color. A small square must be added to every alternate strip before it is stitched into the block.

quilt top can now be cut in a manner of minutes instead of hours or even days, and the strips can be joined accurately by machine into complex patterns involving simple straight-sided shapes or precise angles.

Today, quilters and designers are continually coming up with new ways to use the labor-saving devices on hand to create variations on traditional designs that are easier to assemble, as well as introducing some new patterns of their own.

The pattern used perhaps most often to teach beginners the rudiments of strip-piecing is Log Cabin, an old favorite that was originally worked by hand, often mounted on a block of muslin. The design, which has many variations, first appeared in the 1850s and '60s, leading some historians to relate it to President Abraham Lincoln, the most famous resident of a log cabin.

Amish Bars Quilt

ECAUSE OF ITS inherent simplicity and straightforward design, the Bars quilt is a good project for the inexperienced quilter. The cutting can be done quickly with a rotary cutter, and the piecing is simply a matter of stitching a few straight seams. With a design of such bold simplicity, the colors and texture of the fabric are vitally important.

We chose a luxurious fine wool crepe in strong vibrant colors for this quilt to add warmth and tactile softness. Texture is all important when choosing fabrics for such a simple design. The beautiful finish and drape of pure wool crepe negates the need for elaborate quilting, but if you choose to make the quilt in plain cottons, you could finish it with some simple quilting. The traditional quilting design used for Amish Bars quilts is crosshatching, which can be carried out very quickly and easily on a machine.

For die-hard recyclers, the perfect filling for a wool quilt is an old blanket, or failing that, cotton batting.

YOU WILL NEED

wool crepe in four vibrant colors for the bars

wool crepe in black or a dark color for the border

wool crepe in any of your chosen colors for the backing

wool crepe in a bright color for the binding

either an old wool blanket *or* new cotton batting

sewing thread

knitting yarn for tying

large darning needle

Sizzling Simplicity
A sizzling spectrum of rich reds, pinks, and purples, darkly framed will gladden the eye and provide warmth and welcome on a cold winter's night.

Making the Quilt

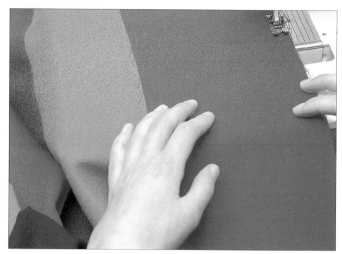

1 Cut the wool crepe for the bars into strips 5in (12.5cm) wide and 54¹/₂ in (138.5cm) long. You will need 12 strips in total, three of each color.

2 Join the strips together along their long edges. If you are using wool crepe, reinforce the seams with a second line of stitching close to the first.

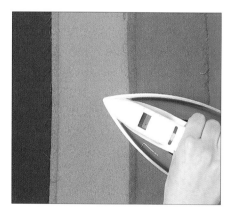

3 Press the seams toward the darker side. You may wish to use a damp cloth for pressing.

4 Using a rotary cutter and ruler, trim the edges so the block is square. The finished block should measure 54¹/₂ in (138.5cm) square.

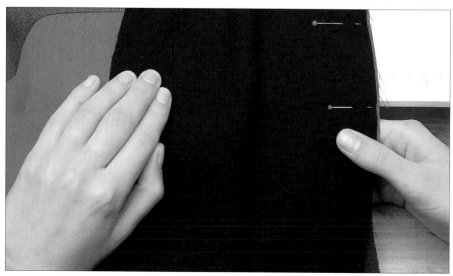

5 Cut four fabric borders 10¹/₂in (27cm) wide from black fabric. You will need two 54¹/₂ in (138.5cm) long and two 74¹/₂ in (189cm) long. Stitch the short border lengths to the top and bottom of the quilt, then stitch the long border strips to the sides. Press seams toward the outside edges.

6 Cut the backing and batting to size, making it 2in (5cm) larger all around than the quilt top. Sandwich the three layers together and pin at intervals to hold in place. Using knitting yarn, tie the quilt at 3in (7.5cm) intervals.

7 Trim the three layers so they are square. Cut the binding fabric into strips 4in (10cm) wide. Join several strips together if necessary to form long strips. Attach a single binding to cover the raw edges of the quilt.

Variation

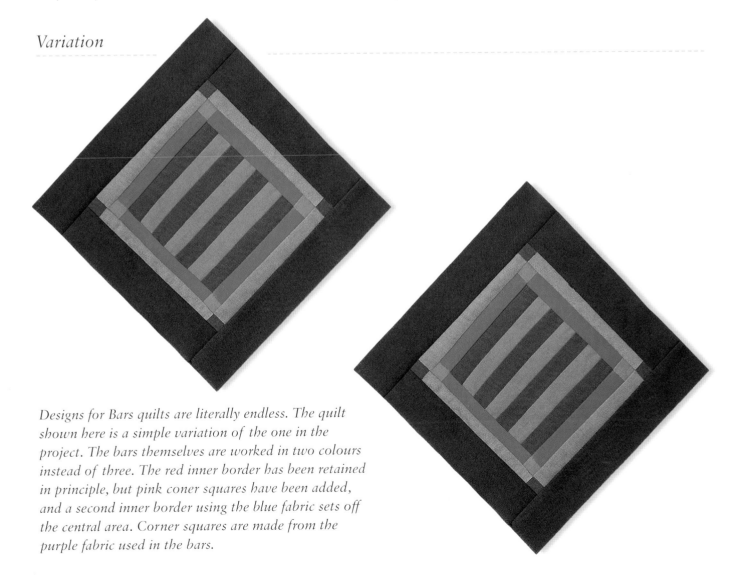

Designs for Bars quilts are literally endless. The quilt shown here is a simple variation of the one in the project. The bars themselves are worked in two colours instead of three. The red inner border has been retained in principle, but pink coner squares have been added, and a second inner border using the blue fabric sets off the central area. Corner squares are made from the purple fabric used in the bars.

Log Cabin Quilt

THIS LOG CABIN quilt is made using a quilt-as-you-go method in which each block is pieced and stitched to a heavy batting at the same time. Even the borders are worked in this quick method before a lightweight batting and backing are added. For more information on quilting-as-you-go, see page 342.

There are a number of ways to make a Log Cabin quilt. One of the quickest is done by cutting strips and chain-piecing in a particular way to make multiple blocks. Log Cabin can be sewn by hand, either by adding strips one by one around a center square, or by applying the square and then the strips to a backing square of muslin or some similar cloth. Miniature Log Cabin quilts on a tiny scale can be fashioned by using narrow strips and a backing of interlining that is printed with a grid pattern.

Log Cabin quilts do not lend themselves to elaborate quilting. Even a strip-pieced Log Cabin quilt has a large number of seams, and most other methods of construction involve more layers than are found in the majority of quilts. The traditional method of holding the layers together is tying, but the quilt-as-you-go technique used here makes a piece that is secure and very warm.

YOU WILL NEED

For the log cabin blocks:
6 dark prints
6 light prints
1 bright, plain fabric
muslin or cotton for block backing
batting for block backing

1 dark print for the outer border

1 dark solid fabric for the inner border

dark fabric for the binding

backing fabric

batting

sewing thread

Making the Quilt

1 Cut the dark and light prints for the pieced blocks into 1¾ in (4.5cm) strips. Separate the strips into light and dark bunches and clip together.

2 Cut twelve 15in (38cm) squares from muslin or cotton and from batting. Mark centers. Pin fabric to batting. Cut twelve 3in (7.5cm) center squares. Pin in place.

Lightning Fast
The rich dark colors contrast with the light-colored calicos in tiny prints to make a quilt with a traditional air in a fraction of the traditional time.

3 *Without removing the fabric strips from the clips, place a light-colored strip face down on the central square. Stitch along the length of the red square, making sure the edge of the strip is parallel with the edge of the square. Lift the presser foot and pull out enough thread to be able to turn the work.*

4 *Trim the first strip even with the central square, open it out, and fingerpress the seam lightly. Pin open on the backing square.*

5 *Place a second light-colored strip face down on the adjacent side of the central square. Start stitching level with the top edge of the first strip and finish level with the bottom edge of the central square. Pull out enough thread to turn, cut off excess fabric, and pin open.*

6 *Make a quarter turn and attach a dark strip on the next side, making sure it is parallel with the first strip. Cut off excess fabric, fingerpress the seam, and pin open on the backing square.*

7 Continue attaching light and dark strips around the central square, working in a clockwise direction and making sure all seams are exactly parallel. Note that piecing and quilting are done simultaneously.

8 When the block has reached the desired size (in this case, 14$\frac{1}{4}$ in/ 37cm square), pull it into shape, then finish the raw edges with zigzag stitch. Trim off excess batting.

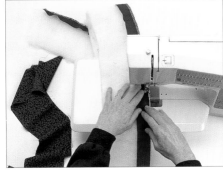

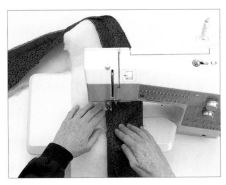

9 Lay the completed blocks on the floor and decide on an assembly pattern. We chose Streak of Lightning, but other combinations are given on page 275. Stitch the blocks into rows with right sides together, matching seams carefully, then join the rows together to finish the quilt top.

10 Cut the fabric for the borders into strips 54in (140cm) long. You will need four 5in (13cm) strips of heavy batting; four 4in (10cm) strips for the outer border; and four 1$\frac{1}{2}$ in (4cm) strips for the inner border. Lay a narrow strip on each piece of batting and zigzag down one long edge.

11 Place an outer border strip face down on each stitched inner border strip. Match the unstitched edge of the inner border strip and stitch through all layers. Repeat to make another strip. Open out, zigzag the raw edge of the border strip to the unstitched edge of the batting. Sew one strip to each side of quilt.

12 Cut two outer border pieces the length of the top and bottom of the quilt plus seams. Add a strip of inner-border fabric and a short length of outer-border fabric to each end of each strip. Cut to length with the insert lined up. Make top and bottom borders as step 11.

13 Cut backing fabric and lightweight batting to the size of the finished quilt and baste the layers together along the edges. Quilt the borders and between each block by hand or machine. Apply binding to the finished quilt.

Triangles

CUTTING SQUARES from corner to corner gives right-angled triangles, known as triangle patches. Although they are trickier to work since one seam must be stitched along the bias, they broaden the scope for creating interesting patterns.

Combining right-angled triangles with squares and strips to make patches for four-patch and nine-patch blocks has provided quiltmakers with ideas for patchwork patterns for centuries.

Many well-known and extremely effective four-patch patterns, such as Pinwheel and its cousin Windmill (see page 287), use patches consisting of two contrasting triangles stitched together along the long side and combined into blocks that look like the blades of a windmill.

The simple four-patch pattern known as Broken Dishes (see page 256) is derived solely from right-angled triangles. When blocks are combined, the effect – or so

Sawtooth
The jagged edges of Sawtooth make it an aptly named block. Constructed here as a nine-patch, it can also be made with the large triangle square as a single piece of fabric. Sawtooth blocks can be combined to create geometric shapes outlined with "teeth" in a contrasting color. The teeth can either point into the center or out toward the edges.

How to Construct a Sawtooth Block

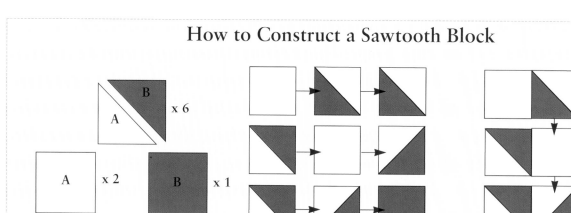

Cutting
Make six triangle squares using fabrics A and B (see page 236). Cut two squares from fabric A and one from fabric B the same size as the finished pieced squares.

Making Strips
Arrange the nine squares and stitch them into three rows, taking a 1/4in (5mm) seam allowance. Press seams in opposite directions on each row.

Joining Rows
Join the assembled rows to make a nine-patch block (see page 258).

the legend goes – is of a pile of broken dishes on the floor. It is certainly fragmented, but much more attractive than the image conjured up by that description. Simple nine-patch blocks such as Ohio Star (see page 295) and Shoofly offer even more variety.

A design of pieced triangles can be a particularly effective way of creating a lively border for a quilt, and some triangle blocks can easily be adapted for use in this way. The jagged "teeth" of the Sawtooth pattern are often seen both in borders, frequently surrounded by narrower borders in a solid color, and in sashing, and can give a feeling of tremendous energy. Flying Geese - triangles set point to base, so that they look like a flock of geese flying in formation – tend to give a rather more formal, controlled feel.

Another way of using Flying Geese triangles is to make strips that are assembled into "strippy" quilts (see page 291). Amish Bars quilts (see page 277) often have

Pine Tree
Most of the pieced blocks depicting trees are formed from triangles and squares, and some are very complex. Most of the squares in this relatively simple example are made from right-angle triangles.

alternating bars formed from the Flying Geese pattern.

Equilateral (60-degree) and isosceles triangles are also used, especially in the Thousand Pyramids design. Here, rows of triangles are joined with the points and bases alternating, and the resulting strips are stitched together to make the quilt. Light and dark colors can be organized to make fascinating and intricate patterns within the piece.

Many of the most familiar and simplest star patterns involve the use of triangles – often combining squares with right-angle triangle blocks, as in Ohio Star, for example. Although their construction is simple, the effect can be stunning. Triangles also form the basis of the Tree of Life and Pine Tree designs that were popular with American quilters in the latter part of the nineteenth century. Indeed, several of the variations that make naturalistic flower and leaf forms are also based on triangles, as are a number of Basket patterns in which the handle is constructed from small triangles and the basket itself from larger ones.

Roman Stripe
This pattern is often found in Amish quilts in which the strips are usually plain, bright colors and the triangle is black or navy. The blocks are joined so the strips face in the same direction. The effect is of patterned and plain triangles facing each other.

Pinwheel Quilt

DRAMATIC PINWHEELS of strong color – plain yellow, vermilion, green, white, and black – have been combined in this geometric design to evoke warmth and faraway places. A chunky scarlet tassel at each corner is a neat, exotic-looking finishing touch. The geometric shapes and contrasting colors make a lively, lightweight quilt.

Quilts similar to this one have been made for centuries in India and Pakistan, and many of the early designs show simple geometric patterns like this pinwheel. Their most striking feature was probably their bold coloring, which was laden with symbolism – for example, the saffron yellow used here recalls the earth, and red is the color of love.

Begin by cutting a 20in (51cm) square from each solid fabric. Place red and yellow squares right sides together. Mark fourteen 3⁷⁄₈ in (9.8cm) squares in pencil on top fabric.

The triangles are stitched by a quick method and then cut, and the pieced triangle blocks are then combined to make a series of four-patch blocks that are joined to make the pattern. Because of the way some black triangles are positioned next to some green ones, an occasional secondary pinwheel pattern can be seen.

Making the Quilt

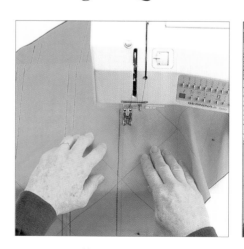

1 Draw a diagonal line through the center of each penciled square. Align presser foot along diagonal line and stitch a 1¹⁄₄ in (5mm) seam first on the right of the line and then on the left.

2 Cut along the marked straight and diagonal lines to form triangles. Open out to form triangle squares and press seams toward the darker side.

Ancient Appeal
The plain cottons of this quilt have been "aged" in tea to give an antique appearance, an effect that is is set off by the block-printed cotton cloth on the back.

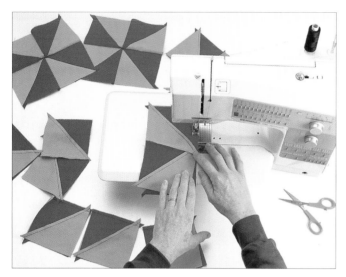

3 Join the pieced squares together in pairs, alternating colors, using the chain-piecing technique (see page 245). Press. Join two sets together to form a pinwheel block, matching center seam. Make 7 pinwheels.

4 Make 8 red and green, and 15 black and white, pinwheels by the same method. Join the blocks into rows, with right sides together, matching seams.

5 Press seams and join the rows together to form the quilt top. Precision is essential, otherwise the seams and corners will not align. For best results, pin seams carefully and stitch over the pin.

6 Cut the border fabrics. The first border is 2¹/₂ in (6.5cm) wide; the second is 1³/₄ in (4.5cm) wide; the third is 1¹/₄ in (3cm) wide; the fourth is 3in (7.5cm) wide. Attach the borders, following the Top and Tail method on page 249. Clip bulky seams and press carefully. Cut the backing fabric and interlining the same size as the finished quilt. Assemble the three layers, following the Bagging technique on page 253.

7 *For the tassels, select four-ply cotton knitting yarn in one of the colors used in the quilt border – here, we have used a strong scarlet. Make the tassels (see below) and attach securely to the corners of the quilt, using matching thread.*

Making the Tassels

1 *Take a strip of cardboard 2¹/₂ in (6.5cm) wide and wind tightly with knitting yarn. Use a short length of yarn to tie the threads together at one end.*

2 *Remove the yarn from the cardboard, holding it tightly at the knotted end with one hand. Cut through the loops at the opposite end to create a tassel.*

3 *Wrap a long length of gold thread tightly around the knotted end of the tassel. Thread onto a needle and fasten with a few small stitches.*

4 *Using a fine crochet hook, fluff up the tassels by teasing out the individual strands of each yarn to give a "crimped" effect.*

Flying Geese Quilt

THE FLYING GEESE pattern probably originated in Britain, where it was used along with other border strip patterns in medallion quilts. It crossed the Atlantic, where the charm of the vigorous triangles lined up in rows gradually became the focus of the quilt itself. It continues to be a good way to use up remnants of fabric.

Strips of Flying Geese were made for the hope chests of young girls from scraps of their gowns, and quilts were created by alternating strips of "geese" with plain, unpieced strips that provided a good ground for elaborate quilting. Eventually strips of "geese", still a favorite way of using up scraps, found their way into the Bars of some Amish quilts.

There are several equally valid ways of creating Flying Geese, but for all of them, it is vital to make sure the triangles are identical in size, and that you keep the correct seam allowance at all times, because a small error repeated over many triangles will compound any discrepancy. The larger "geese" triangles can be as varied as you like, as long as there is a unifying common denominator in color and density of pattern. The small background triangles are best kept to one light color. The completed design works best if you make the sashing strips from a dark color to set off the Flying Geese.

YOU WILL NEED

assorted plaids or stripes for the large "Flying Geese" triangles

light-colored plaid or stripe for the small background triangles

dark-colored stripe for the sashing strips

contrasting stripe for the backing

solid fabric for the binding

batting

sewing thread

Making the Quilt

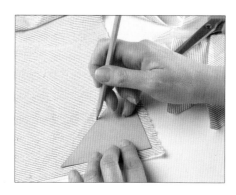

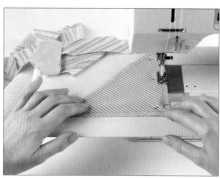

1 Cut 90 large triangles and 180 small triangles (see page 240 for multiple cutting techniques), remembering to include seam allowances of 3/8 in(1cm).

2 With right sides together, pin and stitch the long edge of one small triangle to a short edge of one large triangle. Match corners exactly and take care not to stretch bias-cut seams.

Goose or Gander
The quilt provides a good opportunity to recycle old striped shirts that are worn at the elbow. Choose the color values carefully, however, to accentuate the Flying Geese.

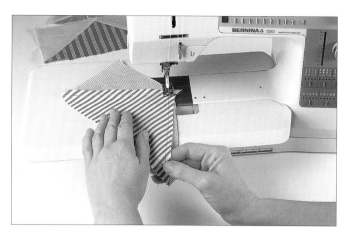

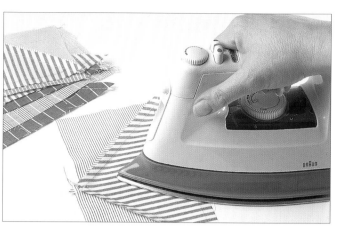

3 Attach the long edge of another small triangle to the remaining short side of the large triangle, right sides together. The corner seam at the point of the large triangle should be 3/8 in (1cm) from the raw edge.

4 Open out the pieced rectangle and presss seams flat on the reverse. Make the remaining Flying Geese blocks in the same way. You should have 90 in all.

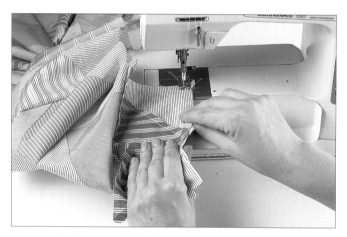

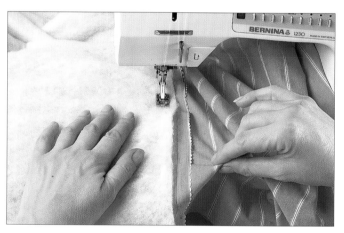

5 Stitch the pieced blocks together along the long side of the pieced rectangle into strips of 18 rectangles each. We used a random arrangement. Press seams toward the point.

6 Cut the backing fabric. We joined two narrow pieces of fabric with a center seam to make a piece 77¼ in (195cm) wide and the same length as the pieced rows. Cut a piece of batting to cover half of the backing fabric and stitch in place along the center seam.

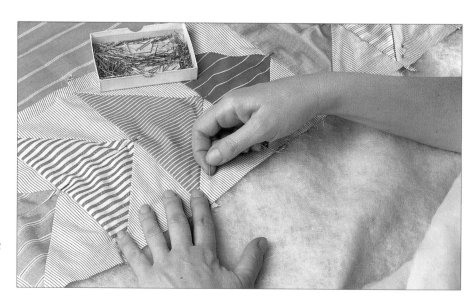

7 Place one of the pieced Flying Geese strips right side up in the center of the batting. Align the triangle points over the center seam of the backing and pin carefully through all three layers.

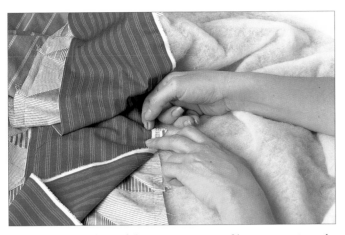

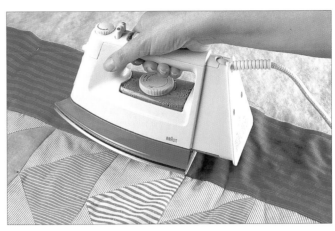

8 Cut the sashing fabric into strips 6³/4 in (17cm) wide and the same length as the pieced rows. Place a sashing strip on top of a pieced strip of triangles, right sides together, and pin, matching raw edges. Baste along stitching line, then sew through all four layers.

9 Remove the basting, open out the sashing strip and press lightly on the right side to remove puckers and wrinkles. Pin open on the batting.

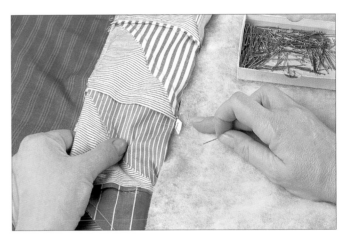

10 Pin a second strip of triangles right sides together on the existing sashing strip. Make sure the triangles point in the same direction as the first and that they line up across the quilt. Stitch in place. Add another sashing strip, followed by a third strip of triangles.

11 When you have completed one side of the quilt, repeat the process on the opposite side. First insert the remaining piece of batting, securing it along the center seam with a row of stitching, then add the sashing strips and pieced strips of triangles.

12 Cut 2in (5cm) wide strips of fabric for the binding. You may need to join several strips to form long strips. With right sides together, pin and stitch the binding in place around the sides of the quilt through all layers. Turn the binding to the wrong side to cover the raw edge and slipstitch in place.

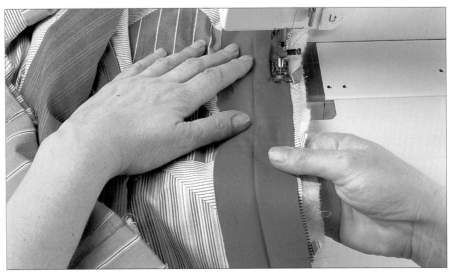

Star Patterns

T HE VARIETY FOUND in Star patterns is phenomenal. Stars can be created from four-patch blocks, or as simple nine-patch patterns such as the ones shown on this page, which are cut from triangle patches and unpieced squares. More complicated "mosaic" stars (see pages 296–97) can be made from diamonds or triangles that require templates.

Star patterns have been a favorite motif for patchworkers almost since the very first patchworks were made. Perhaps their popularity stems from the fact that stars have long had mythical, legendary, and even religious associations; perhaps patchworkers simply relish the technical challenges of piecing some of the more complex designs such as Star of Bethlehem or Mariner's Compass.

Paradoxically, some Star patterns, such as the Friendship Star and Ohio Star shown right and on the facing page, are among the simplest of all patchwork designs to piece. Made from unpieced square and triangle patches, and put together as nine-patch blocks, their success – as always in patchwork –lies in the careful arrangement of colors.

Star shapes made from four-patch blocks are not found quite so often as those made from nine-patch blocks, but they do exist. Some of these patterns, such as North Star, Laced Star, Trailing Stars, Beautiful Star, and Stars and Stripes, are stars by name that look like stars; others, such as Periwinkle, World without End, Clay's Choice, and even Crossed Canoes, which are four-point stars as well as four-patch blocks, have no reference to star in their title and are merely star-shaped.

Prairie Star is another popular design. A six-point star – rather like the Jewish Star of David – the motifs

Friendship Star

This simple nine-patch block forms the basis of a number of interesting patterns. The triangle patches are arranged into a four-point star which gives the block the appearance of tumbling or whirling through the air. It can be combined with plain squares of the same size to create a very simple but vibrant quilt. A dark blue background, combined with a light fabric overprinted with gold or silver gives the look of a night sky.

themselves are usually interspersed with hexagonal blocks in a solid color so the stars appear to float in space. The hexagons are often heavily quilted with wreaths or other circular motifs to offset the angularity of both the pieced blocks and the hexagonal spacers.

Many Star patterns are based on an eight-point star. There are countless four-patch variations, with names like Pierced Star, Ribbon Star, and Martha Washington Star, and even more nine-patch versions, including Braced Star, Variable Star, and Twin Star.

As with the other examples of Star patterns, many of these designs have variations that are starlike in look, but do include the word "star" in their title. One well-known

Ohio Star

Ohio Star is a popular nine-patch block with countless variations. In its simplest form, it consists of five plain and four pieced squares of the same size. The finished blocks are usually alternated with plain ones, although some quilts use simple sashing to separate the blocks.

star block is Feathered Star, in which one of the Star patterns, usually but not always an eight-point version, is edged with small sawtooth triangles. The pattern is usually worked in two contrasting colors and is frequently used as the center in a medallion-type quilt. It is considered one of the most difficult designs to piece – a real test of skill.

There are a number of different ways of setting star patterns. The simplest is to repeat star blocks across the whole quilt (the blocks may be identical or made in different fabrics) and to separate individual blocks with strips of sashing. This works particularly well on relatively simple designs, such as Ohio Star, where bold shapes and colors are the key to the design. Star blocks can also, of course, be set on point, and spacer blocks can be used to alternate between star blocks whether they are set square or on point.

In other designs – particularly the ones that are more complex to construct, or, like Star of Bethlehem, are made from dozens, if not hundreds, of pieces – the central star pattern fills almost the whole quilt top.

How to Construct an Ohio Star Block

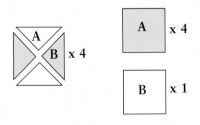

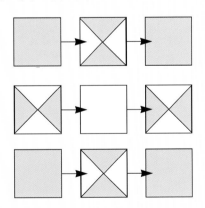

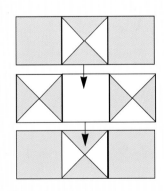

Cutting and Making Squares
For the triangle patches, cut two squares from each fabric and cut them twice across the diagonal. Make the triangle patches, using two triangles of each color. Cut four corner squares from A and one center square from B the same size as the pieced squares.

Joining Squares
Arrange the pieced and plain squares as shown and stitch together in rows, making a 1/4 in (5mm) seam. Press the seams to one side.

Joining Rows
Join the three rows together to form a block, matching corner seams carefully. Press the long seams to one side.

Blazing Star

Also known as Mother's Delight, this four-point star can be simplified by making the corner points in only one fabric, or by eliminating them altogether. When Blazing Star blocks are combined, a secondary pattern emerges – as happens with many patchwork patterns.

Other settings use a central star as the main feature and place smaller stars in the quilt's four corners, and still smaller ones centrally along each side.

Several of the best-known Star patterns are made using templates. They range from four-point versions such as Blazing Star, which is pieced from irregularly shaped diamonds (see left), and all its numerous variations, and the eight-point stars based on diamonds, such as Lone Star (shown opposite) and Star of Bethlehem, to the 16-, 32-, or even 64-point designs found in Mariner's Compass patterns.

Most of these designs are, of necessity, made by the English method of paper piecing, but since they usually have straight seams, many can be pieced on the sewing machine. One can only marvel at the patience of patchworkers in the eighteenth and nineteenth centuries, who pieced designs such as Mariner's Compass by hand!

The main problem with all these patterns is the difficulty of joining the units neatly in the center of the block. Pressing the seams carefully at every stage is vital, and trimming the points as necessary, in the middle particularly, will help reduce the bulk created by having

---

How to Construct a Blazing Star Block

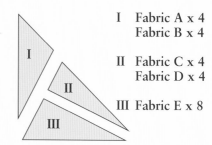

I   Fabric A x 4
     Fabric B x 4

II   Fabric C x 4
     Fabric D x 4

III Fabric E x 8

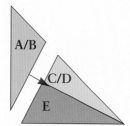

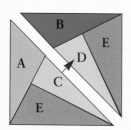

Cutting
Make templates for the three shapes that make up the block. Cut fabrics as follows: shape I – cut 4 x fabric A and 4 x fabric B; shape II – cut 4 x fabric C and 4 x fabric D; shape III – cut 8 x fabric E.

Making the Units
Making a ¼ in (5mm) seam, join a shape II to a shape III. Press seams to one side. Stitch a shape I to the seamed edge. Repeat to make eight units, referring often to the photograph to check the color sequence.

Making the Patches
Join alternate units to make four identical square patches. Join the squares as a four-patch block, matching the seams in the center very carefully.

How to Construct an Eight-point Star Block

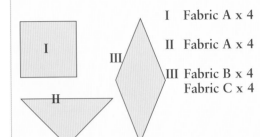
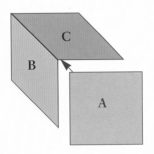
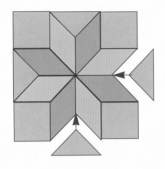

I Fabric A x 4

II Fabric A x 4

III Fabric B x 4
Fabric C x 4

Cutting

Make templates for the diamond and triangle shapes (see pages 284 and 414). Cut four corner squares and four triangles from background fabric, and four diamonds from fabrics A and B; add ¹/4 in (5mm) seam allowances to all.

Making the Patches

Making a ¹/4 in (5mm) seam, stitch a fabric B diamond to a C diamond and repeat to make four pairs. Add a corner square to each unit, stitching from the corner out in each direction. Join units into pairs, then join pairs to make a star.

Assembling the Block

Add triangles in the points to finish the block, stitching from the point of the triangle out in each direction.

so many sharp points all vying for the same space.

The basic construction of Lone Star, shown right, is – in its simplest form – nothing more than eight diamonds in alternating colors, but some quilters have pushed the boundaries further by piecing each of the eight diamonds from dozens of individual diamonds.

By assembling each point using the same fabrics in each row, when the star is finally assembled in all its glory, the effect is of concentric bands of color radiating outward – a veritable kaleidoscope. The technical skill – and patience – required for such a pattern are phenomenal.

The variety found in star patterns, and the challenge they offer to the quiltmaker, guarantee that they will no doubt remain the most popular of all quilt patterns.

Lone Star

The eight-point star is one of the most enduring of all patchwork motifs. Seen here in its simplest form, made from eight diamonds in two alternating colors, it provides the basis for numerous quilts. Careful cutting, preparation, and pressing are essential in the construction of the blocks. To keep all the points sharp in the middle, press seams open to reduce bulk.

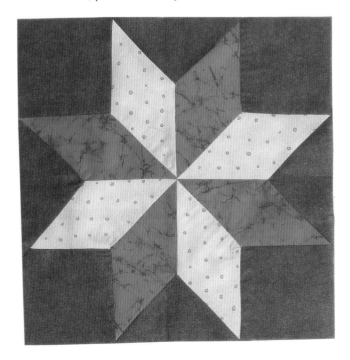

Amish Star Baby Quilt

THE BRILLIANT JEWEL colors of this baby quilt are typical of the work of Amish quilters, as is the center square with its seven separate borders which alternate between light and dark color settings. The corner squares in the second border anchor the center, and the bright-colored sawtooth border – number four – gives the piece a zing.

The central medallion is an eight-point star variation of a traditional pattern called Evening Star. The eight-point star appears in many guises in the middle of similar Amish quilts, especially the Star of Bethlehem, made from myriad diamond-shaped scraps, and the Ohio Star, which looks much like Evening Star but is a nine-patch block rather than the four-patch example shown here.

The borders alternate between dark and light colors typical of those used by Amish quilters. The dark narrower strips have the effect of emphasizing the brighter hues. Above and below the sawtooth border are strips of deep indigo that lengthen the quilt and make it slightly rectangular.

The piece has been quilted simply by machine-stitching along each seam line, but there is scope for more hand quilting like that favored by the Amish, especially along the wider unpieced borders. For quilting templates, see pages 400-29.

Making the Quilt

1 *Make a square template measuring 3⅞ in (9.8cm). Place the two contrasting colors of the fabric that you have chosen for the Eight-point Star right sides together and mark with 6 identical squares.*

2 *Using a ruler, draw diagonal lines across the squares from corner to corner. NB: You only need to mark the top layer of fabric as, with this quick-piecing method, you stitch both layers together.*

Unabashed Brilliance
The brilliant fuchsia of the star shines like a jewel against the deep indigo and blue background and borders, giving the finished quilt an extraordinary brilliance.

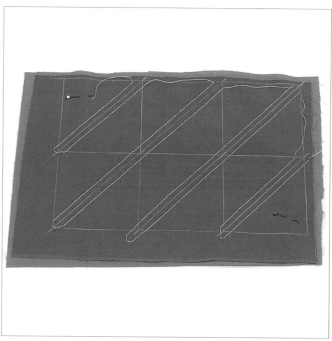

3 *Align the presser foot along the diagonal line and stitch a 1/4 in (5mm) seam first on the left-hand side, then on the right-hand side of the line. Do not cut the thread at the end of each line: simply sew along one side of the diagonal, swing the material around 180 degrees, and sew along the other side.*

4 *When you have finished stitching, your piece of fabric should look like this. As you will see in the stages that follow, this method is far less tricky and time-consuming than piecing the individual squares of the center design one by one!*

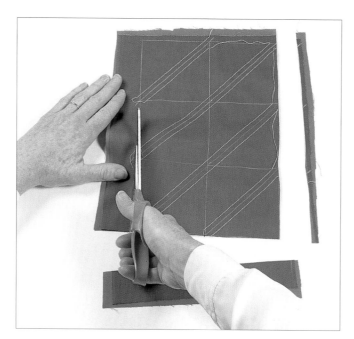

5 *Carefully trim away the outer edges of the block along the marked lines. You can do this with a rotary cutter and ruler, if you have one, or with scissors.*

6 *Cut along the marked diagonal lines between your stitching lines to produce 12 triangles. Open out the triangles and press the seams to one side. You should have 12 pieced squares in total. Cut four plain squares the same size as your pieced squares.*

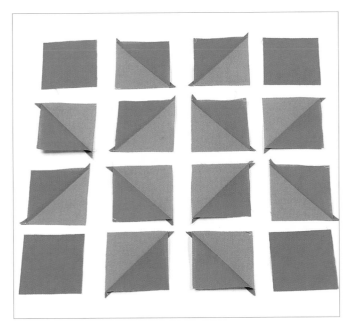

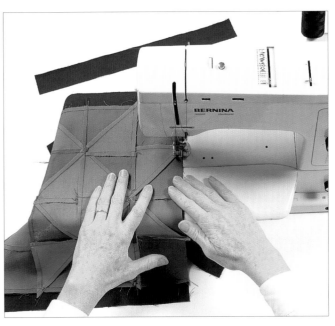

7 *Arrange the pieced and plain squares in your chosen combination. Join the squares together first into rows, then into a block, matching seams carefully. or make four 4-patch blocks and combine them into a double four-patch. Press the long seams to one side.*

8 *The first border band is four strips 1½ in (4cm) wide; the second four strips 3½ in (9cm) wide with a 3½in square at each corner; the third four strips 2½ in (6.5cm) wide; the fourth four strips of pieced triangle patches joined into rows formed from 8 pieced squares, with an unpieced square at one end of each strip. The fifth band is two strips 3½ in (9cm) wide; the sixth four pieces 1½ in (4cm) wide; and the seventh four pieces 3½ in (9cm) wide.*

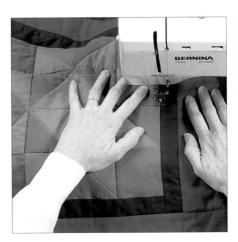

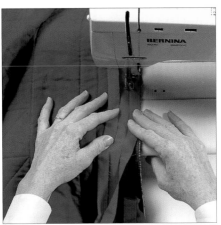

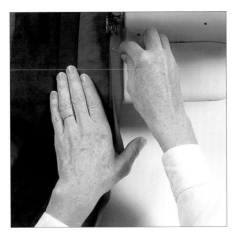

9 *Cut the backing and batting slightly larger than the quilt top and sandwich the three layers together. Pin carefully through all layers. Using a long straight stitch, machine stitch along all seam lines to hold the three layers in place.*

10 *Trim the edges of the quilt, then zigzag to finish. Cut the binding fabric into strips 3in (7.5cm) wide. You may need to join several strips. Attach to the raw edges of the quilt to create a single binding.*

11 *When attaching the borders, particularly the pieced border, to the Eight-point Star block, work on the patchwork side so that you can see the points of the triangle. Start by cutting and stitching the top and bottom borders in place, then cut and stitch the side borders.*

Mosaic and Curved Patterns

MOSAIC PATTERNS HAVE occurred for centuries in art and craft from around the world, and curves are among the most visually appealing of all shapes. While most mosaic designs are based on straight-sided shapes, many of the curved patterns used in quiltmaking also have a mosaic quality.

In patchwork, mosaic patterns are created by joining small pieces of fabric into designs that are regular and repetitive, particularly those based on hexagons and diamonds. The hexagon is one of the most versatile of patchwork shapes, and it has been used to make quilts by the traditional English method of paper piecing since the eighteenth century. Such quilts are still almost always worked by hand, since no one has yet found a way to strip-piece hexagons. The same is true of the diamond, although some larger diamonds can be machine-stitched. If three 60-degree diamonds are combined in a block, a hexagonal shape results, and

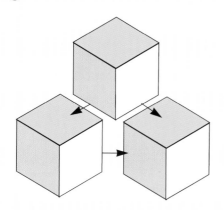

Tumbling Blocks

Also known as Baby Blocks, this charming pattern is highly versatile. The effective three-dimensional feel is achieved by choosing strong color contrasts – light, medium, and dark values – and in careful piecing at the corners. It is usually constructed using the "English" or paper-piecing method, which makes it easier to join the corner points neatly.

How to Construct a Tumbling Block

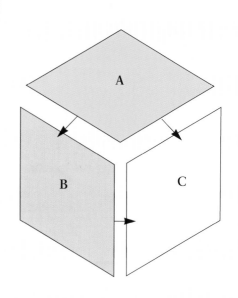

Cutting and Stitching a Unit

Make a template for the diamond shape and use it to cut out paper backing diamonds (finished size), and fabric shapes in the three colors with seam allowances added. Baste each fabric shape to a backing paper, then whipstitch one shape of each color together to make a unit.

Joining Units

Whipstitch along the unit edges. Leave the backing papers in place until the piecing is complete so that the bias-cut edges keep their shape.

hexagons can be combined so the color arrangement creates a diamond shape. Hexagons can sometimes be used instead of squares in creating traditional patterns like Ocean Wave and stars.

Curved shapes have a reputation, not entirely undeserved, for being difficult. They do tend to be intricate and do require careful handling, but because curves are so pleasing to the eye, they are used in a number of popular patchwork patterns. Many of them work best when they are sewn by hand, but careful machine piecing means that some, particularly those that incorporate gentle curves, can be stitched more quickly than in the past.

Many curved patterns work as stand-alone blocks, but others, such as Double Wedding Ring – a favorite challenge for the more experienced quilter – and Drunkard's Path, have a highly mosaic quality that can be used to create beautiful quilts. Fan blocks, for example, can be combined in ways that make repeating mosaic designs, but their nearest relation, Dresden Plate, is usually used as single blocks.

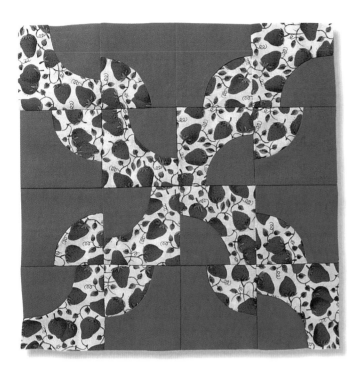

Drunkard's Path

This four-patch block uses curved seams to make a pattern reminiscent of an inebriate staggering home after a jolly night out. The pattern was used in the nineteenth century to make "cause" quilts; designs in blue and white were thought to have been made in support of the temperance movement of the day.

How to Construct a Drunkard's Path Block

I   Fabric A x 8
    Fabric B x 8

II Fabric A x 8
    Fabric B x 8

Cutting and Piecing

Cut eight sections of each piece in fabrics A and B. Join the small fabric A pieces to the large fabric B pieces, and vice versa. Clip into seam allowances before pressing, to encourage seams to lie flat.

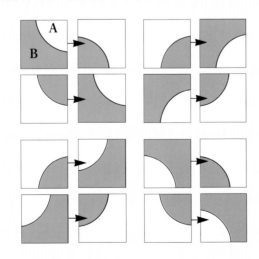

Joining Pairs

Combine the pieced squares into pairs, alternating lights and darks. Then join two pairs together, again alternating colors as shown, to make four patches.

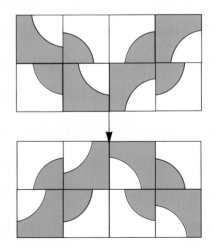

Making the Block

Matching seams carefully, combine the four-patch units into a block.

Baby Blocks Playmat

THIS SMALL QUILT would make a perfect present for a new baby, with its pretty pink and blue color scheme, and its pattern so closely associated with the nursery. It can be used as a crib quilt for a newborn and then as a playmat once the baby is more mobile, but be sure to finish it carefully as it is bound to get lots of hard wear.

Entire quilts can be made from tumbling blocks, but the pattern also works well when it is appliquéd to a background as we have done here. Creating a pyramid emphasizes the diamond shapes on which the pattern is based, and using small groups of floating blocks gives the piece a playful feel appropriate to a young child.

Many people prefer using natural fibers for both fabric and batting in quilts made for children. If you use cotton batting, be sure to wash it first to allow for any shrinkage. The background fabric is widely used for sheets and dust ruffles, and should stand up to heavy laundering.

The machine quilting, a simple outline around the appliquéd shapes, is adequate to hold the layers together securely, but there is plenty of scope for more elaborate quilting if you wish.

YOU WILL NEED

fabric in four colors for the Tumbling Blocks (we used one pale calico print and three solids in strong colors)

fabric for the background

fabric for the backing

batting

typing paper or similar for the backing papers

sewing thread

quilting thread

Making the Quilt

1 *Trace the diamond template from page 414 and cut 175 shapes from plain paper. To make cutting easier and quicker, use a rotary cutter and ruler to cut the fabrics for your blocks into strips 2in (5cm) wide. You will need approximately three or four full-width strips of each color.*

Pretty in Pinks

Alternating two bright pinks adds interest to the blocks patterns. Even though they have entirely different color values, they are both still the middle shade between the dark blue and the light print.

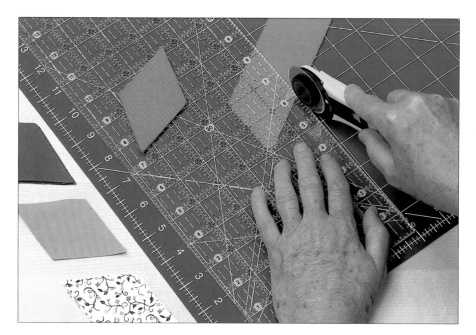

2 Trim one end of each strip at a 60-degree angle. The rotary ruler should include this marking. Cut the rest of the strip into 2in (5cm) diamond-shaped lengths. Repeat to create 175 diamonds in different fabrics.

3 Center a backing paper on a fabric patch, wrong sides together. (The fabric patch should be ¼ in/5mm) larger all around than the paper.) Turn the fabric edges over to the wrong side and baste in place on the backing paper, fingerpressing at the corners before stitching them down. Knot the basting thread on the right side so it is easier to remove later. Prepare all the fabric patches this way.

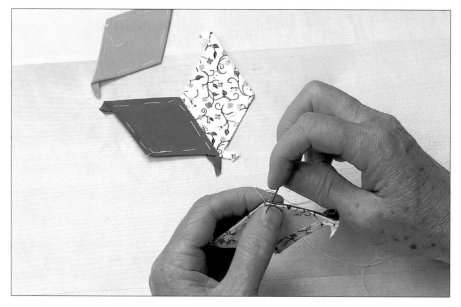

4 The first stage in assembling the Tumbling Block is to join two contrasting diamonds to make a pair. Place two fabric patches right sides together and overcast or slipstitch neatly along one edge. Make sure the seamlines are in the correct position as you work. The "tails" that protrude at each end of the unit will be hidden by the final stitching.

5 Starting in the middle and working out in each direction, overcast or slipstitch the next diamond in place to complete the block. Make 57 blocks in total. Do not remove the backing papers until after the quilt top is complete.

6 Place your completed blocks on a surface and decide on an arrangement. We have alternated blocks of light and dark pink diamonds to create diagonal bands of color throughout the quilt. To assemble the pyramid, start by joining the blocks into strips of 2, 3, 4, 5, 6, 7, and so on, joining the units along one edge only.

7 Then join the strips together to create a tower of blocks. Start at the base of the pyramid with a strip of 8 blocks and join it to a strip of 7 blocks. Continue piecing the blocks together in this way to complete the tower.

Chain Links Quilt

THIS INTRICATE-LOOKING pattern is a variation of Drunkard's Path. It uses the same two shapes to make squares, but the arrangement of these blocks creates a series of ever-increasing rings that can go on and on to make a large square. It can also be pieced by hand, in which case you must mark the seamlines from the template carefully on each patch.

Drunkard's Path and all its numerous variations – with evocative names like Wonder of the World, Falling Timbers, Dove, Love Ring, Snowball, and Fool's Puzzle, to name but a few – are based on a square with a curved "bite" taken out of one corner. Another variation called Robbing Peter to Pay Paul really says it all.

Some of these patterns need half the blocks to be pieced in one combination and half in the other, but Chain Links uses identical blocks to create its effect. Any of the Drunkard's Path designs can be made as scrap quilts, but you must choose your fabrics carefully to keep the color values even through-out the piece or you will risk losing the pattern. The stronger the contrast, the better.

In Chain Links, in particular, the balance between the dark and light colors is crucial. We have used light corners and a dark main square, but a very different look would occur if the colors were swapped.

YOU WILL NEED

light-colored fabric

dark-colored fabric

backing fabric

template plastic

batting

sewing thread

quilting thread

Making the Quilt

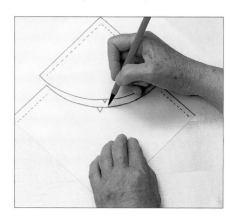

1 Trace your template onto template plastic, or make templates from board. Take care to position the "notch" precisely on each template.

2 Using a rotary cutter and ruler, cut the dark fabric into five strips 6^{1}/2 in(16.5cm) wide, and the light fabric into four strips 4^{1}/2 in (11.5cm) wide.

Links in the Chain
The white-on-white overprinting on the light fabric gives a visual texture that adds interest and depth to a simple pattern.

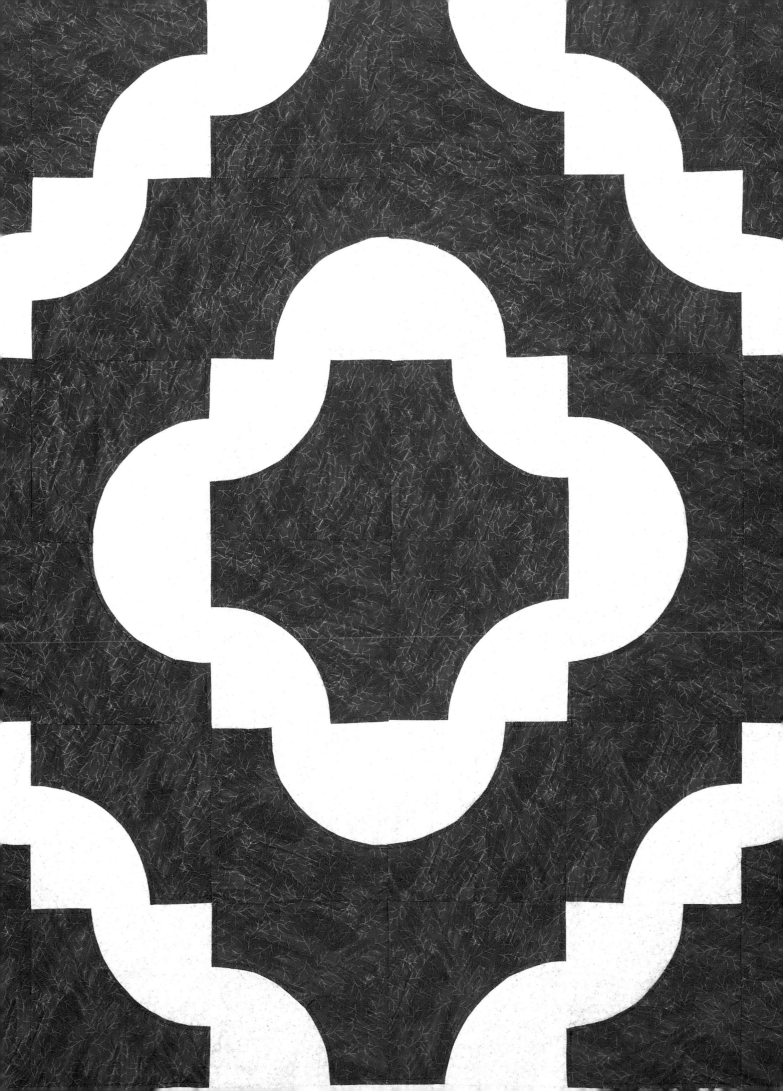

3 *Fold each strip in half right sides together to create a double-thickness layer. Draw around the relevant template to make 18 of each shape (9 of each color). Pin the top and bottom layers of fabric together ready for cutting.*

4 *Carefully cut out the shapes with scissors, paying close attention to the notches. Remove the pins. You should have 36 of each shape (18 of each color).*

5 *Place a large dark-colored patch right side up in front of you. Place a small light-colored "corner" patch on top, right sides together. Align the notches on each patch and insert a pin. Align the side edges and pin again.*

6 *Add more pins along the curved edge, placing them in between the existing pins. Assemble 36 blocks in this way, aligning the notches carefully each time.*

7 *Stitch along the curved edge, making a precise ¹/4 in (5mm) seam allowance, removing pins as you work. You can chain-piece the blocks for speed.*

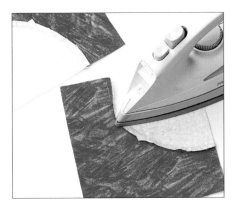

8 *Press the seams on the reverse toward the darker side. If you have cut and stitched accurately, there is no need to clip the curve.*

9 *Lay out the completed blocks to make six rows of six. Rows 1, 3, and 5 are the same configuration, as are rows 2, 4, and 6. Refer to the illustration above to make sure the pattern is correct. Stitch the blocks together in rows and press the seams of each row in opposite directions. Join the rows together.*

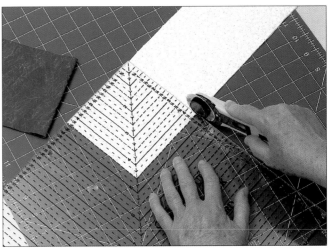

10 *Cut the light fabric for the inner border into strips 1¹/2 in (4cm) wide. Apply to the quilt, following the directions on page 249.*

11 *Cut the dark outer border fabric into strips 4¹/2 in (11.5cm) wide. Cut four 4¹/2 in (11.5cm) corner squares from light fabric. Stitch one to each strip, then stitch the strips to the quilt top.*

12 *Cut the batting and backing to the same size as the finished quilt and assemble the three layers in the following order: batting, quilt top right side up, backing right side down. Stitch around the raw edges through all layers. Turn the quilt right side out and machine quilt in the dark fabric ¹/4 in (5mm) from the seams using matching thread.*

Medallion Quilts

MEDALLION QUILTS, and their close cousins, British frame quilts, are both based on designs consisting of a central panel surrounded by a series of borders of varying widths. They look, and usually are, intricate, and careful planning is essential in making a medallion quilt.

Medallion quilts date from the 1700s in England, and they remained popular through the next century. The design ideas were, naturally enough, imported into North America, and for various reasons, many to do with the availability of certain fabrics that lend themselves to use in medallion quilts, they were widely made until the end of the nineteenth century. The Center Diamond was a popular medallion design among the Amish.

Plain lengths of patterned fabrics are found in medallion quilts, but most versions contain at least one

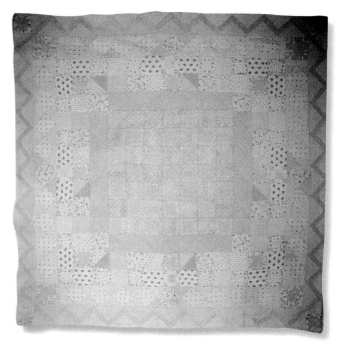

Stars and Spacers
Pieced pink eight-point stars with blue spacer blocks make up the central medallion in this late nineteenth-century quilt from Teesdale in County Durham, England. The five borders are also pieced, with the pink chevrons in the outer border repeated in the first, and the stars used again in the second.

How to Construct a Medallion

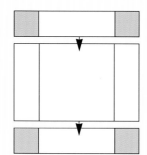

Making Block I
Cut the center panel, making sure the edges are straight and the corners square. Add a border to opposite sides and make and apply strips with corner squares for the top and bottom.

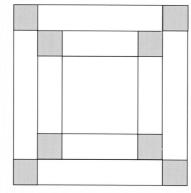

Making Block II
Continue adding borders by your chosen method until you reach the edge of the quilt.

Medallion Borders
The borders found on medallion quilts can be pieced or plain, and the corner squares used can be simple pieces of fabric or can be versions of patchwork blocks or appliqué patterns. The Round Robins so beloved of quilt groups are versions of medallion quilts in which each quilter adds another border to the original maker's center square.

or more pieced borders. The center panel can also be pieced, and the form offers great potential for the appliqué enthusiast. There are many surviving historical examples, and these can be wonderful sources of inspiration to anyone who wishes to embark on a new medallion quilt.

Because medallion quilts generally have a plethora of pattern as well as many seams, quilting is usually limited to stitching along seamlines to secure the layers together. Any quilting done on highly patterned fabric tends to be lost, so apart from outlining and quilting in the ditch, medallion quilts do not need to be heavily stitched. The exception is any version that shows intricate appliqué mounted on a plain background. Such quilts are usually greatly enhanced by carefully planned and executed quilting that flows around and through the shapes.

Squares within Squares
The double medallion is pieced from printed cotton squares and surrounded by two diamond-and-hourglass borders, then more squares. Each border strip is quilted separately.

Sqaure on Point
Both this quilt (1835-50) and the one above (1860-90) were made by a member of the family who lived at Snow Field Farm at Stanhope near Weardale in County Durham. The diamond at the centre of this design is a single piece of floral chintz set on point in a square of small print calico.

Center Diamond Quilt

THE CENTER DIAMOND quilt, the quintessential Amish design, is complicated slightly by its long bias-cut seams, which must be sewn carefully to avoid stretching them. However, the heavy quilting traditionally worked on these quilts, such as dense areas of crosshatching, eases the impact of any distortion and enhances the bold, simple spaces provided by the design.

The seeming simplicity of the Center Diamond pattern, also known as Diamond in the Square, belies its potential. Most Center Diamond quilts consist of the large central panel with its enclosed diamond shape and two borders, the inner one narrow and a wide outer one. But the number of possible variations are endless. The diamond can be a plain piece of cloth, or it can be pieced – into stars or Sunshine blocks – or bordered with sawtooth edges. Sometimes the diamond contains a separate square. The borders can float – that is, have no corner squares – or they can be anchored by squares in coordinated or contrasting colors. And the quilting possibilities are positively mind-boggling. The large plain areas cry out to be given texture and pattern like no other design on earth. For a selection of quilting templates, see pages 400–29.

YOU WILL NEED

solid fabric in two colors for the center diamond and background triangles

solid fabric in four colors for the borders and corner squares

solid fabric for the binding

solid fabric for the backing

batting

sewing thread

Making the Quilt

1 *Cut out the center diamond and background triangles. The diamond measures 14¹/2 in (37cm) square; the four right-angle triangles are cut from a 15¹/4 in (39cm) square, which is cut twice across the diagonal to form four right-angle triangles.*

2 *Cut out the borders and corner squares. The inner border uses four strips 2¹/2 in (6cm) wide and 18in (45.5cm) long and four 2¹/2in (6cm) squares; the outer border uses four strips 7in (18cm) wide and 23in (58.5cm) long and four 7in (18cm) squares.*

Diamonds and Hearts
The rich hues of this quilt are made more emphatic by the black areas, which make the jewel colors stand out dramatically.

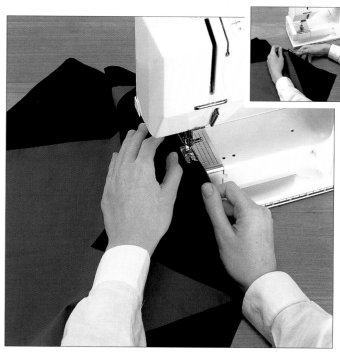

3 Match the center of the long side of a black background triangle to the center of one side of the center diamond and mark with a pin. Make a ¼ in (5mm) seam. Attach another triangle to the opposite side. Inset: Press seams toward the outside edge.

4 Add the third and fourth triangles to the center diamond, as in Step 3. Press seams toward the outside edge. Inset: Using a small pair of scissors, trim the overlapping points of black fabric at the corners of the blue square.

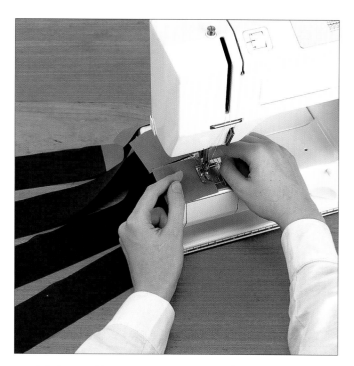

5 Making a ¼ in (5mm) seam, stitch a pink corner square to one end of each inner border strip. For speed, follow the chain-piecing method. Cut the strips apart and press seams to one side.

6 Following the method used in step 5, chain-piece the larger corner squares to the outer border strips. Cut the strips and press the seams to one side.

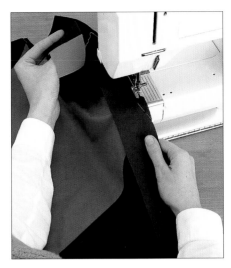

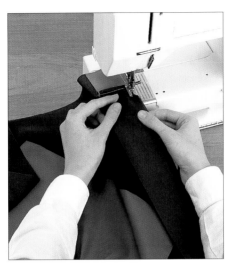

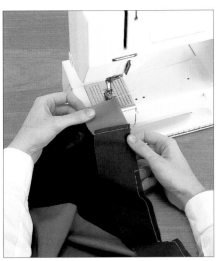

7 Apply the first inner border strip to the pieced center square, right sides together. Line up the strip so the corner square at the end of the strip overhangs the top edge of the center section. The end of the strip should align with the edge of the center. Begin stitching approximately 3in (7.5cm) below the corner square.

8 Add the second and third inner border strips, stitching them in place using a 1/4 in (5mm) seam. Match the seams precisely where the corner squares meet the center section.

9 Stitch the fourth inner border strip in place, then return to the overhanging corner square on the first strip. Matching the seams precisely as before, finish stitching the seam to complete the inner border.

10 Add the outer border, following the method in steps 7-9 Trace the heart quilting template from page 406 and mark the patterns on the quilt top.

11 The quilt top will look like this. Cut backing and baste the layers together. Using quilting thread, quilt along the lines marked by hand. When the quilting is complete, remove the basting and bind the quilt.

Provençal Quilt

THIS CHARMING QUILT would make a good project for a beginner, since it does not require any complex piecing. The only tricky procedure is mitering the corners, which need close attention for a professional finish. The machine quilting is easy to do, consisting of parallel rows of stitching around the border and simple crosshatching in the center.

The French have a tradition of simple patchwork using plaids and prints, but where they really excel is in their Provençal quilts of block-printed cottons in radiant colors with wide borders and fine quilting.

The region of Provenc e is known across the world for its colorful prints, known locally as "les indiennes," named for the wood-block printed cloth that was imported into the area from India in the seventeenth century.

The tradition still flourishes today, and vibrant fabrics in glorious colors can be found at the many outdoor markets throughout the region. Most of the fabrics available today are no longer printed by hand, but many of them still emulate the brightness and subtlety of the original designs.

Provençal cottons have an extraordinary capacity to coordinate well together and no where is this more evident than in this quilt, where geometric prints and floral borders blend into a beautiful whole in perfect harmony.

Making the Quilt

1 *Cut a rectangle for the center panel 24 x 30in (61 x 76cm). Cut the fabric for the outer border into strips 5½ in (14cm) wide. You will need two pieces 57in (145cm) long, and two pieces 52in (132cm) long.*

2 *Cut strips 4½ in (11cm) wide for the middle border, two 41in (104cm) long and two 47in (119cm) long. Cut floral fabric strips 4½ in (11cm) wide – two 33in (84cm) long and two 38in (97cm) long.*

French Style
When you are combining several different prints in a quilt, it is important to have at least one unifying element. Here, the geometric print in the center is repeated in the outer border.

3 The floral border is made from two narrow strips that have been joined right sides together along the entire length. This doubles the border width and gives a mirror image of the pattern when the fabric is opened out.

4 Stitch three side border strips together along their length. Repeat. Stitch top and bottom borders. Press the seams to one side. Cut the ends of each strip across the diagonal at a 45-degree angle.

5 Measure and mark a point 1/4 in (5mm) in from the corner on the center panel. Mark a point 1/4 in (5mm) in from the corner of the inner border. Using a rotary ruler, mark the stitching line – a precise 45-degree angle – along the diagonal edge of the borders.

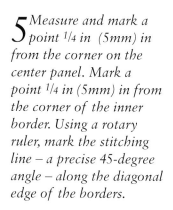

6 Pin the top border to the center panel, first in the middle, then at each side, matching marked points. Stitch in place, starting and finishing precisely at the marked points. Working in a counterclockwise direction around the center panel, add the side border and pin in place. Begin stitching the border, starting at the base of the quilt and finishing exactly on the marked point at the top. Leave the needle in the machine and lift the presser foot.

7 *Without breaking off the threads, rotate your fabric 45 degrees and position the two diagonal pieces of fabric for stitching.*

8 *Continue the row of stitching, matching border seams and stitching carefully along the marked lines only. Add the bottom and side borders in the same way, again paying close attention to the marked points.*

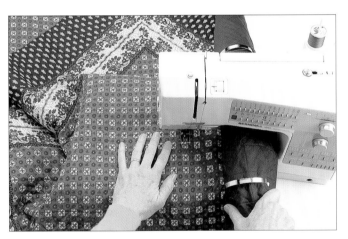

9 *Cut batting and backing the same size as the quilt and assemble the layers. Anchor the layers together for quilting by basting or pinning. Stitch the diagonal lines of crosshatching across the center panel.*

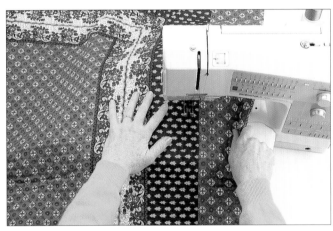

10 *Quilt the borders with parallel lines 1–2in (2.5–5cm) apart, working around the quilt in a clockwise direction.*

11 *Cut the binding fabric into strips 3in (7.5cm) wide. You may need to join several strips together. Attach them to the raw edges of the quilt, following the directions on page 252.*

Crazy Gallery

LTHOUGH "CRAZY" PATCHWORK was probably the first method used to make lengths of fabric from small scraps, as a decorative fabric craft using scraps of fine fabrics like silk and velvet, or even cotton, to make bedcovers and throws is associated firmly with the Victorian era. To begin with, it was almost certainly practiced as a necessary way to preserve and recycle tiny pieces of a valuable fabric.

Victorian stitchers almost always applied their crazy scraps by hand to a backing of a lightweight foundation fabric. Various methods were used to hold the scraps in place, from simply basting them down and using decorative stitches to embroider over the raw edges, to fitting small pieces around a centrally positioned one, to turning the edges under and slipstitching them in place like appliqué.

A century or so later, there are several quicker and more secure ways of creating a piece of crazy patchwork. They all still need a foundation fabric, but can be sewn by hand or machine, or they can be pressed on a backing of fusible webbing, the method used to create the jewelry pouch on the following pages.

It is possible to make a crazy quilt by cutting a piece of backing large enough to cover the bed and applying

Curved pieces
Laying scraps out on a foundation is the best way to decide which ones to use where. It can be tricky to work with curved pieces, and they should be incorporated at a fairly early stage in the construction of the block if at all possible.

Coping with obtuse angles
Using scraps of fabric cut with obtuse angles, such as the bottom of the large red scrap in the top right-hand corner is difficult and may make it necessary for you to turn under an edge or two by hand. Alternatively, the piece could be appliquéd in place.

the scraps directly to it, but it is much easier to work with smaller blocks that can then be put together, either edge to edge or with sashing, to make a quilt or throw. To make clothing from pieces of crazy patchwork, cut foundation pieces that are roughly the same shape as the garment pattern pieces, but make them slightly larger to allow for the shrinkage that occurs when so many seams are sewn. Crazy patchwork for clothing is best worked by machine.

Sewn crazy patchwork can be worked as a hand technique, and for those who love the feel of fabrics, it is a satisfying method, especially if you are using fine material like velvet, satin, or silky textiles, but piecing by machine is quick and not difficult. Whether you work by hand or machine, you may find that some raw edges are not turned under as you work and must be hemmed or slipstitched in place. If you keep straight edges as you work and make sure all the raw edges are covered under the newest piece to be sewn, you should avoid the

problem. If you end up with spots where the foundation shows through, simply cut a piece of fabric roughly the same shape as the blank space and appliqué it in place with the edges turned under.

Using scraps of any shape or size, you can use a stitch-and-turn method to make crazy patchwork. You can position the first scrap in the center of the foundation fabric and sew odd-shaped pieces around it, working out toward the edges. Or you can start in one corner of the foundation block and work out in a fan shape, from the bottom edge to the one adjacent to it, until you reach the opposite corner of the foundation. New pieces are sewn on with right sides together. Once you have sewn a seam, trim its raw edges to reduce bulk and keep things neat. When you finish a block, baste around the outside edges.

Decorative stitching can also be worked by hand or machine. Outline stitches can follow the seams, and individual motifs can be embroidered in separate scraps. Let your imagination run wild.

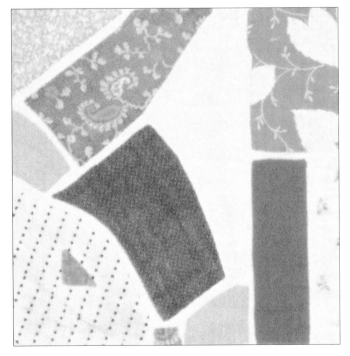

Complementary colors

The use of blue in each of these samples shows the effect of incorporating a complementary color into a block. In the first three of these samples, the blue scrap is the one that jumps out visually.

Cut Fabric to Fit

If you use the brown floral scrap in the middle of this block as the starting point and apply the others around it, you will still have a raw edge that needs to be turned under by hand along the seam joining the red dotted piece above and the gold one on the right.

Crazy Patchwork Jewelry Pouch

THIS ATTRACTIVE YET practical pouch is perfect for keeping your treasured items of jewelry safe and sound. Lined with a hand-quilted piece of silk, it will protect your favourite earrings, rings or necklaces from damage. Making the pouch also provides excellent practice in one of the popular methods for making crazy patchwork.

One of the most popular methods for making crazy patchwork makes good use of fusible webbing. Silk is notorious for raveling, and it can be difficult to make use of small pieces before they disintegrate, but scraps backed with webbing can be bonded to a lightweight backing fabric in a way that covers up all the backing without any overlap and secures all the raw edges so no raveling occurs. Just make sure the edges of each scrap are cut straight and that the pieces fit together, and remember that the webbing makes the pieced fabric a little thicker and slightly more difficult to embroider by hand.

We have hand-quilted a piece of silk for the lining. You can use a piece of prequilted fabric if you prefer – but silk gives such a luxurious feel; and you need such a small amount for a project this size, that it is well worth the additional expense.

Making the Jewelry Pouch

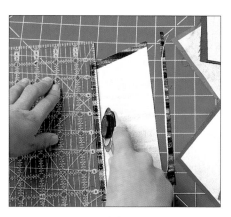

1 *Select scraps that you feel work well together and lay them out on a piece backing fabric cut to size, here 8¹/2 in x 24¹/2 in (21.5 x 62.5cm). Try out different combinations until you have a pleasing arrangement.*

2 *Iron a piece of fusible webbing to the wrong side of each chosen scrap. Make sure the webbing is smaller than the fabric, so that the glue does not get on your ironing board cover. Trim the raw edges from each scrap.*

Travel the World
The pouch can be used on a dresser to keep jewelry handy, and it is a very useful and attractive way to carry your trinkets when you travel.

3 Working in sequence, peel off the backing paper and bond each scrap to the backing fabric in order. Butt each scrap up to the next. Do not leave any gaps, but try not to overlap scraps either. Using a variety of stitches, decorate each edge of every fabric scrap.

4 It is unlikely that the patchwork rectangle will need to be trimmed to even up the edges. Make sure you do not embroider beyond the edges – if you cut throught the embroidery thread, it will unravel.

5 To make a flap, cut two 4 x 6in (10 x 15cm) pieces of lining fabric and stitch them right sides together along the sides and one long edge. Trim the edges and turn the piece right side out, then press. To make pockets, cut two 8½ in x 10in (21.5 x 25cm) pieces of lining fabric and stitch them right sides together along both long edges only. Turn right side out, press, and topstitch a double line along each stitched edge.

6 Cut batting and lining fabric 9 x 25 in (23 x 63.5cm). Mark diagonal lines 1in (2.5cm) apart on the fabric, and baste or pin the layers together. Quilt a grid. Cut a 3in (7.5cm) length of cord and secure it, looping downward, in the center on the right side o f the quilted lining.

7 Place pocket piece 1in (.5cm) up from the bottom on the right side of the lining. Stitch along center from raw edge to raw edge. Then stitch at a right-angle through the center of top half to make a small double pocket. Baste flap to bottom edge of lining piece.

8 Making sure the edge of the large pocket is not caught in the basting that secures the flap, place the crazy patchwork piece right sides together on the quilted lining piece. Pin or baste it in place.

9 Stitch around all sides, leaving a 4in (10cm) gap in one side edge. Rounding the corners will make a neater finish. Turn the pouch right side out and slipstitch the gap to enclose all raw edges. Notice that the flap hangs free at the bottom edge.

10 Press the edges carefully, using a pressing cloth. Fold the pouch and check the position of the button loop, then sew on a button to correspond.

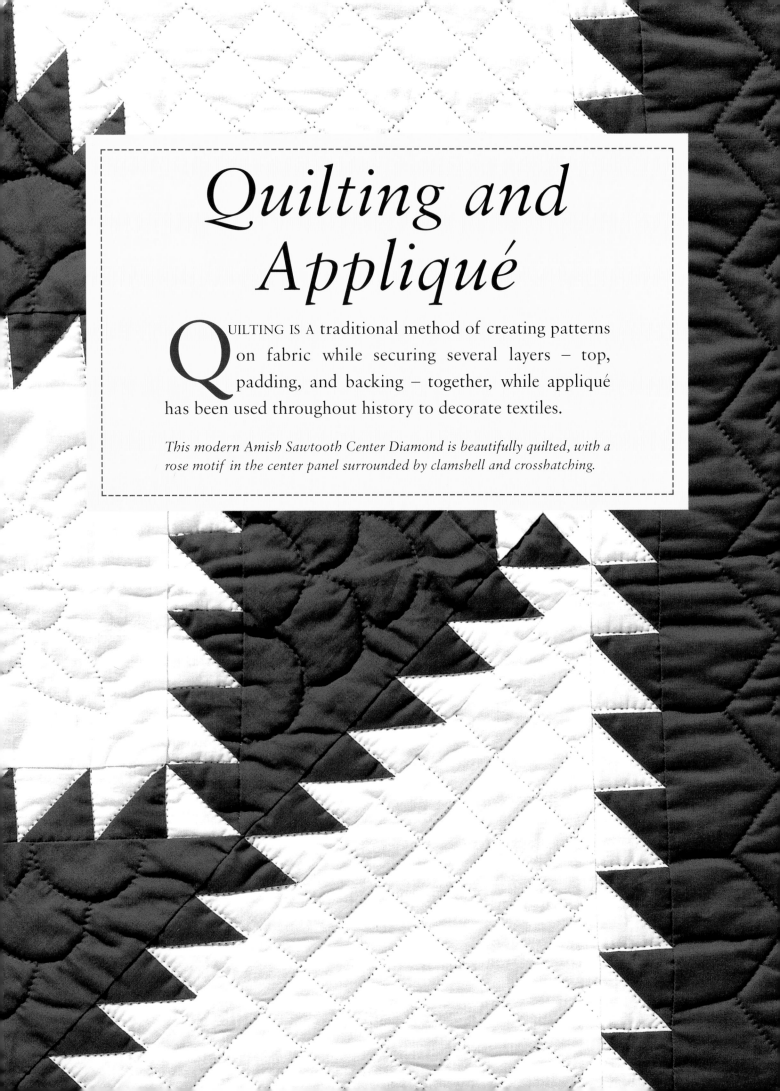

Quilting and Appliqué

QUILTING IS A traditional method of creating patterns on fabric while securing several layers – top, padding, and backing – together, while appliqué has been used throughout history to decorate textiles.

This modern Amish Sawtooth Center Diamond is beautifully quilted, with a rose motif in the center panel surrounded by clamshell and crosshatching.

Quilting and Appliqué Techniques

Tʜᴇʀᴇ ᴀʀᴇ ᴠᴀʀɪᴏᴜs techniques used in quilting and appliqué. The ones that follow are only a selection, and there may be other ways to approach projects.

The concentric circles in this quilt, made in Pennsylvania in about 1860, are quilted following the rings. The triangles in the outer circles and the Sawtooth shapes in the sashing strips are outline-quilted, while double diagonal lines create a background pattern.

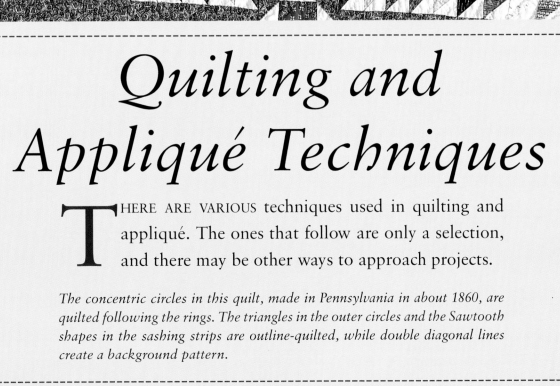

Tools and Equipment

STITCHERS THROUGHOUT THE world have quilted for centuries with limited equipment. While many of the same simple tools used by dressmakers, tailors, and patchworkers are also used by quilters, specialized or adapted items help make both quilting and appliqué quicker and easier.

Sewing

Both the quiltmaker and the appliqué worker need basic sewing equipment, including scissors, needles, thread, straight and safety pins (and somewhere to keep them close at hand and safe), and thimbles. Lots of people use a sewing machine for appliqué work as well as for piecing the top and adding the borders, and many quilt by machine as well.

Ordinary sewing thread is used for appliqué work, and it can also be used for quilting, especially by machine. There is now a choice of thread available in a reasonable choice of colors and especially spun for hand quilting, which is waxed to make it heavier and stronger than sewing thread.

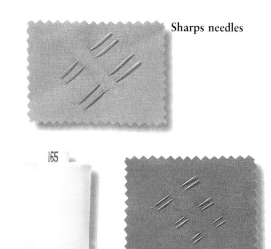

Sharps needles

Quilting thread

Betweens needles

Pins and needles

ABOVE AND BELOW: Needles used for quilting are known as "betweens," and can be used for appliqué, allowing you to make tiny stitches not possible with sharps. Pins are used at several stages in quiltmaking. Quilter's pins are longer than ordinary straight pins. Rustproof safety pins can be used to "baste" the layers of a quilt together for hand-quilting.

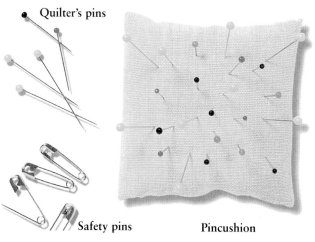

Quilter's pins

Safety pins

Pincushion

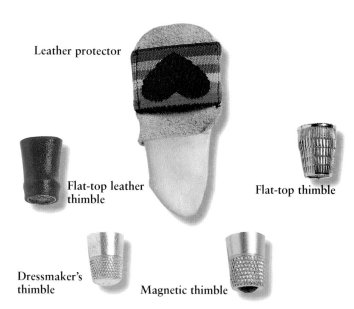

Leather protector

Flat-top leather thimble

Flat-top thimble

Dressmaker's thimble

Magnetic thimble

Thimbles

LEFT: Should you use a thimble or not? Some quilters refuse to wear them; others cannot stitch without them. To execute a rocking quilting stitch without some form of protection is an invitation to pricked fingers, however, and the choice these days is enormous.

Measuring and Drawing

Accurate measuring is essential at all times when you are creating a quilt. To make stencils or determine the spacing between lines of quilting, you may need to use a variety of tools or equipment, much of which can be found in a sewing box or desk, while the rest can usually be borrowed from the workshop or a handy student.

A compass, protractor, and set square are utilized for measuring angles and drawing regular curves.

The flexible curve (also known as a French curve) is an artist's tool used for making curves that hold their shape while you reproduce them. A

A ruler, tape measure, T-square, and seam gauge are used for determining measurements and distances, and drawing straight lines.

Tracing paper is pretty well an essential drawing material; in addition, squared and isometric graph paper can be useful for drafting accurate templates and patterns for quilting and appliqué.

Useful tools

BELOW: *Almost all the drawing and measuring equipment you need for quilting and appliqué is readily available from good stationery stores. The items shown here would all be useful and inexpensive additions to your workbox.*

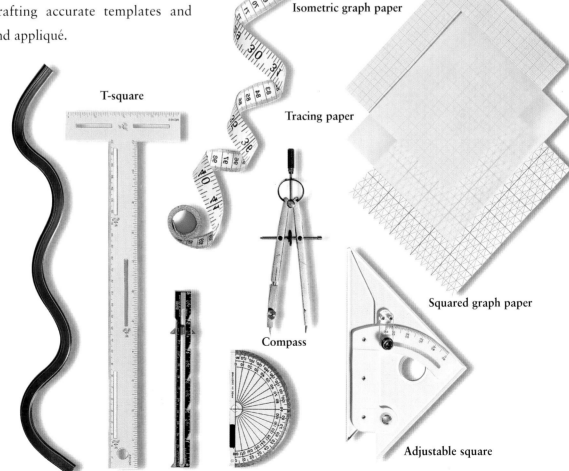

Tape measure

Isometric graph paper

Tracing paper

Squared graph paper

T-square

Compass

Adjustable square

Metal ruler   Plastic ruler   Flexi curve   Seam gauge   Protractor

Stencils and Templates

Ready-made templates and stencils for appliqué and quilting come in an array of styles and sizes, and while they can be expensive, they are also highly accurate and long-lasting. If you prefer to make your own, make sure you measure and cut accurately. Sheets of see-through template plastic that can be cut easily with a craft knife are available, and firm cardboard can be used to make stencils and templates that will not get heavy use.

Self-adhesive film, cardboard, and freezer paper

ABOVE: *Self-adhesive film (left) can be cut into shapes and positioned to give a clear, long-lasting outline. Freezer paper (right) can be ironed to the wrong side of fabric and used to create a firm edge for cutting and basting appliqué pieces.*

Templates

LEFT: *Templates are used as outine patterns and can be any size or shape. Ready-made versions are usually made from plastic or metal; you can easily make your own from cardboard.*

Stencils

BELOW: *Ready-made quilting stencils can be expensive, but because they are made from good-quality clear plastic, they are usually sturdy and hold up under repeated use.*

Frames and Hoops

Quilting frames and hoops are specialized for their task. The familiar wooden varieties are thicker than ordinary embroidery hoops, and have a sturdier and longer tightening bolt, specifically to cope with the layers of fabric and batting.

Frames and hoops that are made from white plastic tubing with grip pieces are adjustable and lightweight. They come in a variety of sizes, from small square shapes to larger, floor-standing versions, and are easy to dismantle and store when they are not in use. Full-size floor frames are also available to the dedicated hand-quilter.

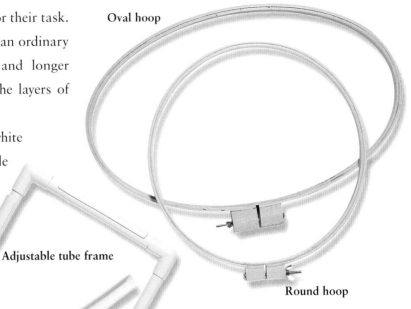

Oval hoop

Adjustable tube frame

Round hoop

Marking Equipment

Tools for marking fabric for quilting and appliqué have become highly specialized in the past few years. Some quilters still prefer ordinary lead pencil or a tailor's pencil used lightly, or tailor's chalk. However, none of these options washes out, and the chalk can be difficult to manipulate. Among the newer options are chalk and soapstone pencils, silver quilter's pencils, and air- or water-soluble pens, most of which can be erased from many fabrics. For quilting straight lines, narrow masking tape can be laid on the fabric and removed after stitching.

Dressmaker's carbon

Masking tape

Tailor's chalk
and chalk wheel

Marking equipment
RIGHT: *(left to right) chalk pencil; lead pencil; soapstone pencil; transfer pencil; silver quilter's pencil; fade-away pen; water-soluble pen; watercolor pencil; tailor's pencil.*

Hand Appliqué

THERE ARE MANY ways to approach hand-appliqué work. The traditional method involves cutting a shape, pinning it to the background fabric, and turning under a small seam allowance using the point of the needle.

Other methods that can make appliqué neater and quicker, as well as being more accurate, have also been devised and adapted over the centuries. Turning under and basting the edges of a fabric shape, or basting shapes over paper, similar to so-called English patchwork, helps create sharp edges to sew along. Both of these techniques take a little longer than needle-turning, but are widely used.

Turned-edge appliqué
A wall hanging made in Christmas colors is based on the Amish Lancaster Rose design, one of the few appliqué patterns used by Amish quiltmakers.

1 *Make a template and cut the shape from fabric. Cut the shape, minus seam allowances, from a support paper such as typing paper or freezer paper.*

2 *Pin the paper shape, or iron the freezer paper onto the wrong side of the fabric shape. Turn under and baste fabric to support. Clip the seam allowance if necessary.*

3 *Press the basted shape to make a good crease on the edges and pin it in place on the background fabric. Mark the background to make positioning easier if you wish.*

4 *With thread to match the appliqué, secure the shape to the background with small slipstitches through the fabric edges. Here, the bottom of the shape will be covered by the next layer of appliqué work, so it is left unstitched.*

5 *Remove the pins and basting and carefully remove the backing paper. Freezer paper will peel off easily, and plain paper should slide out. If you are stitching all the edges, leave a gap to remove the paper, or slit the background fabric and take it from the back.*

Hawaiian Appliqué

HAWAIIAN APPLIQUE is a unique phrase that is applied both to a specific type of quilted item, and to the technique used to create such textiles.

As used for making quilts, Hawaiian appliqué must be done by hand. Beautiful wall hangings and pillows can be made by machine using fusible webbing, but the stiffness of the bonding material makes the method inappropriate for bedcovers. Designing a motif is a bit like cutting out paper snowflakes from folded paper, and can be done on a small or large scale. Here, the background square is 12in (30cm), and the motif is cut from an 8in (20cm) square.

Starting simply
Designing and applying a simple mofit is a good way to practice before attempting a full-scale quilt.

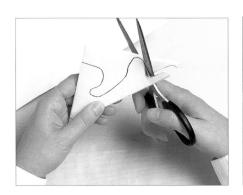

1 *Fold a paper square diagonally into eighths. Draw the design and cut it out.*

2 *Unfold the template and cut out one quarter.*

3 *Fold and press the smaller contrasting fabric square into quarters. Repeat with the larger background square.*

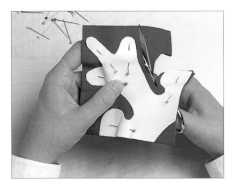

4 *Pin the quarter pattern on the small square, straight edges on the folds. Cut out, leaving a 1/4in (5mm) seam allowance.*

5 *Open out the motif and use the quarter pattern to mark a basting line around all raw edges.*

6 *Position the motif on the background and baste using a contrasting thread. Turn the raw edges under and slipstitch in place.*

Reverse Appliqué

REVERSE APPLIQUE can be intricate and complicated, and built up of many layers of contrasting fabrics, but it can be just as effective when it is used to make simple, colorful shapes.

The method of reverse appliqué is most familiar in the form of molas, the lively panels made by the San Blas tribes of Panama, but it is a useful decorative technique for the quiltmaker. Entire quilts can be made this way, or separate sections can be incorporated into other types of appliqué and patchwork. Remember to wash and press the background fabrics before you begin.

Revealing layers

Three layers of lightweight cotton – dark blue on top, turquoise in the center, and orange as the bottom – have been used to create a simple tropical fish reminiscent of mola work. To help reduce bulk and to save fabric, the yellow eye is inserted as a separate small piece of cloth, which can be only a scrap.

1 *Cut out fabric pieces. Draw the main pattern on the top piece and baste layers together 1/4in (5mm) outside the marked line.*

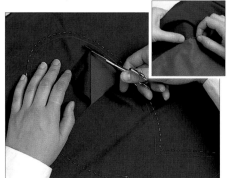

2 *Cut away the first layer 1/4in (5mm) inside the marked line. Inset: Turn under the seam allowance and slipstitch raw edges.*

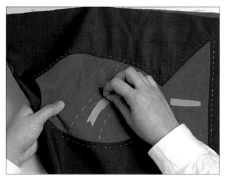

3 *Draw the patterns for the next layers and baste between sections. Cut out and stitch the second layer.*

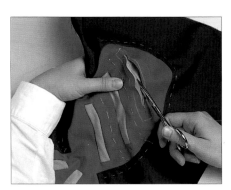

4 *Cut out the third layer the same way. Always be very careful not to cut through the back layer.*

5 *Continue stitching the elements for the third layer until the design is complete.*

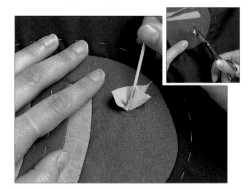

6 *Insert a small square, baste layers and clip allowance. Stitch eye and remove basting. Inset: Draw the eye and cut a small opening.*

Machine Appliqué

A SEWING MACHINE with a zigzag function is a useful tool in some types of appliquéd work. Several of the outline stitches on many modern machines can also be used to good effect.

There are several ways to hold pieces in place as you stitch around them. Pinning or basting are traditional, but are not always suitable for machine work. Basting spray, which allows pieces to be repositioned, and craft glue secure fabrics while you work. Both can be washed out of the fabric easily when the piece is complete. If you have an open embroidery or appliqué foot, it is easier to see what is happening while you work.

Decorative stitching

Because the cat's tail is tricky to work, it has been secured with fusible webbing, positioned to cover the place where the body stitching began and ended. This creates a permanent bond and does not wash out.

1 *Trace each piece of the design. Machine-applied pieces do not need seam allowances.*

2 *Glue each tracing to cardboard and cut it out. Alternatively, use template plastic.*

3 *Draw each piece on its chosen fabric. Make sure they are the right way up.*

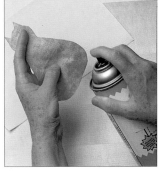

4 *Spray wrong side with basting spray and place on background. Iron tail fabric to fusible webbing.*

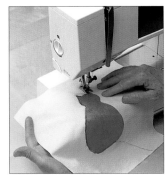

5 *Stitch the first shape, beginning in a place that will be covered by another place if possible.*

6 *Zigzag all around the body, working carefully in tricky areas like sharp points.*

7 *Peel the paper backing from the tail piece and iron it in place on the body.*

8 *Stitch around the tail. We have used a more open, decorative stitch instead of zigzag.*

Hand Quilting

QUILTING BY HAND has been practiced for thousands of years in some form in almost every culture known to historians and anthropologists. What probably began as a way to hold layers of clothing together for warmth became a decorative art that has been used to embellish clothing and home furnishings in a tradition that continues today.

Marking straight lines

Quilting patterns can be transferred to the finished quilt top either before or after the layers are basted together. Straight-line designs, including grids of squares or diamonds, are the easiest patterns to stitch and to mark. They are useful for filling large background areas, and look good on borders.

Straight lines can be drawn straight onto fabric using a ruler and a suitable marker, such as the water-soluble one shown here. Indelible lines should be dotted or dashed.

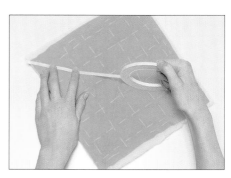

Narrow masking tape can be applied to the quilt top after the piece has been basted to delineate straight lines. Stitch along one or both edges and remove the tape.

Transferring with tissue paper

1 *Some intricate designs, especially for corded quilting, are best transferred by basting a tissue-paper tracing of the pattern to the fabric. Working in contrasting basting thread, use small running stitches to mark the solid lines only. Knot the thread on the top side of the fabric for easy removal later.*

2 *When all the lines have been stitched, run the point of the needle gently around the drawn lines. This will tear the paper along the stitching line so that the outside part of the tissue paper pattern can be removed.*

3 *Continue working along all the lines of stitching to remove all the pieces of the paper pattern. Always pull gently so that you don't loosen the stitches.*

Quilting stitch

This is not an ordinary running stitch, and it requires practice. Ideally, quilting stitches should be small and the same length on the front and back of the quilt. Use a single thread.

1 *Insert the needle through all layers and tilt it up, again piercing all layers. Repeat to take two or three more even stitches, then pull the thread through to the end.*

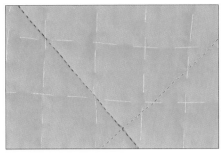

2 *Continue working along the marked lines, using small, closely spaced stitches.*

Travelling

To move the needle a distance of several inches without taking a stitch, you can "travel" through the batting. Be careful not to pull the thread too tight when doing this or you may cause the surface to pucker.

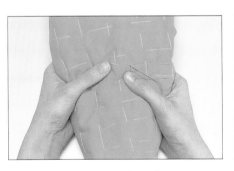

1 *Start your row of quilting stitches and bring the point of the needle – and only the point – through to the top.*

2 *Turn the needle over inside the batting so that the threaded eye points in the direction you want to go. Push the eye out through the top.*

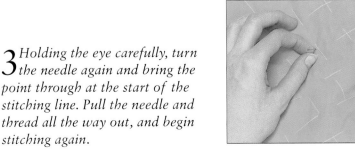

3 *Holding the eye carefully, turn the needle again and bring the point through at the start of the stitching line. Pull the needle and thread all the way out, and begin stitching again.*

Templates

The quilting patterns in this book can be enlarged or reduced on a photocopier and traced onto template plastic or cardboard ready for marking on the quilt top.

1 *Using a soft pencil, trace your chosen design onto template plastic or tracing paper. Transfer paper tracings to plain cardboard.*

2 *Cut out the shape with a craft knife and lay it on the fabric. Mark around the design in pencil with a dotted line.*

3 *Use chalk or a white pencil to mark the dark areas of a quilt, making your marks as light as possible.*

Machine Quilting

Q UILTING BY MACHINE was traditionally the ugly stepsister of the art, but the advent of sewing machines designed to cope with the layers – and especially the speed possible – have brought the skill into its own in recent years. Well-worked machine quilting is attractive and versatile, aided by the range of machine embroidery threads. Always make a test sample first.

Straight lines

Straight lines can be marked on the fabric and stitched. You can simply mark one line and then use the foot as a guide. A special walking foot is available that helps to keep the layers moving at the same speed.

Curved lines

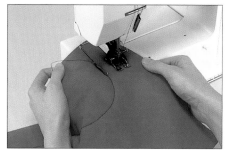

Curved lines can be marked on the fabric beforehand and stitched, or the curve can be followed using a special bar – found on many machines – that measures the distance from one line to the next as you work.

Meander Stitch

The machine version of stippling, this stitch gives a lovely close stitched texture as it winds its random way through the area to be quilted. This method works best if lines are not overstitched.

Quilt-as-you-go

1 *Cut fabric strips the desired width, and a piece of batting 2in (5cm) bigger all around than the finished size of the block. Place two fabric strips right sides together and wrong side down on the batting. Stitch the right-hand edge of the strips through all layers.*

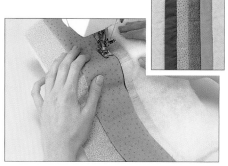

2 *Fold back the top strip and place a third strip of fabric right side down on the second strip. Stitch in place along the right-hand edge. Repeat to cover the batting.*

Rolling

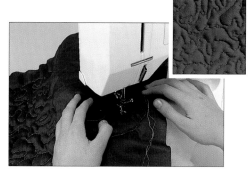

A large quilt can be difficult to handle under the machine. Roll up the edges of the area to be stitched, to distribute the weight and make it easier to move the piece around. Bicycle clips can be used to hold the roll in place.

Types of Quilting

THERE ARE A NUMBER of types of traditional quilting techniques that are used for decorative effects. Corded work and stuffed work have been used in many places for centuries to give unusual texture to clothing and bedcovers, while sashiko is a time-honored method of making thick, warm fabrics from several unbatted layers of cloth.

Corded (front and back)

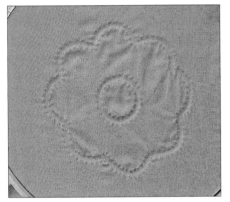

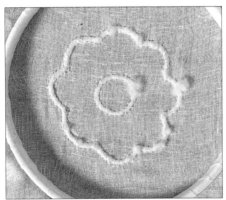

This elegant version of quilting, known as Italian quilting, is suitable for curved and flowing lines, but does not work so well on sharp angles.

The fabric is backed with cheesecloth onto which the pattern has been transferred. A channel is stitched in running stitch or backstitch, and a cord is inserted through the channel.

Sashiko

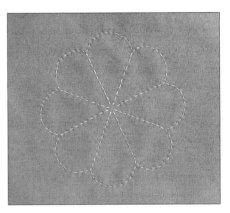

This Japanese technique, used to hold several layers of fabric together for worker's clothing, uses thick thread and large stitches. It is traditionally worked white on blue or red fabric.

Stuffed Work (Front and Back)

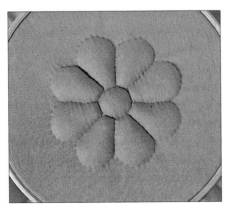

This padded method of quilting provides interesting texture and a background for embellishment with beads or embroidery. Careful marking of the design is essential.

The fabric is backed with a thinner one, the marked lines are stitched with running stitch backstitch. Slits in the backing are filled with scraps and sewn back together with herringbone.

Kantha

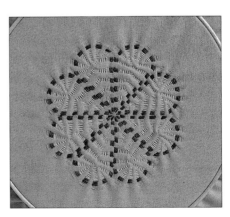

This heavily stitched technique from Bangladesh originated as a utility method of securing thin layers of fabric, usually worn saris, together for warmth.

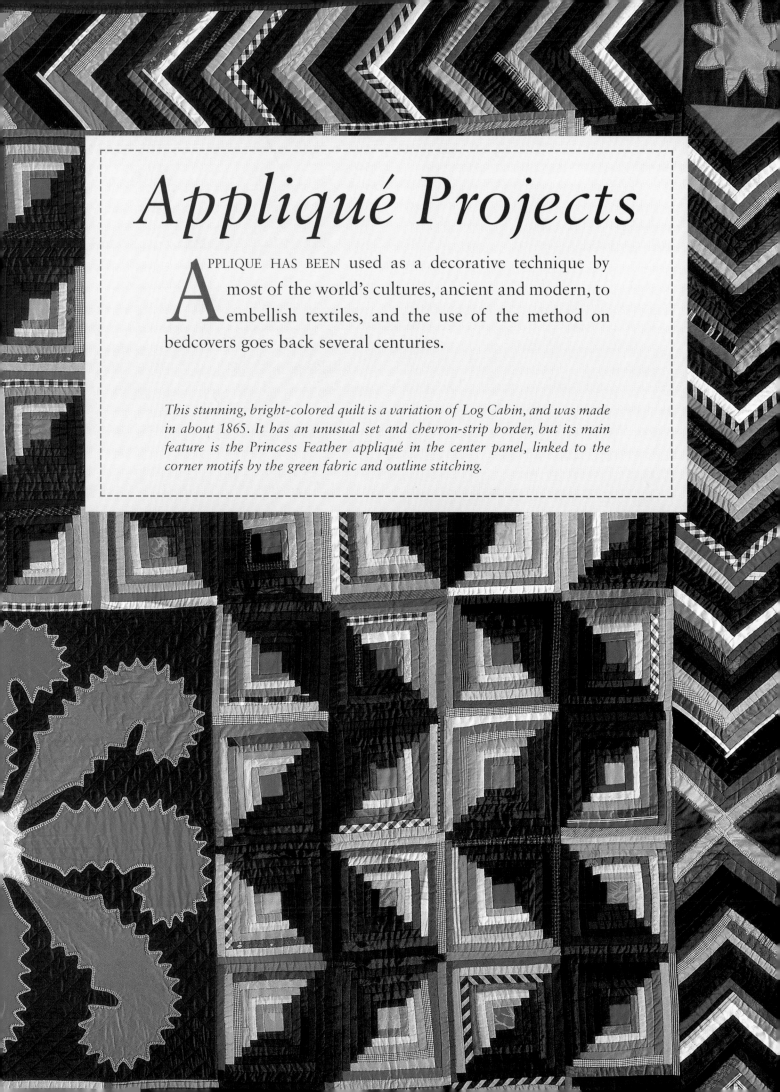

Appliqué Projects

APPLIQUE HAS BEEN used as a decorative technique by most of the world's cultures, ancient and modern, to embellish textiles, and the use of the method on bedcovers goes back several centuries.

This stunning, bright-colored quilt is a variation of Log Cabin, and was made in about 1865. It has an unusual set and chevron-strip border, but its main feature is the Princess Feather appliqué in the center panel, linked to the corner motifs by the green fabric and outline stitching.

Appliqué

THE SIMPLEST AND most often seen method of working appliqué by hand involves cutting a design from one fabric and stitching it to another, usually larger, background piece, made from another fabric.

Appliqué can be worked in a number of ways, some traditional and some modern. In the most basic method, the appliqué piece is cut with a seam allowance, which is then turned under and stitched in place. It is much easier to work curves and intricate shapes using appliqué techniques than in patchwork. Designs can be fashioned by cutting pieces from different fabrics and combining them to make a pattern, or pieces of patterned fabric can be cut out and applied to different background. Pieces can also be enhanced with decorative embroidery stitches, such as blanket stitch and feather stitch, around the edges.

Freezer paper from the supermarket has become the quiltmaker's friend, and it can be used to stablilize appliqué pieces while they are being stitched and then

Bold shapes

ABOVE: *Plaid eight-point stars and a center square are appliquéd by needle-turning and then decorated with blanket stitch around all the edges.*

removed from the final piece. The sharp edges of the paper, which can be ironed onto the wrong side of most fabrics, makes it easy to turn under the edges of the design piece.

Any sewing machine with a zigzag function can be used to make machine appliqué. Pieces are cut without seam allowances, secured with washable glue or basting spray, or with fusible webbing, and applied to the

Decorative beading

LEFT: *A bold yellow path cuts across the corner of a fire-engine red rectangle to make a vibrant abstract design. Its needle-turned edges have been outlined with French knots and coral stitch, and small silver beads are evenly spaced along each side.*

Golden glitz

LEFT: *Three different striped fabrics – the background pale two-tone silk, the middle black and white voile, and the top pinstriped shirt fabric – have been layered to create a series of square frames. The raw edges have all been machine-stitched with gold metallic thread.*

Colored stitching

BELOW: *Red cotton strips on a tobacco-brown background have an earthy feel. They were basted in place with the edges turned under, and then blanket-stitched in place to give a secure, firm edge. The use of a different color along the bottom edge of the lower strip adds to the ethnic effect.*

background with a close satin stitch around the edges. This technique can also be used for small, tricky pieces and on fabrics that are thin or liable to ravel easily. Other decorative machine stitches can be used as well.

Appliqué is often seen in conjunction with patchwork: Baltimore album quilts, of which many superb nineteenth-century examples survive, are perhaps the ultimate in terms of both skill and design flair. They often incorporate broderie perse, a type of appliqué in which printed fabrics are cut out for use as motifs.

Pieces of appliqué can be stuffed – to make berries, for example – or padded with batting before they are finally secured to give an interesting texture and three-dimensional effect to the finished piece.

The technique known as Hawaiian appliqué (see page 337) was developed by native Hawaiian stitchers in the nineteenth century, and has become a standard part of the art of appliqué. The best-known variation of appliqué is the method known as reverse appliqué (see page 338), in which at least two, and usually more, layers of fabric are placed one on top of another and the design is cut through to expose the contrasting colors below.

Madcap Throw

THIS LIVELY LAP QUILT or throw is perfect to snuggle under when you are reading or napping. We have used a fairly heavy waffle-finish cotton that makes it light in weight but still warm. Using a lighter fabric would create a summer-weight cover.

This throw is assembled like a strippy quilt, but it has no batting and the strips are decorated with appliqué instead of the traditional elaborate quilting. The top and backing are stitched together by quilting in the ditch along the seam of each strip, which holds the layers together and makes the back more decorative and longer lasting.

You could, if you wish, cut out the appliqué squares and simply turn under and press a hem on all sides before stitching them in place, eliminating the fusible webbing. However, they will be much more secure if they are bonded to the throw. Try placing the squares in different positions until you achieve a look that appeals to you.

YOU WILL NEED

fabric for strips in three colors

fabric for squares

fusible webbing

backing fabric

Binding fabric

20 buttons

quilting thread

Autumnal glow
The warm earth colors give this throw an autumnal feel, but you could use bright primaries for a child's throw, or calico prints for a summer look. The squares could be made in assorted colors, or used prints on solids, or vice versa.

Making the Quilt

1 *Bond the wrong side of the fabric for the appliqué squares to a piece of fusible webbing and cut twenty 6in (15cm) squares. Do not remove the backing paper at this stage.*

2 *Using a rotary cutter, cut four strips of fabric 5¹/₂in (13cm) wide from each of the three solid colors. Each strip should be 64in (162cm) long.*

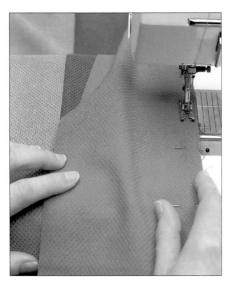

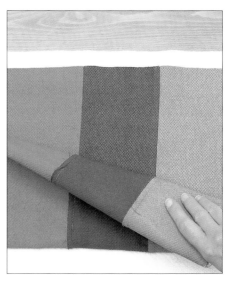

3 *Pin the strips with right sides together, referring to the photograph on page 349 for the correct color sequence. Join them together with a generous ¹/₄in (5mm) seam.*

4 *Cut the backing fabric 1in (2.5cm) bigger all round than the joined strips. Place the throw centrally, wrong sides together, on the backing fabric, and use basting spray to hold the layers together.*

5 *Machine quilt in the ditch down each seam to hold the top and the backing together. Alternate the direction in which you stitch on each row.*

6 Remove the backing paper from each fabric square and turn under a ¼in (5mm) single hem on all four sides. Press the edges only. Be sure not to let the iron touch the webbing, or you will be left with a sticky mess on both the fabric and the iron.

7 Lay the squares on the right side of the throw, spacing them more or less evenly across the surface, and bond them in your chosen positions.

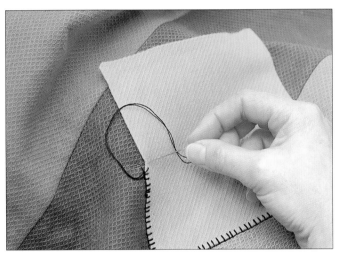

8 Using a double length of quilting thread, blanket stitch around all four sides of each square to secure them firmly to the throw and add an informal decorative detail.

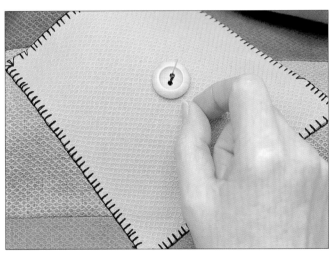

9 Continue the decoration by sewing a button in the center of each square.

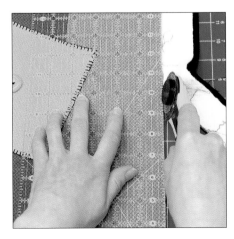

10 Carefully trim the excess backing fabric from around the edges of the throw.

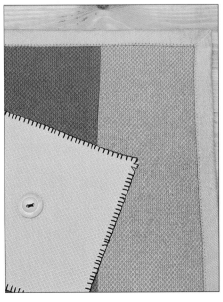

11 Apply the binding. The corners are mitered, and we have topstitched around the inside edge to secure and decorate the binding.

Hearts Quilt

H EARTS AND MONOGRAM letters are appliquéd to plain squares of muslin to make a charming crib quilt for a new baby. Baby quilts generally need to be laundered often, so be sure to wash the fabrics before you start work, to make sure that the colors don't run and the material doesn't shrink.

The appliqué shapes are all applied using fusible webbing to hold the layers together, and are machine-stitched in place. This method creates a strong bond that will withstand many trips through the washing machine, but the webbing is permanent and creates a certain amount of stiffness where it is used, so it is best applied to limited areas of a quilt like this one. If you wish, you can cut the shapes with a seam allowance and apply them by hand – kinder to delicate young skin!

This idea is very easy to adapt: you could use colorful balloon or teddy-bear shapes in place of the hearts, or spell out the baby's name, or even design and make a different motif for each square.

Making the Quilt

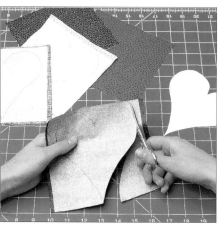

1 Cut the muslin and the fabric for the hearts into strips 7¹/₂in (19cm) wide, then cut the strips into squares. You will need 20 muslin squares and 20 plaid/print squares. Cut twenty 6in (15cm) squares from fusible webbing.

2 Center a square of fusible webbing on the wrong side of every plaid/print square and iron in place. Trace the heart shape from page 406 and make a template. Draw around the template on every square and cut out the shape.

Have a heart
The plaid sashing coordinates with the fabrics used to make the hearts and letters, making a lively-looking quilt for a baby's bed. It could also be used as a play mat for a toddler.

3 *Remove the backing from one of the fabric hearts or initials and center it on a muslin square. Iron in place to fuse the layers together, taking care not to stretch the fabric. Repeat with the remaining hearts or initials.*

4 *For a personal touch, use your child's initials in place of two of the hearts. Simply draw a letter or make a template, draw around the initial onto the fabric, and cut out the shape.*

5 *Pin a piece of stabilizer to the wrong side of every muslin square. Working from the right side, zigzag or use machine blanket stitch around the raw edges of every heart or letter shape, then carefully tear away the stabilizer.*

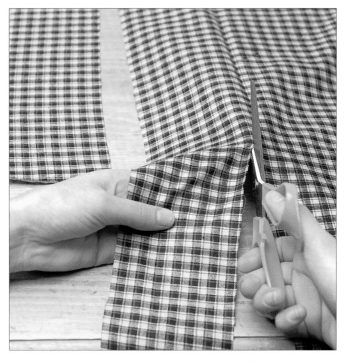

6 *Cut 12 strips 3½in (8.9cm) wide × 44in (112cm) long from sashing fabric. Cut three of the strips into rectangles to give 5 rectangles per strip, each measuring 3½in × 7½in (8.9 × 19cm).*

7 *Arrange the heart or initial squares in five rows of four. Insert a sashing rectangle between every square on each row. Join the squares and sashing together to make rows, making a 1/4in (5mm) seam. Press the seams toward the sashing (the dark side).*

8 *Cut six of the remaining sashing strips so they are the same length as the rows. Insert a sashing strip between each row and stitch together. Press the seams toward the sashing.*

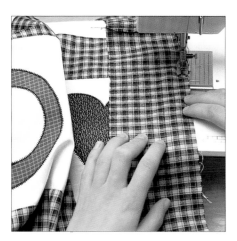

9 *Cut two 12in (30cm) lengths from remaining strip. Attach to other strips to make two lengths. Cut to same length as top. Stitch in place.*

10 *Cut the backing and batting the same size as the quilt top. Sandwich the three layers together, trim the edges even, then baste with pins or by hand. Quilt by stitching around the edges of the muslin squares, using matching thread.*

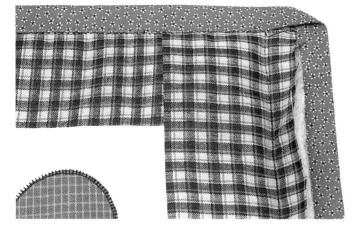

11 *Cut the binding fabric into strips 3in (7.5cm) wide and attach to the sides of the finished quilt, taking care to miter the corners neatly as shown.*

Cabana Pillow

THIS SIMPLE, COLORFUL project provides a good way to practice your machine appliqué skills. Made from small pieces of fabric, it also gives you the opportunity to use up scraps left over from other projects. The cabanas are lined up side by side like the huts or tents in which swimmers change into bathing suits on European beaches.

Brightly colored cabanas – small huts that are permanent but very basic structures – are a feature of many beaches in northern Europe. Many of them have been in the same family for generations. They are used as dressing rooms by swimmers and sunbathers, as shelter during wind and rain storms, and as storage sheds for deckchairs, towels, and picnic equipment.

In the interpretation shown here, fusible webbing secures the colorful shapes to the background fabric, and variegated machine-embroidery thread, which changes color as you stitch, is used to outline and define the shapes.

Only small amounts of fabric are needed. Each piece can be bonded to fusible webbing, and the shapes can then be drawn on the backing-paper side of the webbing and cut out. When the backing paper is removed and the shape ironed onto the background fabric, a permanent bond is achieved.

Bewcause fusible webbing is used, the whole piece can be laundered without coming unstuck. Nonetheless, it is best to machine-satin stitch the raw edges to prevent them raveling.

Satin stitch or other decorative stitches can be added to enliven the finished piece.

A Welcome Shelter
The design used here to make a lively pillow could also decorate a tote bag to carry things to the beach or home from the supermarket. Fusible webbing is generally used sparingly in quilts and throws because it is somewhat stiff.

Making the cushion

1 *Draft the pattern on a large square of paper. The measurements we used are given on the opposite page, but you could easily adapt the measurements to suit your own design if necessary. Draw or trace a template from your pattern for the roof triangles and the rectangles for the huts.*

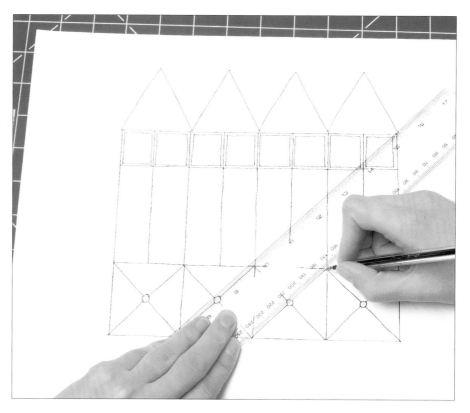

2 *Iron each piece of gingham and solid fabric to fusible webbing. On the paper side, draw around the relevant template and cut out the shape. Make four gingham rectangles and four roof triangles. Then cut two strips ¹/2 in (1cm) wide from each gingham fabric.*

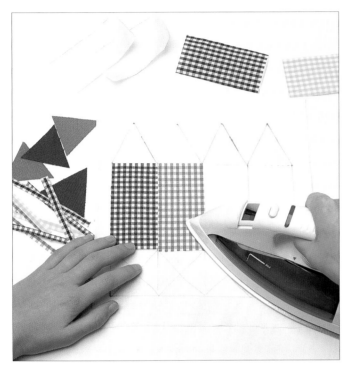

3 *Draw or trace the full pattern on the background fabric using water-soluble pen. Remove the backing paper from each fabric piece in turn and iron it on the background to bond it in position. Apply the rectangles first, then the roof shapes, and finally the diagonal strips at the bottom of the design.*

4 *Using variegated machine-embroidery thread, satin stitch the edges of the appliqué. Start with the left-hand roof and carefully work all the way around the outside edge.*

5 *Then fill in the internal shapes. (Note that the gingham strips in the bases are merely bonded into place in step two and left unstitched.) The circles are worked as several rings of straight stitch on top of each other. Remove any pen marks that are still visible.*

Measurements

Cabanas: 3 X 5-1/2 in (7.5 X 13.5cm)
Draw four rectangles side by side and draw a vertical line down the middle of each one. At the top of each tall rectangle, draw windows 11/2 in (1.5cm) square, and draw a line 1/8 in (3mm) inside each one.

Bases: 3 in (7.5cm) square
Draw one square at the bottom of each rectangle. Then draw a diagonal line from each corner in both directions in each square and draw a small circle in each square where the diagonal lines cross.

Roofs: 3 in (7.5cm) equilateral triangles
Draw one triangle with sides measuring 3 in (7.5cm) on top of each cabana.

Hawaiian Wall Hanging

HE INTRICATE DESIGNS found on traditional Hawaiian appliqué quilts can be reproduced to make hangings and pillows as well. This one is bonded to the background with fusible webbing and stitched by machine, but could be made by hand if you wish.

If you ever experimented with paper cutting as a child, you will relish the creative challenge of this project. Directions for working Hawaiian appliqué by hand are given on page 337 if you prefer to work in the traditional way.

Traditional echo quilting used on Hawaiian appliqué quilts is worked by hand, and ripples out from the edges of the motif in even rows. It is not difficult to work, but it can be time-consuming. The quilting here is

machine-stitched, which not only speeds up the process, but also looks very attractive. Following the edges of the central motif with a row or two of outline quilting before starting to meander-quilt gives the hanging an authentic feel, and the closely worked meander quilting creates an interesting texture in the background. Remember that quilting by machine needs a steady hand; you should always make a test piece before you start working on the piece itself.

Directions for working Hawaiian appliqué by hand are given on page 337 if you prefer to work in the traditional way.

YOU WILL NEED

solid fabric in two colors for the quilt top, appliquéd motif, and backing fabric

fusible webbing

several sheets of medium-weight paper, 28in (71cm) square

soft pencil

craft knife

basting spray

batting

Making the Wall Hanging

1 Fold a piece of paper 28in (71cm) square in half, then in half again to make a small square. Fold in half across the diagonal to make a triangle. Trace the template and transfer to the paper. Cut out the shape through all layers with a craft knife, and iron flat.

2 Cut out a 30in (76cm) square of red fabric. Iron a piece of fusible webbing to the wrong side. Lightly spray the template with basting spray and lay it squarely on the interfacing. Trace around the edges of the template with a soft pencil.

Red and white

The classic color combination in an extrovert Hawaiian design gives a wall hanging maximum impact.

3 Place the bonded fabric on a cutting mat and cut out the marked design, using a rotary cutter for straight lines and small, sharp scissors for curves. Cut a 36in (90cm) square of white for the background.

4 Fold background across diagonal twice. Press to make guidelines. Cut batting same size, and baste or spray to wrong side. Peel away motif backing paper and bond to right side of background. Align along pressed lines.

5 Zigzag around all raw edges with red thread in the needle and white thread in the bobbin, adjusting the tension if necessary to make sure no bobbin threads show on the right side.

6 Cut the backing fabric the same size as the quilt top and position it with basting spray.Using a darning foot and matching thread, meander quilt the white areas of the cloth with all-over pattern.

7 Thread the needle with red thread and echo-quilt the red areas, following the natural contours of the design.

8 *Trim the raw edges through all the layers to form a neat square. Pull any loose threads through to the back of the quilt, thread them onto a needle, and darn them in invisibly.*

9 *Cut binding strips 3in (7.5cm) wide. Join several strips together if necessary, and attach it to the sides of the quilt top, finishing on the right side with narrow zigzag stitches.*

Alternative designs

You can either copy the template at the back of the book, or you can design a Hawaiian motif yourself for a more personal touch. You could incorporate images taken from nature such as leaves, flowers, and fruit, or you might prefer to design an abstract image. The process is rather like making a paper snowflake: first fold a large square of paper in half several times before you mark your design to produce an exact mirror image in each quarter.

Mola

COMPLEX AND TIME-CONSUMING, though much speedier than a hand-stitched mola, this wall hanging is a splendid example of ethnic-style decoration made using the reverse-appliqué technique. Directions for working the technique by hand can be found on page 338.

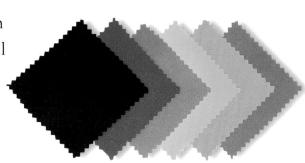

Molas originate in among the Kuna tribes in Panama, where they are traditionally stitched by hand. They consist of a foundation of strong cotton fabric, often black, covered with several layers of lightweight cotton that are cut away to reveal the colors below, and then hemmed with invisible stitches. Fine details are worked by hand, using tiny embroidery stitches.

Molas can be abstract and regular, designed using folded paper cutouts, or showing complicated, maze-like patterns. Usually, however, they depict people, animals, plants, fish, or corals. The Kuna keep up with the times and add rockets, advertising slogans, and other lettering in their work. The traditional color palette includes yellow, orange, red, purple, green, blue, white, and black.

YOU WILL NEED

solid fabric in six colors

heavyweight iron-on interfacing

fusible webbing

craft knife

two sheets of acetate

china marking pencil

water-soluble pen

sewing thread

embroidery thread

Making the Hanging

1 *Cut your chosen fabrics into 20in (50cm) squares. Iron a piece of interfacing to the wrong side of the background square (here orange). Iron a piece of fusible webbing to the wrong side of the other five squares. Trace the templates on page 365 and transfer to the wrong side of the top fabric (here red).*

2 *Do not cut along the marked lines; instead cut a seam allowance (¼in/5mm) width outside the marked lines.*

Mola magic
A piece of virtuoso machine work, this mola depicts a bird and a nattily dressed cat.

3 *Place the red cut-out square of fabric on the next layer of fabric (here black) as a guide. Center the templates in the cut-out areas of the cloth and draw around the shapes onto the black fabric.*

4 *Cut out the marked shapes on the black cloth through webbing and fabric. The cut-out shapes should be the same size as the paper templates.*

5 *Lay red fabric right side up on black fabric. Peel away the paper backing from the red fabric and place squarely on the black fabric. Check there is a 1/4in (5mm) margin of black showing behind the red fabric.*

6 *Use an iron to bond the two fabrics together carefully. Keep the pieces in alignment and avoid stretching the material.*

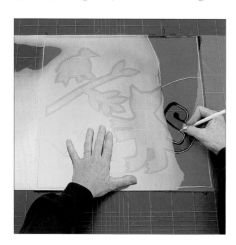

7 *Trace outline for each shape on separate sheets of acetate. Add lines for background. Cut a template for each shape from acetate; keep second acetate as guide.*

8 *Use the cutout cat template to draw its outline in position on the right side of the orange fabric. Choose the color for the other templates, and draw around them in reverse on the webbing backing paper.*

9 *Cut out background pieces in the chosen colors. Position them on the orange fabric so they do not overlap. Check by laying them on the red/black fabrics.*

10 *When everything is correctly positioned, peel off the backing paper for each individual shape, and bond them to the orange background fabric. The cat outline will remain orange.*

11 *Place the acetate guide over the red/black fabrics. Lift and mark lines between the colored areas with a water-soluble pen.*

12 *Remove the acetate, and use a water-soluble pen to draw regular lozenge shapes on red within the marked lines of the color areas. Cut out the lozenge shapes with a craft knife. When the red/black fabrics are laid on the bonded fabrics, these holes will reveal different colors underneath.*

13 *Remove the paper backing from the black fabric and bond it carefully to the orange piece. Using matching thread, zigzag around all raw edges of the red fabric.*

14 *Decorate the figures with embroidery. Cut black binding 1³/4in (4.5cm) wide and attach to the sides of the hanging. Zigzag in place around all edges.*

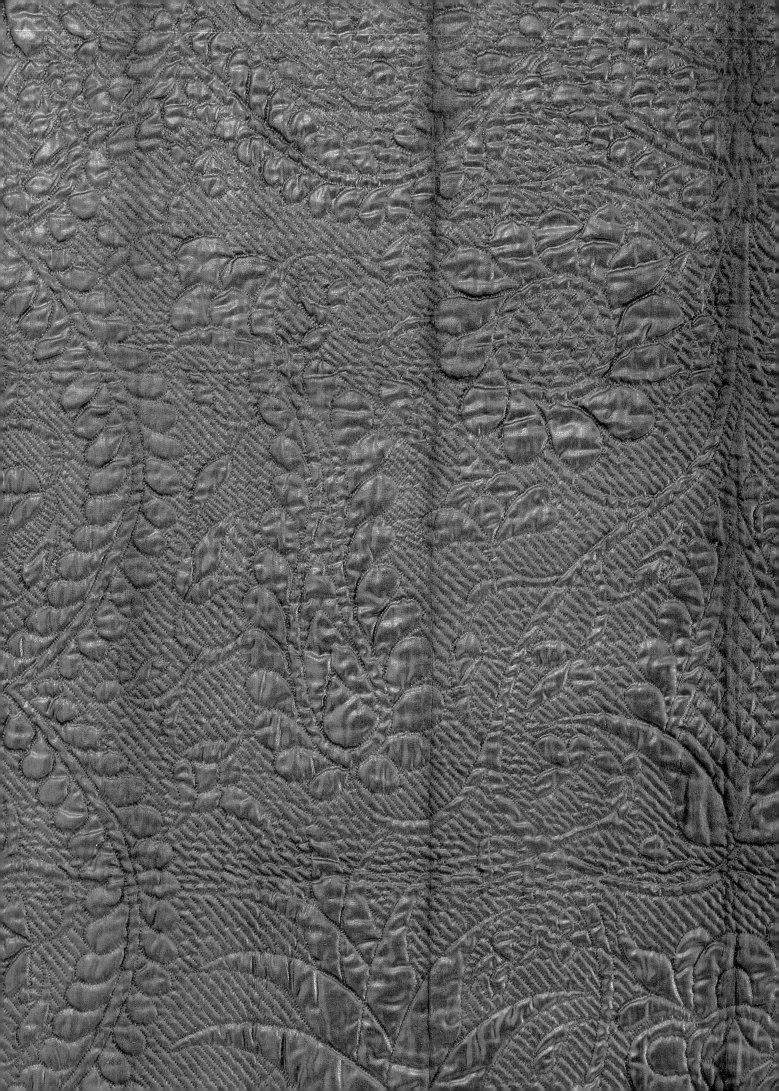

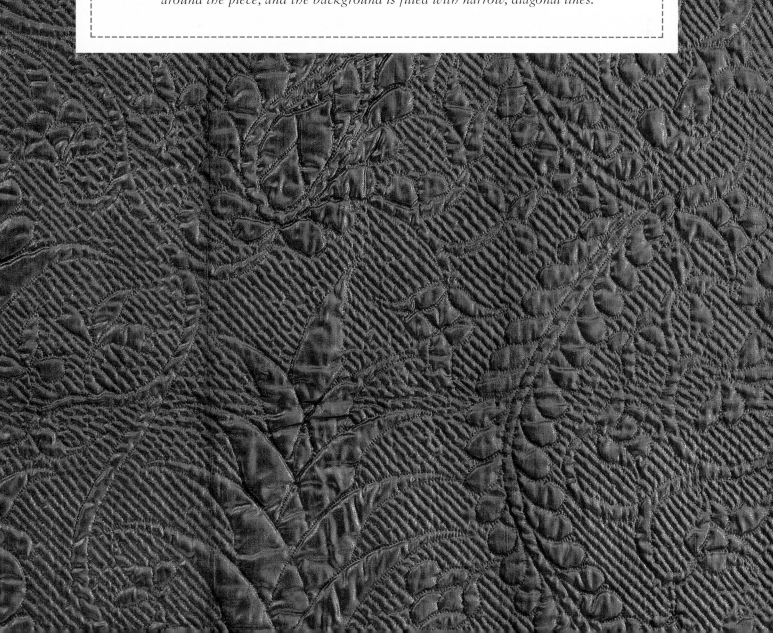

Quilting projects

QUILTING IS – quite literally! – what holds a quilt together. In the hands of an accomplished needle-worker, it also holds the quilt together visually, complementing and enhancing the design of the top. The following projects allow you to practice different techniques.

The dark, glazed surface of this wool calamanco wholecloth quilt has been close-quilted with a selection of floral motifs. A narrow feather loops its way around the piece, and the background is filled with narrow, diagonal lines.

Quilting Techniques

THE SIMPLEST OF stitches is used for quilting, whether the pattern being worked is highly intricate or easy lines. Making quilting stitches that are small, evenly spaced, and the same on both front and back is more difficult than some might think.

Quilting, of course, ranges from large utilitarian stitches to the finest of lines. In the earliest days of quilting, quilted textiles were put to useful purposes, and were almost certainly not made to be seen, but instead were used as padding and protection by soldiers on the battlefield, as warm undergarments for women, and as bedcovers to keep out the drafty cold of unheated homes, from castles to cabins.

By the eighteenth century in Europe, and even earlier in certain Eastern countries like Japan and the area that is now Bangladesh, quilting had become highly decorative, and the stitching itself was refined into stylized forms and patterns.

As needleworkers became more proficient and their tools and materials more sophisticated, quilting became

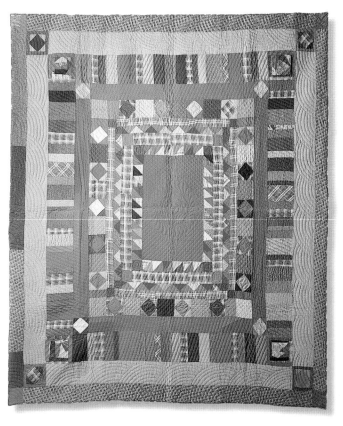

Complex border
ABOVE: *In this Americal medallion frame quilt, the center is a Feathered Wreath, and the border quilting has concentric waves, diagonal lines, and crosshatching.*

an art in itself, resulting in large numbers of quilts as we know them, many of which have survived the ravages of time and the elements to end up in public and private collections, where they can be enjoyed and studied today.

The technique sounds simple enough. The only essential requirements for quilting are two or more layers of fabric and/or batting to stitch together, a needle (quilters prefer the type called betweens), a length of thread, ideally one that is waxed, either by the manufacturer or by you using a block of beeswax, a design to quilt, and an implement for marking it on the

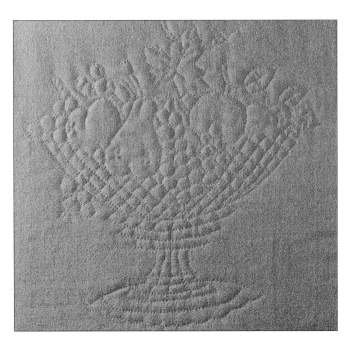

Hand stitching
LEFT: *Motifs like this overflowing fruit bowl are generally marked using a stencil or template, and then filled in by hand. Such an intricate design would be almost impossible to work by machine, but by hand it is an effective way to fill an area of solid-color fabric.*

Stuffed quilting

LEFT: *This fabulous white wholecloth quilt, made in New York, is emphatically dated "1796" in the center bottom. The unique pattern is mainly stuffed work, beautifully executed, especially the double Running Feather around the outside.*

Maple Leaf

BELOW LEFT: *This brightly colored Amish-made Maple Leaf lap quilt was bought new at a fund-raising auction in Lancaster County, Pennsylvania, in 1994. The leaf blocks are set on pont, while the spacer blocks are filled to the edges with beautifully stitched roses. The border is decorated with interlocking hearts.*

cloth. Many quilters like to work using a special quilting hoop or a frame. Large pieces are almost always stretched on a frame, but small pieces can often be worked "in the hand," that is, without being set in a hoop or frame.

Designs can be marked in a variety of ways, and these days many of the tools draw lines that can be removed fairly easily without leaving a mark. Stencils and templates specifically made for quilting patterns are available for purchase, and the sewing machine, once anathema to the serious quilter, has come into its own for creating effective quilting quickly.

Quilting beautifully by hand is tricky, even for highly experienced stitchers, but it is a skill that is certainly worth mastering. Those who enjoy hand sewing almost always find the rhythm of hand-quilting a soothing – and extremely enjoyable – process.

Windmill Baby Quilt

THIS RED, WHITE, AND BLUE cotton crib quilt, composed of ten different calico prints and quilted by machine, makes an intricate pattern. Made with a combination of Pinwheel and Hourglass blocks, when finished, the whole piece fairly spins before your very eyes just like the windmaill from which it takes its name.

This lively baby quilt provides a good way for you to practice machine-quilting. All the stitching is done "in the ditch" around the edges of the elements that make up the pattern, not necessarily along each seamline. For instance, where the Hourglass blocks meet the dark Pinwheel shapes, the quilting is worked around the resulting pointed blade shapes, and the Hourglasses that are in the outside edges are quilted as rectangles.

The method of stitching along the diagonal of square pieces of fabric and then cutting them apart, to form either pieced triangles or pieced squares, is a wonderful way to speed up the construction of this complicated-looking piece. Both the Hourglass blocks and Pinwheels are made this way.

Making the Quilt

1 Cut an 18in (46cm) square from A, B, C, and D. Pair A with C and B with D, right sides together. On the light fabrics, mark sixteen 3¹/₂in (8.9cm) squares diagonally in both directions. Make a ¹/₄in (5mm) seam on the left-hand side, then on the right, of one set of lines only.

2 Trim away any uneven raw edges and cut along both sets of marked diagonal lines to form triangles. Open out and press seams toward the darker fabric. Arrange in piles of blue and red pieced triangles.

Spinning blades
This variation of the Pinwheel block has Hourglass blocks inserted in the design in a way that creates a Windmill pattern with alternating red and blue blades.

3 *Stitch each red pieced triangle to a blue pieced triangle along their long edges. This can be done using the chain-piecing method on page 245 to save time.*

4 *Press open patch seams to one side. Cut 20 plain squares the same size as the pieced squares, 6 from E and 14 from F. Cut a 16in (40cm) square from G, H, I, and J. Place right sides together, light to dark. Mark twelve $3^7/8$in (9.5cm) squares on the light fabric. Stitch diagonal lines in one direction. Cut apart, cut two triangles from each square, open and press.*

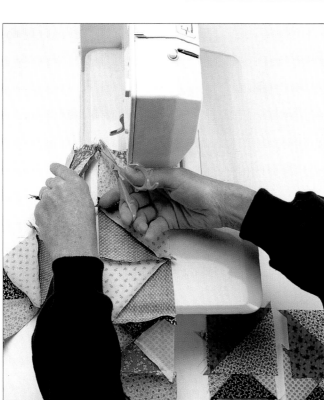

5 *Cut six $1^3/4$in (4.5cm) squares from fabric F and fusible webbing. Bond a webbing square to the wrong side of each fabric square. Center a small square wrong side down on the right side of each red square cut in step 4. Remove the paper backing and press to fuse them together. Arranged pieced and plain squares as in the illustration on the previous page, and stitch four rows of thirteen squares each.*

6 *Join the first two rows, matching the corners carefully so the points of each triangular shape do not get caught in the seam.*

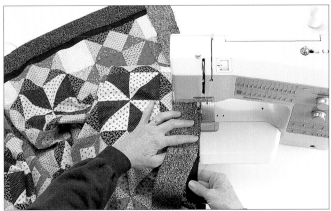

7 *Join the rows together, matching seams carefully, to complete the quilt top.*

8 *Cut 1¹/₄in (3cm) wide strips for the inner border. Stitch to the top and bottom edges first, then the side. Cut 2¹/₂in (6.5cm) wide strips for the outer border and stitch in place (see page 248).*

9 *Cut batting and backing the same size as the quilt top and baste the three layers together. Trim the raw edges level, then zigzag the edges together. Using matching thread in the needle and bobbin, machine-quilt in the ditch along seamlines to match the pattern.*

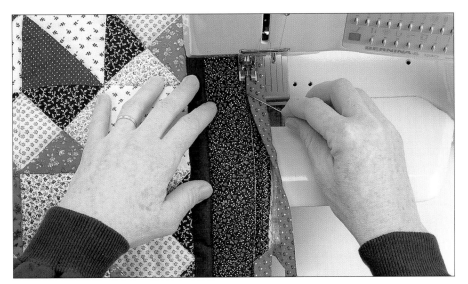

10 *Cut the binding fabric into strips 3in (7.5cm) wide and attach to the wrong side of the quilt, right sides together. Fold over to the right side and stitch in place by hand or machine.*

British Strippy Quilt

THE PARTNERSHIP OF FABRICS – block-printed floral calico and pale peppermint-green cotton – used to make this classic strippy quilt evokes strong feelings of the style of the 1930s. The simplicity of the strippy quilt, one of the undervalued examples of great British design, makes it a good piece for a novice to make and quilt.

One of the great advantages in making a traditional-style strippy quilt is the ease with which you can adjust the size to suit yourself. Cut the strips shorter and narrower, and you can make a crib quilt in no time. Alternatively, by making the strips longer and cutting more of them, you can make as large a king-size quilt as you wish.

The quilting shown here is somewhat intricate, as befits the traditional strippy, but for those who feel its complexity is beyond your grasp, or perhaps more than your machine can cope with, there is a wide choice of alternative patterns you could use.

Any of the classic cable or border patterns – see pages 421–27 for a selection – will work well, provided it fills the strip almost to the edges. Strippys can also, of course, be quilted by hand.

YOU WILL NEED

solid and printed fabrics for the strips

contrasting fabric for backing and binding

batting

template plastic

craft knife and cutting mat

water-soluble pen

Making the Quilt

1 *Fold the solid fabric along the lengthwise grain into accurate 8in (20.5cm) folds and press. The creases will act as cutting guides.*

2 *Fold the floral fabric along the lengthwise grain into accurate 8in (20.5cm) folds and press. Cut along the marked foldlines to make three strips 72in (183cm) long.*

Floral stripes

The floral-pattern strips in this twin-bed quilt have not been quilted. You can fill these areas with simple crosshatching or a plain cable border pattern if you wish.

3 *Cut the solid fabric along the marked crease lines to make four strips 72in (183cm) long.*

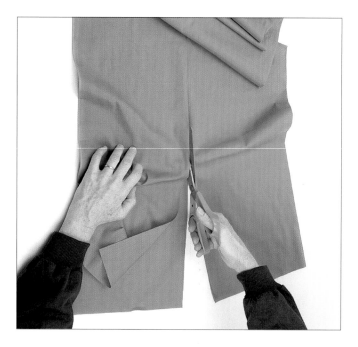

4 *Stitch the strips together along their long edges, alternating colors as shown. Press seams toward the solid fabric.*

5 *Cut backing and batting the same size as the top quilt. Sandwich the three layers together, and baste using your preferred method. Trim the outer edges so they are even, then zigzag around all sides to stop the edges from raveling.*

6 *Trace the quilting pattern on page 377 and transfer it to a piece of template plastic. Cut out the shape with a sharp craft knife, leaving plenty of bridges to hold the design together.*

7 Use a water-soluble pen to transfer the quilting design to the solid strips only, repeating the design at regular intervals.

8 Thread the needle to match the floral fabric and the bobbin to match the backing. Machine-quilt in the ditch along the seamlines on the floral strips.

9 Quilt carefully along the marked lines and tie the threads on the back. Remove pen marks. Cut the fabric for the binding into strips 3in (7.5 cm) wide and apply it around all four edges.

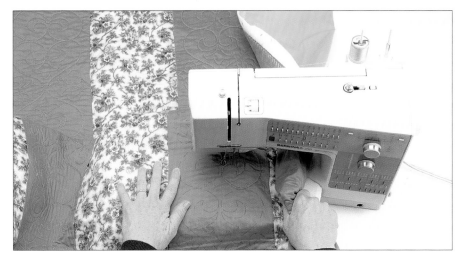

Practice first!

Practice on a layer of scrap fabric and batting first, to check the tension and "warm up" your technique. Then thread the needle to match the solid fabric and put on a darning foot to quilt the main design.

Corded Pillow

CORDED, OR ITALIAN, quilting is a simple but highly effective way of adding texture to fabric. It works best on plain fabric with no pattern or textured weave of its own. Combining it with trapunto, as we have done here, gives the piece extra dimension, since it introduces areas of deep padding around the narrow, delicate channels.

The channels are formed by parallel lines of evenly spaced running stitches, which are filled with lengths of quilting wool or thick yarn to produce a raised effect which picks out the design.

The channels are usually stitched the same color as the background fabric, but colored yarn can also be used to work the channels, and this technique produces a subtle, attractive contrast.

When cording, the stitches should be as even as possible and close together – but take care not to pull the thread too tight, as this will cause the fabric to pucker. When you have finished cording, make a few small cross stitches to anchor the tails of cord in place.

The trapunto areas on the cushion illustrated opposite are too small to cut and fill in the traditional way. Instead, they have been filled with small amounts of quilting wool from the wrong side to achieve the desired depth of padding.

Use only tiny pieces of wool for the padding – it is very easy to over-estimate and put in too much, and this distorts the top fabric and spoils the overall effect.

YOU WILL NEED

light solid fabric for the pillow front, back and borders

dark solid fabric for the borders

butter muslin for backing the pillow front

embroidery hoop

quilting wool

tapestry needle

Making the pillow

RIGHT: This close-up detail of the pillow opposite shows the added depth that can be achieved with a combination of corded and trapunto techniques.

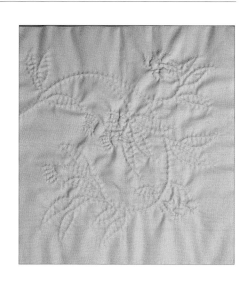

Cool cording
Stitched in the same color as the background fabric, this corded pillow is subtle and elegant. The triple border draws attention to the central design.

1 *Cut two 18in (47cm) squares from light colored fabric and butter muslin. Trace your chosen pattern and enlarge it on a photocopier if necessary. Transfer the full-size pattern to the right side of the muslin square, positioning it centrally.*

2 *Baste the marked square to the fabric, wrong sides together, working from the center out in all directions. Mount loosely on a hoop, placing your marked design on top.*

3 *Using an evenly spaced running stitch, work the marked lines of the design. The double lines of stitching form channels for the cording; the small areas between the single rows of stitching are stuffed with wool. Make sure that all the lines have been stitched.*

4 *Thread a length of quilting wool in a long tapestry needle. Working on the wrong side, slide the needle into the end of a stitched channel.*

5 Guide the needle along the stitched channels, working on one area of stem at a time. Bring the needle out on the wrong side of the fabric. Below: There is no need to knot the ends. Simply trim the wool, leaving small tufts at each end. The lower of the two photographs shows the work from the right side.

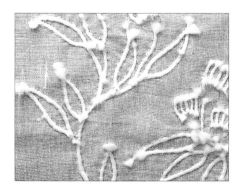

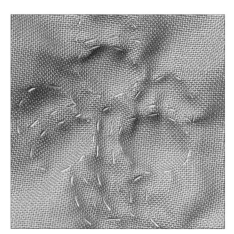

6 Press carefully, avoiding the padded areas. Center the design and trim the edges to 10in (25cm). Cut four dark-fabric strips 10in (25cm) long × 1in (2.5cm) wide. Cut four light-fabric corner squares, 1in (2.5cm) plus seam allowances. Stitch a square to both ends of two strips, then stitch the strips in place on the pillow front.

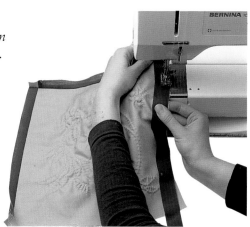

7 Repeat for the second border, reversing the colors so that the border is in light fabric and the corners dark. Repeat for the outer border, again reversing the colors, but this time cut strips 4in (10cm) wide. Back with dark fabric.

Tied Tailor's Quilt

THIS CRISP-LOOKING quilt is a natural for speedy machine-piecing, and the tied quilting makes it quick and easy to finish in a hurry. Made from samples of wool suiting like that used by made-to-measure tailors, it is also a great example of making much of limited resources – continuing the thrifty, utilitarian tradition of these quilts.

Using suiting samples or scraps of wool to make simple but warm quilts did not orginate with Australian quiltmakers. Such quilts had been pieced by quilters in the Scottish Borders and Wales, and no doubt the idea was carried by some of them as they emigrated, or were sent, to the other side of the world in the eighteenth and nineteenth centuries. However, the tradition of tailor's quilts is associated with the make-do-and-mend principles embraced by the isolated Antipodeans in the mid-twentieth century after two world wars and an economic depression.

The quilts made in Britain were usually heavily quilted with intricate patterns, to keep in place the loose wool used as batting. The rugged style of life in Australia meant that quilts served as throws and comforters, and provided perfect cover for nights under the stars for hunters and herders.

Making the Quilt

1 *Cut 28 light and 28 dark rectangles from assorted fabrics, each measuring 5 × 7in (13 × 18cm). Divide the light rectangles into two piles of 14.*

2 *Draw a diagonal line from top left to bottom right corners on each light rectangle in one pile. Repeat from top right to bottom left for the other pile.*

Tied in knots

Australian quilts were rough-and-ready pieces. They were usually batted with an old blanket, so tying provided an adequate means of securing the layers.

3 Pair the light rectangles right sides together with the dark rectangles, aligning the diagonal line on each light piece with the opposite corners of a dark piece asymmetrically. Pin at right angles to the diagonal line.

4 Align presser foot with diagonal line and stitch 1/4in (5mm) seams first on the left side, then on the right side of the marked line. Cut along the marked line.

5 Open out and press seams open. Divide pieced rectangles into two piles, one containing the mirror image of the other, so when they are paired, they form light and dark pyramids.

6 Arrange the pieced rectangles following the photograph on the previous page. Using an accurate 1/4in (5mm) seam, stitch the rectangles together to make 7 rows of 8 pieced rectangles, matching seams carefully.

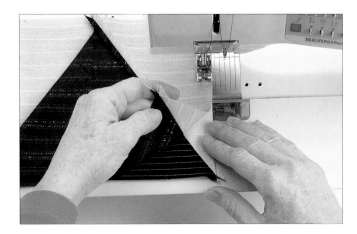

7 Make sure you match the seamlines exactly. Press all seams open.

8 Join the rows to complete the block, this time making a 1/2in (1.3cm) seam. The seamline should align exactly with the tops of the pyramids. Press seams to one side.

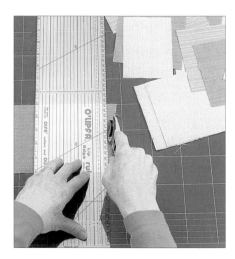

9 Cut the fabric for the pieced border into strips 5in (13cm) wide. Trim the ends, then cut into assorted short lengths from 2in (5cm) to 8in (20.5cm).

10 Join the lengths together at random, to make four pieces long enough to extend around the quilt. You will need two pieces the same length as the top and bottom edge, and two pieces the same length as the sides plus $1/2$in (1.3cm) seam allowances. Press seams to one side. Cut four 5in (13cm) corner squares, and attach to each end of the side borders. Cut the fabric for the inner border into strips 2in (5cm) wide.

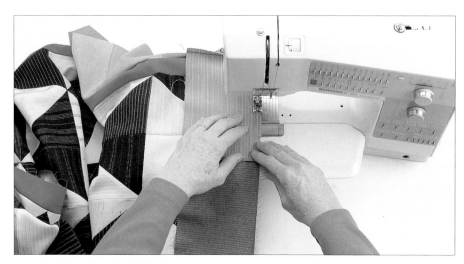

11 Attach the inner border to the sides and top of the quilt. Then attach the pieced border in the same order. Cut the fabric for the outer border into strips 4in (10cm) wide and stitch in place.

12 Cut batting and backing the same size as the top and sandwich the three layers. Trim, then zigzag raw edges. Cut binding into 3in (7.5cm) strips and stitch in place.

13 Thread a large darning needle with knitting yarn. Tie the quilt at the apex of every pyramid by taking the needle from top to bottom, then to the top again. Leave an end on top and tie a double knot; then cut the yarn and repeat at each triangle. Cut the ends to $3/4$in (2cm), then tease out the individual threads.

Yogi Mat

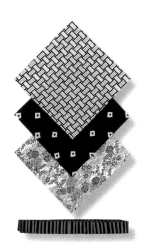

THIS JAPANESE-INSPIRED PIECE is not so much a quilt as a floor mat. Similar to a futon, it can be used as a playmat for a child or even for a pallet for an overnight guest to sleep on in comfort. The fabrics look authentically Japanese, but are easy to find in the West. Geometric weaves are commonly found in men's kimonos; small prints, too, are popular.

Japanese quilts evolved from thick, padded kimonos, sometimes several layers of them, that were worn to sleep in. This proved to be the best way of keeping out the bitter cold of snowbound nights spent in drafty wooden houses, where the only heat came from a central wood-burning stove and the only mattress was a futon on a floor that was covered with tatami matting.

These early quilts were often made from old kimonos, and they frequently retained their characteristic shape. The thick batting was held in place with large basting stitches, usually made using thick white thread, on the back, which meant that the entire construction of the quilt could be dismantled to make washing and drying easier.

YOU WILL NEED

3 indigo-print fabrics, one dark and two light, for the quilt top

backing fabric

1 bright stripe for the binding

thick cardboard

heavyweight batting

masking tape

soft embroidery cotton (not stranded floss)

sewing thread

Making the Quilt

1 Make a 12in (30cm) square template from thick cardboard. Cut 14 squares from the dark print and 7 squares from each of the light prints.

2 Alternating colors as shown opposite, join the squares into four rows of 7 squares each, making a 1/4in (5mm) seam. Press the seams toward the dark squares.

Comfortable utility
The big-stitch quilting used on this mat is worked from the back with thick soft embroidery cotton. It provides a fine example of true utility quilting.

3 Matching the seams carefully, stitch the rows together to complete the top. Press the seams to one side.

4 Baste the three layers together (see page 251). Cut batting and backing slightly larger than the quilt top. Baste and then zigzag around the edges through all the layers.

5 Trim away any excess batting or backing fabric around the edge of the quilt top to form a neat rectangle.

6 Measure the exact center of every square and mark with a pin.

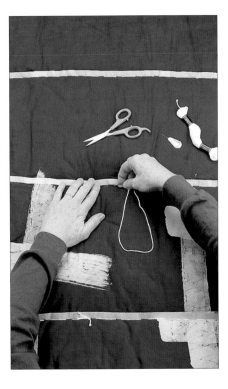

8 Thread a needle with soft embroidery cotton and quilt along the marked lines. Work from back to front, taking long 1½in- (4cm-) long stitches on the back and tiny stitches on the quilt front. Keep your work flat at all times.

7 Working on the back of the quilt, position lengths of masking tape from pin to pin so that they act as a guide to stitching.

9 When you run out of thread, join a new piece to the end with a double knot, then rethread the needle and continue. Trim the ends of the knot to 1in (2.5cm).

10 Quilt along all the marked lines this way, then remove the masking tape. Viewed from the front of the quilt, your stitches should be tiny.

11 Cut the fabric for the binding into strips 6in (15cm) wide. You may need to join several strips together to fit around the sides of the quilt. Stitch to the sides of the quilt, finishing on the right side with a neat straight stitch.

Shaker Comforter

OBJECTS MADE BY the Shaker communities of the eighteenth century were, almost without exception, timeless and uplifting classics, showing perfect proportion, grace of line, and respect for the natural materials.

A wide piece of wool plaid is backed and bound to create a bedspread reminiscent of the spirit of the best of Shaker design.

Like everything made by the Shakers, from furniture and agricultural implements to eating utensils, their textiles were plain but good. By the beginning of the nineteenth century, Shaker communities manufactured almost all their own cloth – not only wool, but cotton, silk, and linen as well, in stripe designs, checks, plaids, and twill.

In addition, they did their own dyeing, using sources that had been used by Native Americans for centuries, such as butternut bark, indigo, fermented sorrel, aleppo galls, brazilwood, and sumac berries.

The layers of this old-fashioned Shaker-style comforter, with its padding of flannel or lightweight batting, and its backing, are secured by simple tying. If you cannot find wool wide enough to make this quilt from one piece, purchase a double length of fabric and join the pieces.

YOU WILL NEED

plaid wool for the front

solid wool for the backing

flannel or lightweight batting

solid wool in a contrasting color for the binding

knitting yarn for the tufting

thread

Making the Quilt

1 Cut the fabric for the front and the back, plus batting the same size. Our quilt measures 74 x 84in (188 x 214cm). Sandwich the three layers together: backing wrong side up, batting, quilt top right side up. Smooth any wrinkles, and pin the layers in place.

2 Pin carefully around the edges with the fabric flat, then baste through all layers.

Classic simplicity
Using a contrasting knitting yarn to tie the top to the backing gives this cozy cover a traditional look.

Making the Coverlet

3 *Cut the fabric for the binding into strips 5¹/2in (14cm) wide. Join several strips together to make four pieces that will fit around the sides of the quilt. We needed two strips 74in (188cm) long for the top and bottom and two strips 88¹/2in (225cm) including seam allowances to fit down the sides. Press any seams open.*

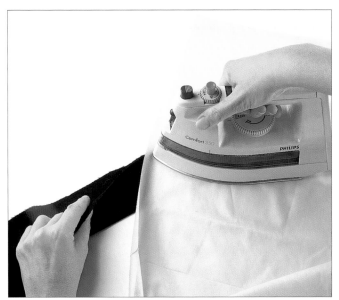

4 *Fold the binding strips in half lengthwise and press them flat, using a damp cloth to protect the fabric.*

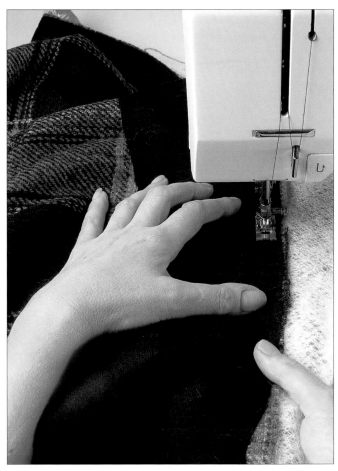

5 *With right sides together, join the two short strips of binding to the top and bottom of the quilt.*

6 *Trim away any bulk close to your stitching line, then fold the binding to the wrong side. Turn under the raw edges and pin, then sew in place.*

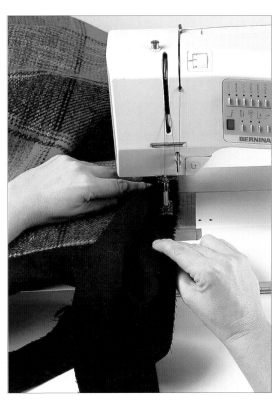

7 *Stitch the two longer strips of binding to the quilt the same way. At each corner, fold the end of the strip to the inside and square off the corner. Pin and stitch in place.*

8 *Strengthen the corners by topstitching them close to the folded edge.*

9 *Lay out the finished comforter on a flat surface and mark the position of the hand tufts with pins. We have spaced ours at 10in (25cm) intervals, following the pattern of the plaids. Using a double thickness of yarn, make a stitch through all layers and tie on the right side with a square knot. Cut the ends to 1in (2.5cm) and tease out the individual threads for a crimped effect.*

Sashiko Pillow

SASHIKO IS A TRADITIONAL form of Japanese quilting in which the simplest of running stitches are used to most elegant effect. Stitching is usually worked in thick white thread on a navy background, but red is also used, both thread and cloth. This throw pillow (opposite) and a geometric version (demonstrated below), are simple to make.

When it comes to design, the Japanese are masters of the art of the minimal. Many classic motifs date from the sixteenth century, a period of high refinement. Sashiko has a long history as a hard-wearing textile that began as a practical way of strengthening loosely woven fibers and binding them together.

Traditionally, sashiko garments were thick and stiff, and had a ridged texture. Cotton batting or layers of cotton cloth were quilted together to make warm winter worker's clothing. As time went by, the utilitarian nature of the stitches was forgotten, and patterns were gradually stylized into representations of traditional kimono prints or natural forms such as plant and animal life, and ocean motifs, which still make beautiful decoration for quilts and other textiles.

Making the Cushion

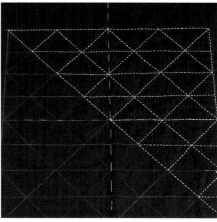

1 *Cut a 25in (64cm) square from indigo fabric and interlining. Place wrong sides together and baste around the edges. Fold in half, then in half again and press lightly. Baste along marked fold lines, then press flat. Mark a centered 16in (41cm) square with tailor's chalk.*

2 *For a geometric design, mark 4in (10cm) points at intervals around the outside of the square. Join the marked points together, both horizontally and diagonally to reveal a diamond pattern.*

Stylish stitching
Two symmetrically placed chrysanthemum flowers contained within a neatly stitched frame – the success of this design lies in its restraint.

3 *Thread a needle with four strands of embroidery cotton and stitch along the marked lines, taking small, even stitches.*

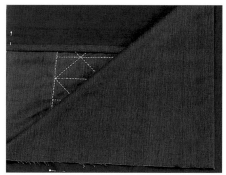

5 *To make the pillow back for either design, cut two pieces of fabric 25 × 14¹/2in (64 × 37cm) and 25 × 19¹/2in (64 × 50cm). Hem one long edge of each piece. Place on top of the pillow front, right sides together, so that the hemmed edges overlap in the center. Pin the layers together around the outside, then stitch ¹/2in (13mm) from the edge. Zigzag the raw edges to neaten them. Turn the pillow right side out and insert the pad.*

4 *For the chrysanthemum pattern shown on the previous page, trace the template from page 397 and transfer to thick cardboard. Center the template in the top right square and draw around the motif with tailor's chalk. Repeat in the bottom left square. Mark the center of the motif, then draw in the cross-secting lines. Quilt over the marked lines.*

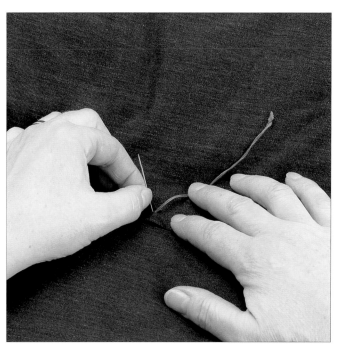

6 To make the corner tassels, thread a needle with a long piece of embroidery thread. Sew eight loops 4in (10cm) long at each corner and knot the thread. Trim the ends level.

7 For the tassel, wind embroidery thread eight times around closed fingers, tie one end and trim level. Push a threaded needle through the pillow. Thread the tassel onto the needle on the right side. Return. Tie the ends.

Alternative designs

Even spacing of the stitches is the key to successful sashiko. Sashiko stitches are regular and rhythmical, usually spaced at about six to the inch. Traditionally, geometric patterns, such as the ones shown on the right, were used for sashiko, but in more recent years figurative images of trees and flowers have been used, too.

Many geometric patterns are simple enough to make without using a pattern, provided you take care to keep the pattern repeats evenly spaced, but if you don't entirely trust your measuring skills, try using one of the quilting grid patterns shown on pages 410–17.

Blocks

THE QUILTING MOTIFS shown here are all classic and much-loved designs that are particularly useful for filling large spaces, like plain spacer blocks. The pattern you choose will, of course, depend largely on the shapes of any other elements in your quilt top. It is often best to go for contrasts of shape: if you are quilting a plain block that is surrounded by very angular, geometric pieced shapes (stars, for example), a rounded, flowing motif such as a clamshell, heart, or wreath might work well.

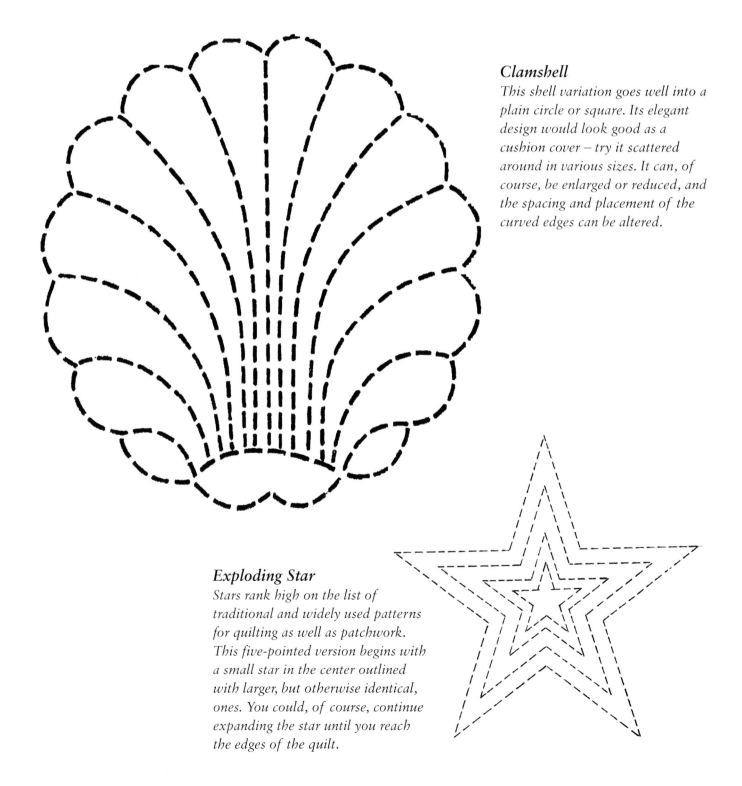

Clamshell
This shell variation goes well into a plain circle or square. Its elegant design would look good as a cushion cover – try it scattered around in various sizes. It can, of course, be enlarged or reduced, and the spacing and placement of the curved edges can be altered.

Exploding Star
Stars rank high on the list of traditional and widely used patterns for quilting as well as patchwork. This five-pointed version begins with a small star in the center outlined with larger, but otherwise identical, ones. You could, of course, continue expanding the star until you reach the edges of the quilt.

Fan

This pattern can be used to fill the corner of a plain square. The tops of the fan blades can be rounded, pointed or straight, or alternated, as shown here. Combining two of these motifs edge to edge creates a fully opened fan. Combining four fan shapes along the straight edges creates a traditional plate design.

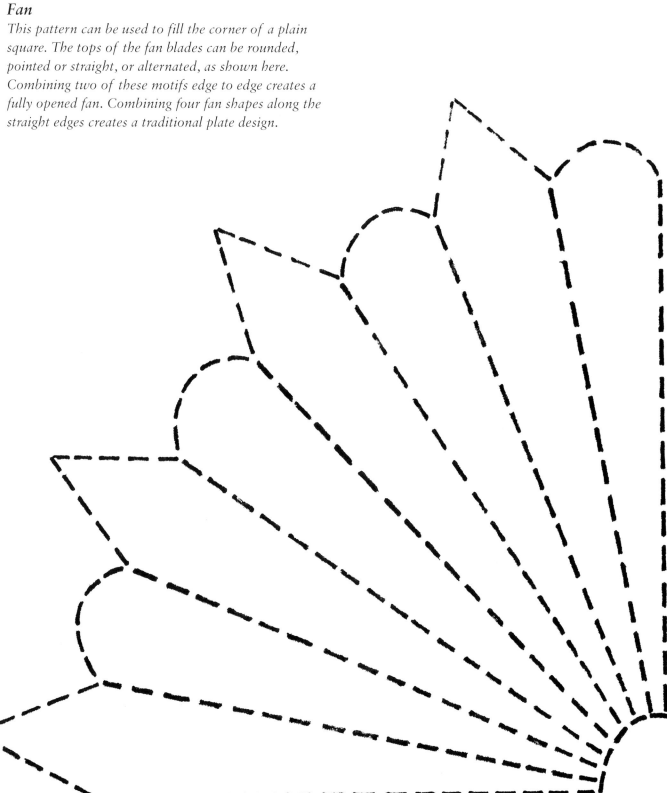

Feathered Circle

Virtually any line you can draw can be enhanced with feathers, and this circle is no exception. It can, of course, be made larger or smaller; in addition, the size and shape of the feathers can be changed to suit other elements in an overall design.

Feathered Cross

This cross-shaped motif is often seen filling the plain blocks on Irish Chain quilts, but it is obviously far more versatile than that. It can be made longer or shorter, thinner or wider, and the shape of the cross can be altered as the space to be quilted dictates. It is tailor-made to enhance plain areas on a patchwork piece, but can also be adapted to form an overall design on simple quilts.

Feathered Heart

This traditional pattern combines two of the most widely used motifs into a charming design that can fill a plain square or circle to perfection. It is simple to design your own: just add single feathers to a heart shape, altering the size and shape as you work around the outline of the heart.

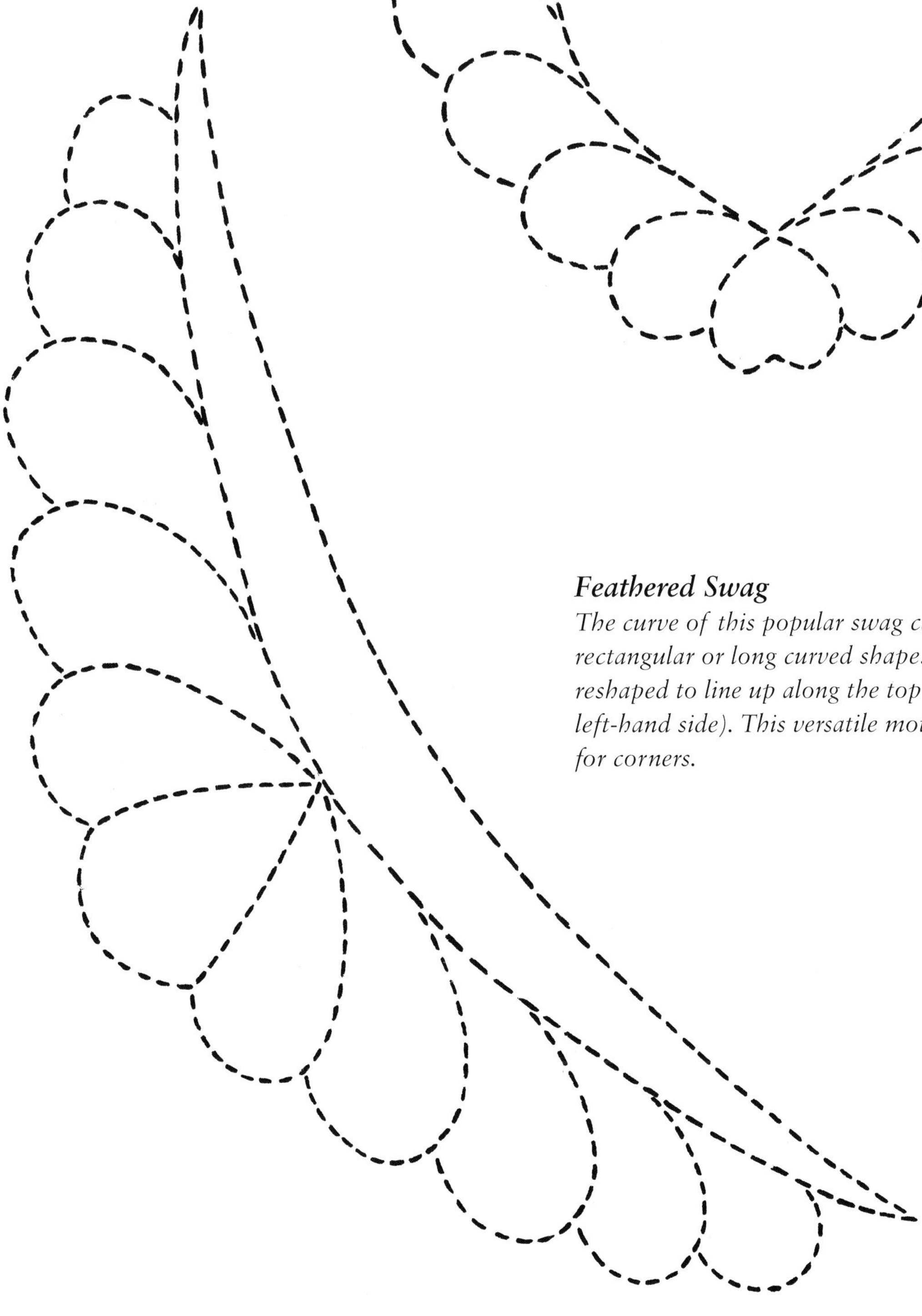

Feathered Swag

The curve of this popular swag can be varied to fit a rectangular or long curved shape. The feathers can be reshaped to line up along the top edge (seen here as the left-hand side). This versatile motif is also very useful for corners.

Five-pointed star

This star is fashioned as five irregular diamonds which meet in the center and are then outlined on the inside of each individual shape. It works well on a star-studded quilt, or as a motif in a plain square or circle.

Fleur-de-lis

The traditional fleur-de-lis pattern appears in many form on quilts from all eras. Here, it consists of a simple outline that is easy to stitch, but it can be made more complex by making four copies and placing the bases together to make a square shape, as in Four Hearts, opposite.

Grape Leaf

This traditional broken leaf consists of an S-shaped central stem with thin leaves that are graduated in size along it. It has many possibilities, in both its variety and its uses. The stem, for instance, could be corded and the leaves stuffed to make an interesting and unusual wholecloth pattern.

Four Hearts

This more complicated heart pattern makes a beautiful filling for a plain block. If the top indentations of the heart shapes are rounded off, a four-leaf clover shape can be created.

Grapes

This cluster of fruit, another example of a natural motif adapted for design, is a good pattern to use for trapunto, as well as a simple block pattern for quilting. Try combining it with a grape leaf or two (see opposite).

Heart

The familiar heart shape has been used in patterns for as long as design has been known. It is simple and straightforward and capable of enormous variation. To use it for corded quilting, simply draw a second line $\frac{1}{4}$ in (5mm) inside or outside the shape.

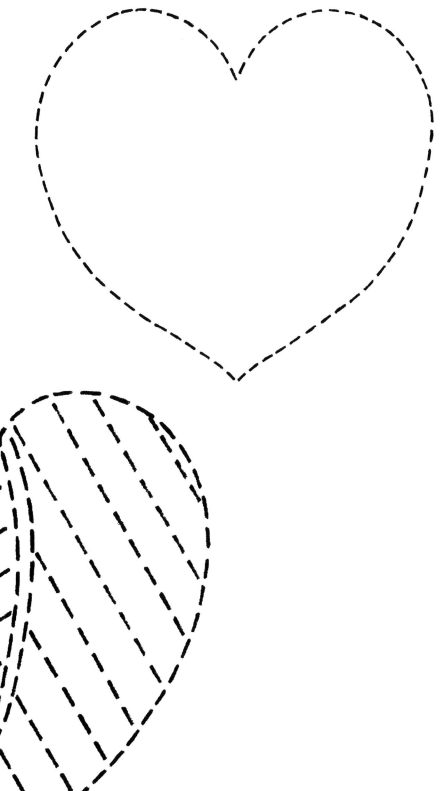

Leaf

This simple shape has been embellished with parallel lines of quilting from the outside edges to the central stem, giving a feeling of movement to an otherwise static image. The curving outline without the straight lines could easily be adapted for corded quilting.

Oak Leaf and Reel

This traditional twelve-pointed star is based on a double hexagon and can be used to great effect in plain square or circular patches. It can be altered in any number of ways – try making the outer points longer or eliminating the central circle.

Shell

There are endless designs taken from nature, and variations on shell patterns are almost infinite. This form, probably based on a nautilus shell, looks intricate but is actually quite straightforward to stitch – just take care to keep the spiral evenly spaced. Shell patterns are useful for filling irregular shapes or creating texture – particularly on quilts with a nautical theme.

Tulip Ring

Tulips are another motif widely used on quilts, especially appliquéd work. Their pleasing shape is simple to quilt, and the ring shown here is a good pattern to use for filling a plain block. An individual tulip shape can easily be turned into a design for corded quilting or trapunto.

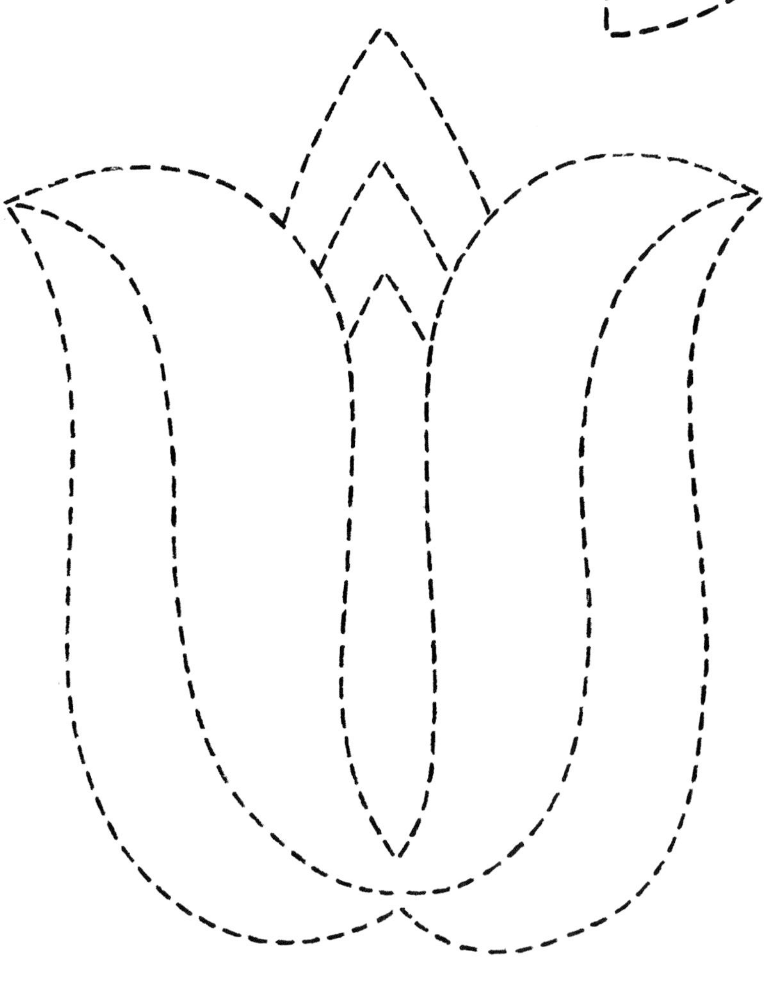

Tulip

The ever-popular Tulip makes a stunning single motif for a plain block, and it also works well as a design for corded quilting. Simply double the outlines, $1/4$ in (5mm) apart, or eliminate all but the outside outlines first.

Lover's Knot

This pattern would make a stunning central medallion for a wholecloth quilt. It also looks wonderful in a plain square or circle.

Square Swirl

This design, based on a simple feather shape, is ideal for filling a plain square shape, or it could be used to make an overall quilting pattern. Its potential is limitless – it can be made more intricate, with more blades, and the corner shapes can be made larger or smaller.

Simple Grids

GRIDS ARE REPEATING patterns that are generally used over a background area. The straight-lined ones in particular are good for novice quilters to start with, since – provided your measuring and marking are accurate – they are relatively easy to stitch. Remember that fine, detailed quilting will not show up well on a heavily patterned fabric or an elaborately pieced top. It is also more difficult to quilt such tops, simply because of the number of seams that you need to stitch over.

Clamshell

This traditional design is very effective when used with patchwork patterns based on straight lines, or as a background for a medallion or appliquéd quilt. A single basic clamshell shape is outlined in a solid line in the middle of this pattern; this can be traced and enlarged or reduced to fit into the space to be quilted.

Chevrons

These stepped lines make rectangles that are three times as long as they are wide. If the short edges at the bottom of the vertical shapes and on the right-hand side of the horizontal ones are eliminated, the zigzag pattern is even more clearly defined.

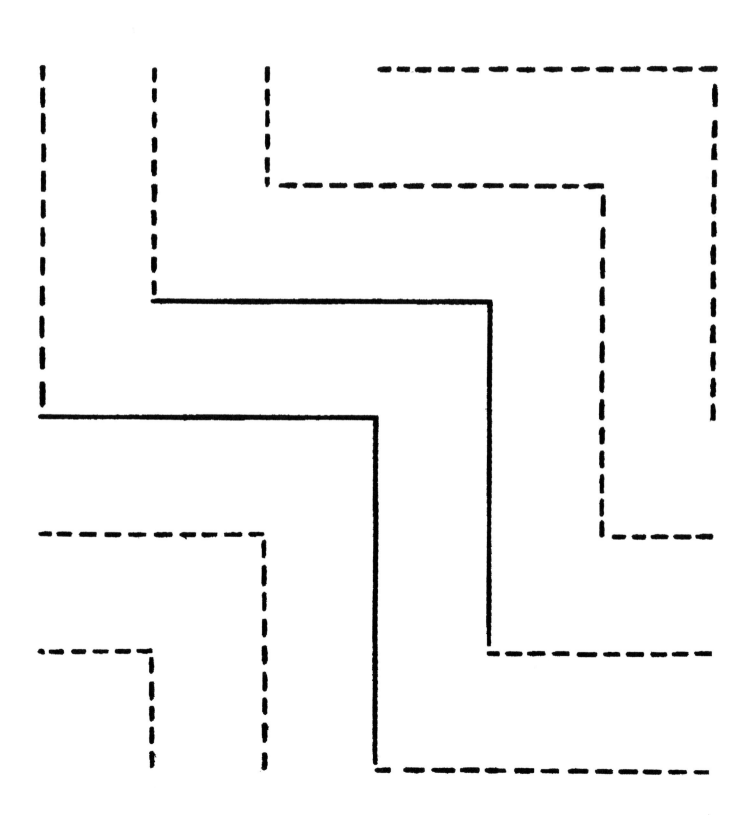

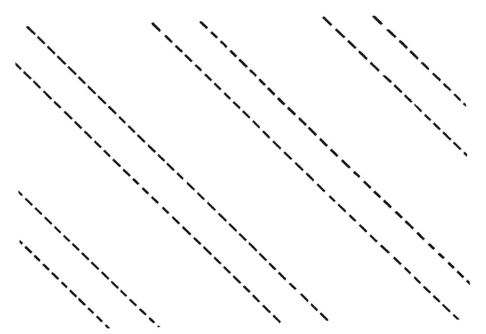

Diagonal

These simple diagonal lines run in one direction only, but lines running on the opposite diagonal could be added and would give a completely different feel to the finished quilt. Single lines in one direction are not as effective as the double lines shown here or triple ones. Accurate marking is essential.

Diagonal into the Center

The center lines cross in the middle and subsequent rows meet along the axis on which they are located. If the entire piece is marked in a grid, this pattern can be combined with the one on the opposite page to give alternating up and down diagonal lines that work very well on simple quilt designs.

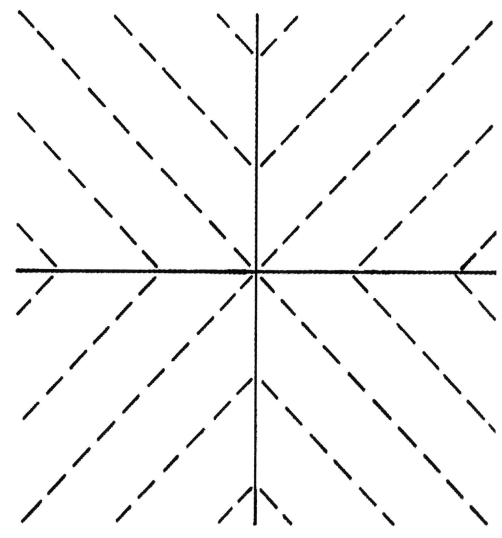

Diagonal out from the Center

Diagonal patterns add movement and vitality to all art forms, and quilting falls into this category. Here, the lines that radiate out from the center in concentric squares are evenly spaced, but the spacing can be varied if you wish. This design works very well on traditional patterns such as Trip Around the World.

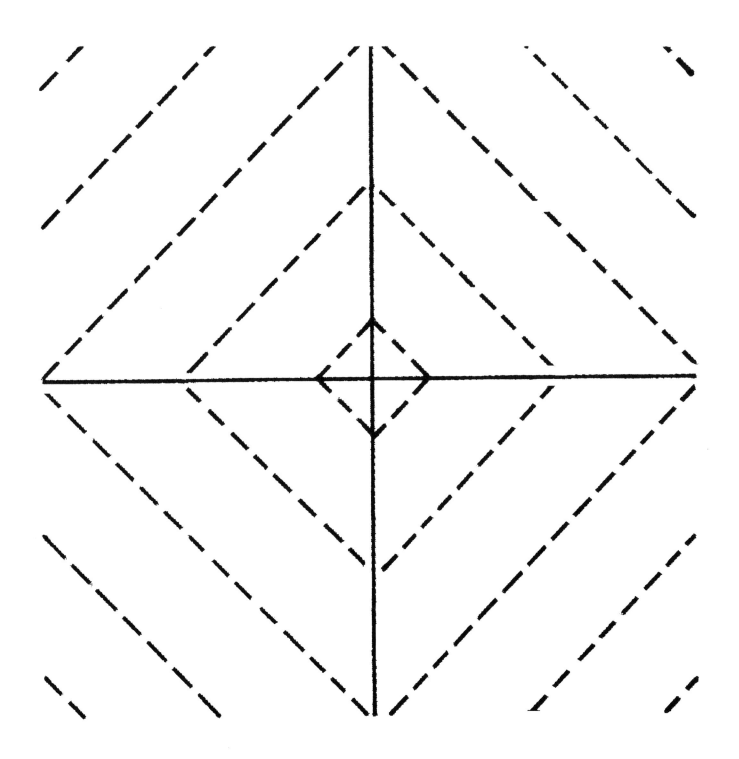

Diamond

Single, evenly spaced diagonal lines running in both directions give a simple, but very effective, diamond pattern. If double or triple lines are used, the texture of the finished piece becomes even more marked. Diamonds work particularly well on overall square patchwork patterns.

Hexagon

Another traditional design, the basic hexagon shape is very versatile. It works well as an outline or in the ditch with Hexagon patterns. It also makes an interesting background for many other designs, both traditional and non-traditional. Trace the solid shape shown in the center of this illustration and enlarge or reduce it to make a template.

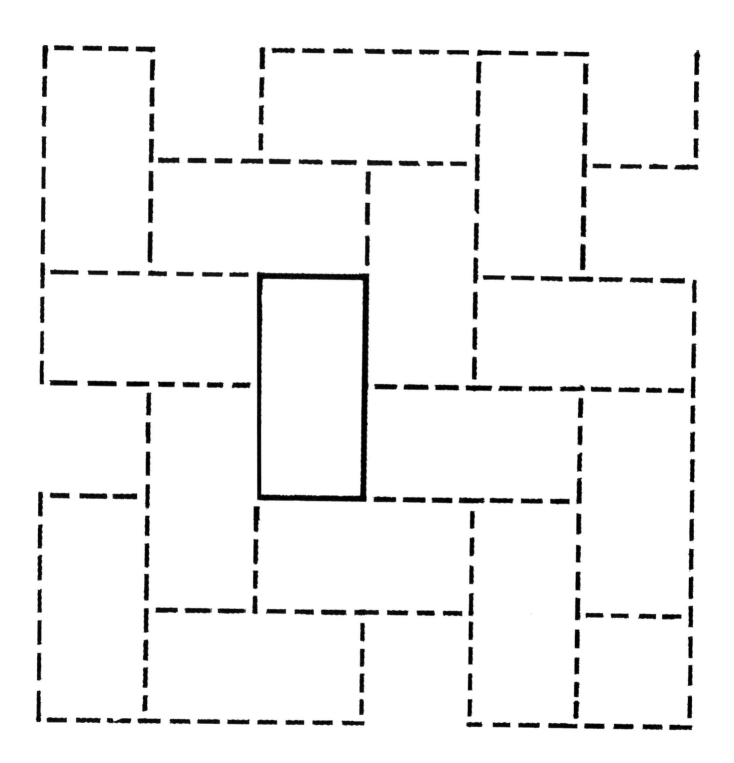

Steps

In this grid pattern, the lines form rectangles that are twice as long as they are wide. Alternated vertically and then horizontally, they create a stepped effect. Careful marking is essential, and although working with a template can be tricky, it is probably easier than drawing the lines with a ruler.

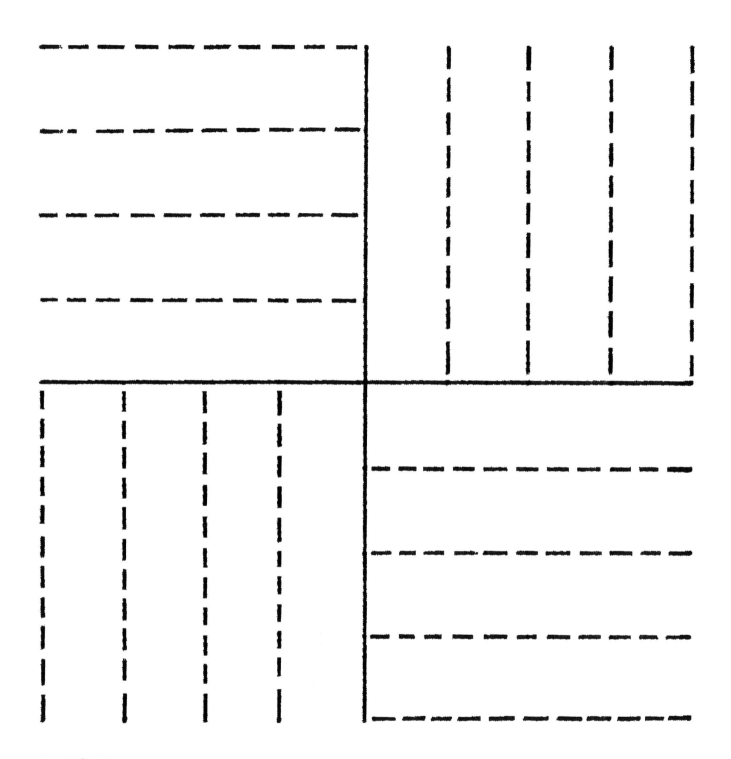

Straight Lines

The simplest of all quilting patterns is, of course, straight parallel lines. They can be stitched vertically or horizontally, and can cross each other to make a giant grid, or they can be stitched checkerboard fashion, as shown here. The stitches can be large or small, but for best effect they should be even and all the same size.

Wine Glass

This curved square in a circle can be drawn using a circle of your chosen size. Perhaps wine glasses were used for drafting in the past? It is certainly easier to see the overlaps if the marking is done in this way. The visual reversal of the pattern is a four-petaled flower shape.

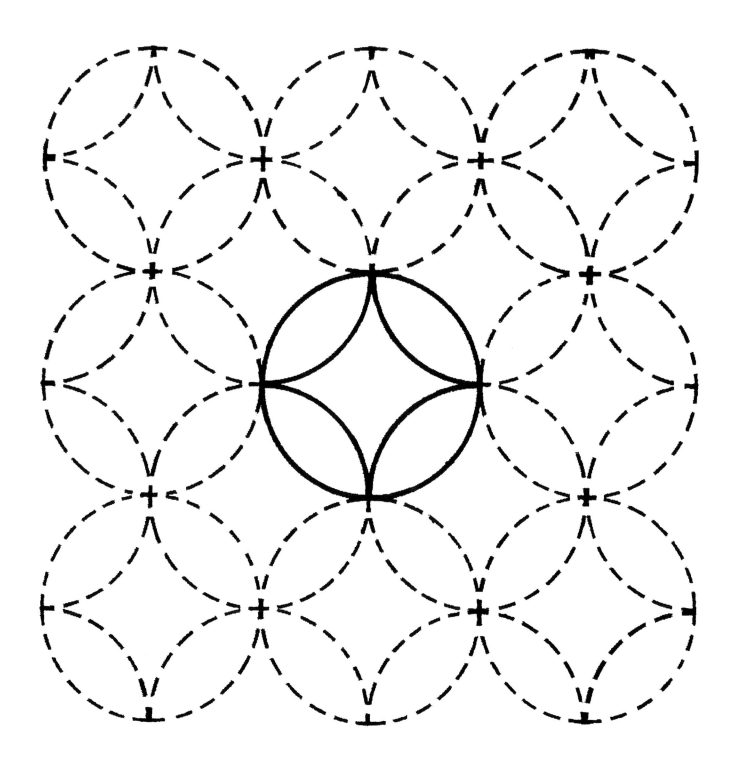

Simple Motifs

THESE MOTIFS ARE a versatile addition to any quilter's repertoire, since they can either be used in individual blocks, or joined end to end and repeated as necessary to form continuous borders. The ones shown here are predominantly curved in shape, and they combine well with the overall straight grid patterns on pages 410–419.

They are particularly good for beginners to stitch because their clean, simple lines are so straightforward to follow.

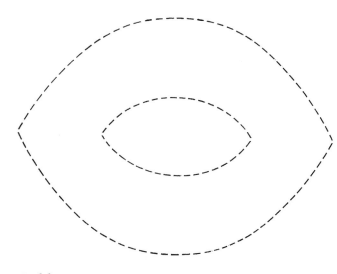

Cable

The cable is one of the most popular of all quilting motifs, and it is renowned for its versatility. Based on a pointed oval, it can be elongated or made more circular. It can be made more intricate and even combined with feathers or diamonds.

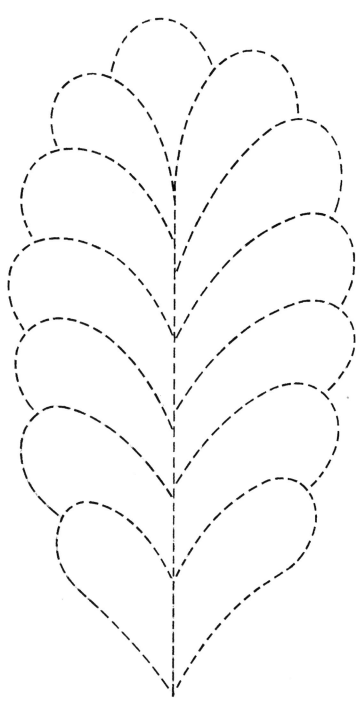

Double Feather

This pattern, like all feather designs, is made up of a number of single feathers which have been re-sized and assembled into a pleasing arrangement. Some are bigger than others, some thinner, some overlap. But all are based on the same motif.

Fan Blade

Another motif that can be used alone or in combination, the Fan Blade here has been given a choice of three tops – straight, curved, or pointed. Placed side by side, Fan Blades can be repeated to produce a right-angle, semicircular, or round motif to fill a plain square or circle.

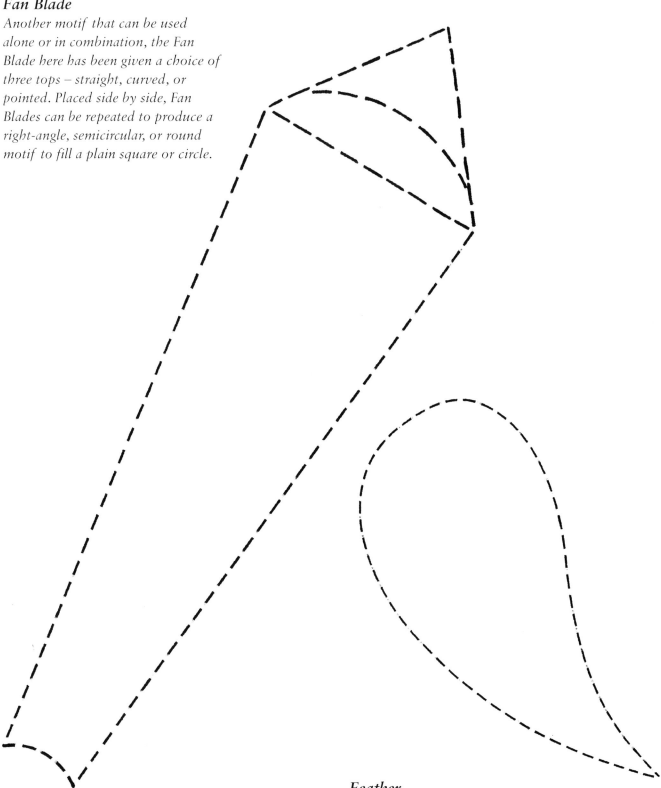

Feather

Like the cable shown opposite, the feather is a highly versatile image for quilting designs. This single frond can be re-drawn, re-sized and combined with others to make a straight feather. It can be made into a flowing cable, a heart or a circle of feathers, or a Feathered Cross or Feathered Swag.

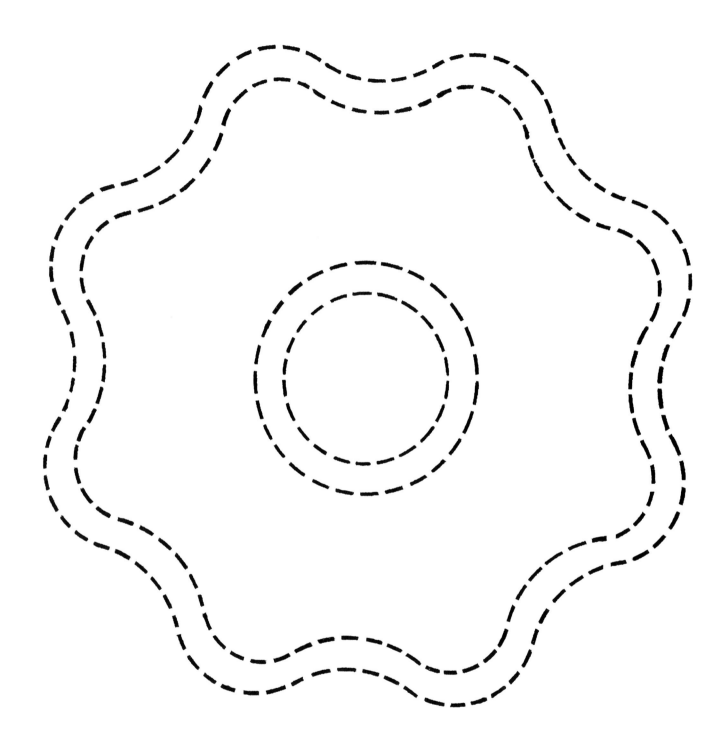

Flower

Flower patterns abound in traditional quilting. This one is traditionally known as a rose, and with the double lines as shown it makes an excellent design for corded quilting. In fact, many of the motifs shown in this section can be used for corded quilting if the outline is drawn double in this way.

Simple Cable

Cabled patterns of all types are very effective on borders or sashing. Here, the single cable winds down the pattern, overlapping as it goes. To make it longer, simply overlap the open end with the top shown here until the entire border has been marked. To finish, turn the template upside down and draw around the rounded end.

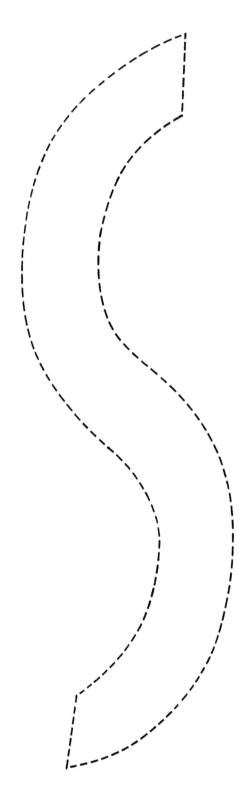

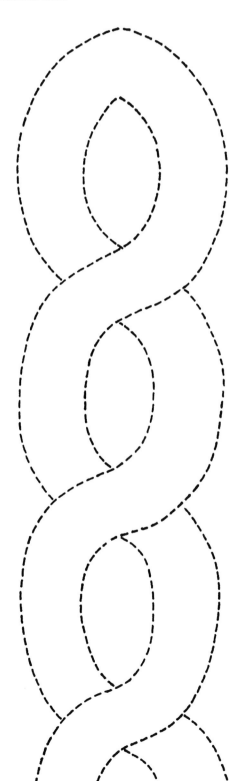

S-Curve

This motif is really half of a Simple Cable (right), but it can be drawn easily using an artist's flexible curve. Draw one line of the curve, then repeat the same curve a measured distance away from the first. To make a series of S-curves, make a template and place the top straight edge of the template against the bottom straight edge of the previous curve.

Borders

ORDERS ARE THE 'frame' for a quilt, and are as important a part of the overall effect as the piecing of the quilt top.

They are often made in solid colors, and it is in situations like this that quilting really comes into its own. With no competition from patterned fabrics or intricately pieced patches, the viewer's eye is free to linger on the fine stitching.

The patterns shown here can all be repeated as necessary to fill the available space.

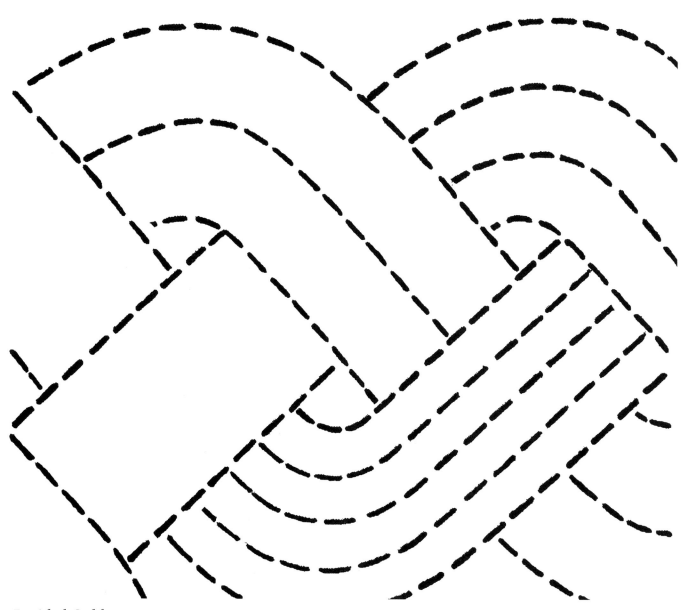

Braided Cable
Three ropes are plaited together to create an intricate cable that can also be altered by adding lines within the channels.

Diamond Border

Here, the lines intersect in both directions to create a series of contiguous small diamonds inside pointed peaks and troughs. The look is very angular.

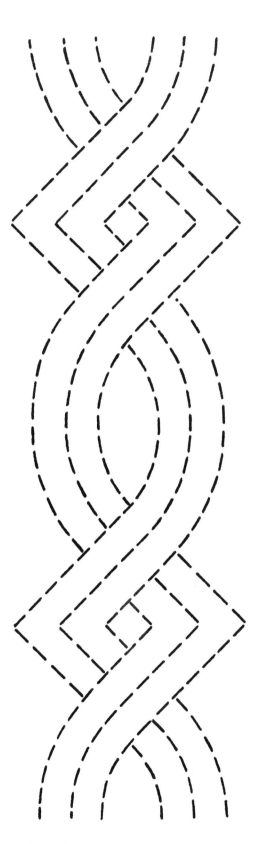

Diamond Cable

This elegant pattern combines a standard cable with the Diamond Twist shown on the next page. Equally effective without the center line, the border can be made even more complex by altering the size and shape of the ovals and squares.

Double Interlocked Squares

Based on overlapping squares, an attractive chain effect is created by threading the interlocked lines under and over each other. The same technique can be used with circular and oval shapes.

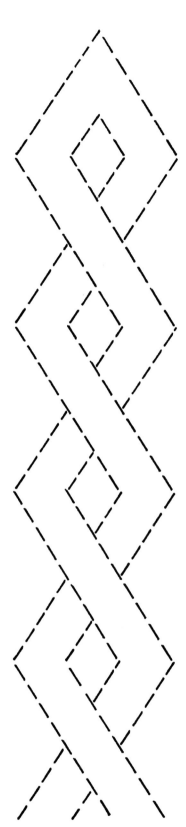

Diamond Twist

A doubled straight line that bends at just over 90 degrees each time it hits the side of its imaginary channel creates a wide diamond pattern. The chain is fluid and sinuous, without a curved line in sight.

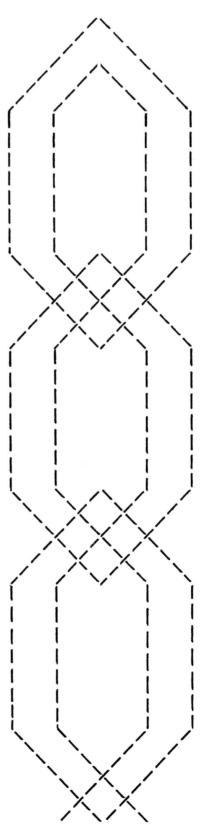

Interlocked Hexagons

These hexagons interlock in the same way as the square pattern opposite, but the crossover here creates a square on point that divides into four sections. Eliminating one of the intersecting lines reinforces the chain link; leaving the square blank means the interlocking disappears.

Feathered Twist

One of the most popular of all cable patterns, this twist combines a simple cable with a continuous Running Feather. The cable is the basis of the design, and the size of the central oval determines the width of the pattern and the size of the feathers.

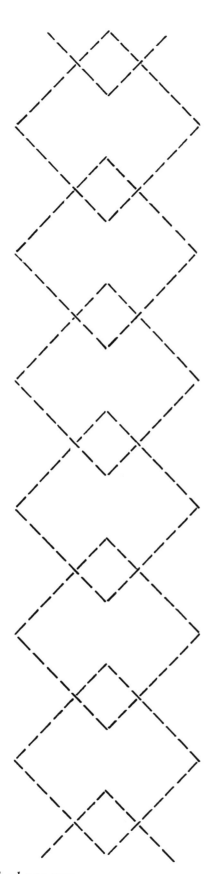

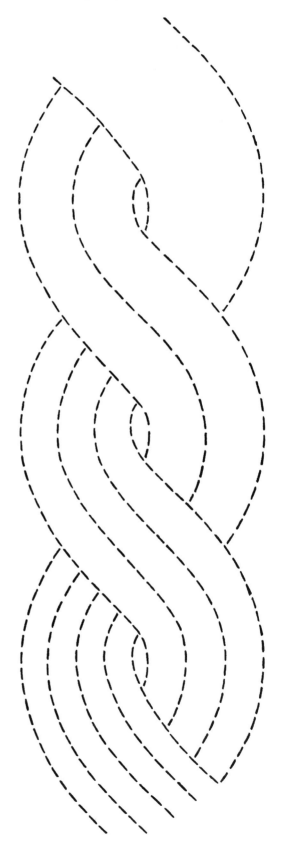

Cable
The simple cable consists of curved parallel lines that weave their way over and under each other. The pattern can be varied in the width of the cable itself, and by adding lines between the cable lines – here we show sections with one, two, and three central lines.

Interlocked squares
The square is turned on point and interlocked with its partner on either side to make a diamond-patterned border. The depth of the crossovers can be altered – small squares can be made tiny or can touch corners.

Tulips

The stems of this pattern can be lengthened to give more space between the flowers, and the leaves can be altered or eliminated. An effective variation could be made by substituting a rose, or another floral or leaf shape, for the tulips.

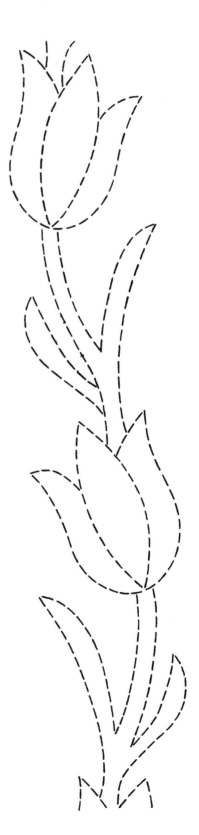

Pumpkin Seed

This is an adaptable pattern widely seen on Amish quilts, and can be accomplished surprisingly easily on a sewing machine, since the seeds are constructed as figures of eight, and the lines that enclose them can be worked up one side and down the other.

Corners

MANY OF THE border designs shown on pages 422–427 can be adapted to continue around corners, but visually, it is far more satisfying if the corner is turned smoothly, with flowing lines. All the designs shown here are based on repeating patterns that can be extended to fill the whole border. Any border pattern can be given a right-angled corner by drawing a line at a 45-degree angle across the design and reproducing its mirror image. Use a small mirror to decide the point at which the corner should occur.

Cable Twist Corner
Here, the two strands of the cable diverge at the corner to keep the flow of the pattern. One goes up into a steep curve to round the corner, while the other flattens out to slide under it. Reverse the pattern to make the corner bend the opposite way.

Diamond Cable Corner
This pattern consists of two arching outlines that cross each other to make the ovals and the diamonds. Here, the corner is formed by joining the ends of the inside arc in a point and simply rounding off the outside arcs to pass through the resulting thin oval shape.

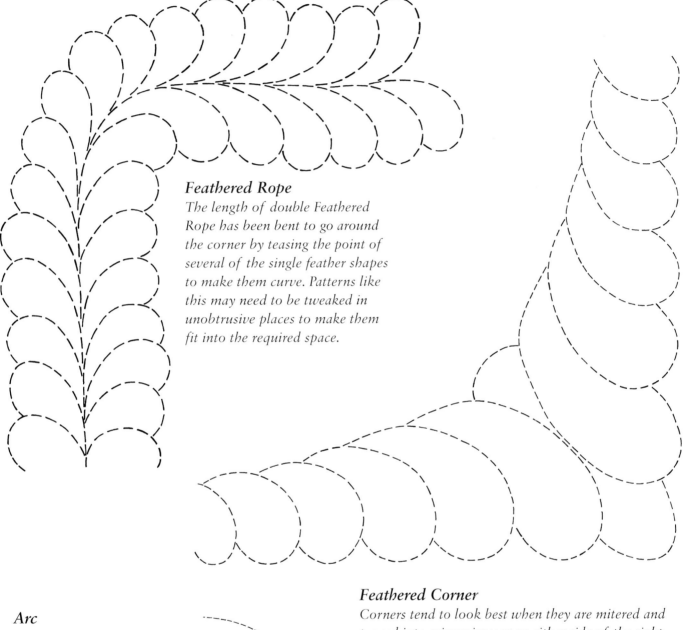

Feathered Rope
The length of double Feathered Rope has been bent to go around the corner by teasing the point of several of the single feather shapes to make them curve. Patterns like this may need to be tweaked in unobtrusive places to make them fit into the required space.

Feathered Corner
Corners tend to look best when they are mitered and turned into mirror images on either side of the right angle. Using a mirror standing on its edge you can visually bisect any pattern at any point along its length. When you find a miter that you like, mark the point, fold the pattern to a 90-degree angle, and trace it in the opposite direction.

Arc
Also known as Shell or Fan, this pattern is most appropriate as a corner on its own, perhaps on a wide border with simple vertical and horizontal stitching. The section in the corner itself is based on a quarter-circle, while the other motifs are parts of a half circle.

Project Templates

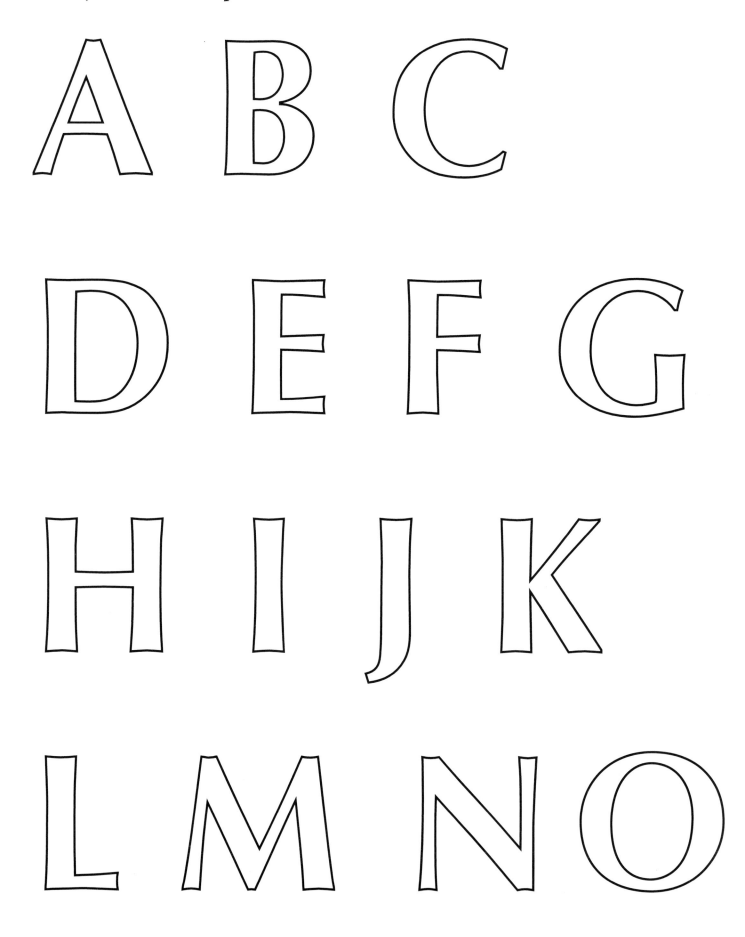

***Plaid Baby Quilt (pages 262–265);
Hearts Quilt (pages 352–355)***
*Alphabets are always useful in appliqué as a
way of personalizing your work –
particularly if you are making a piece to give
as a gift. Many quilters "sign" their work by
embroidering or appliquéing their initials
in one corner.*

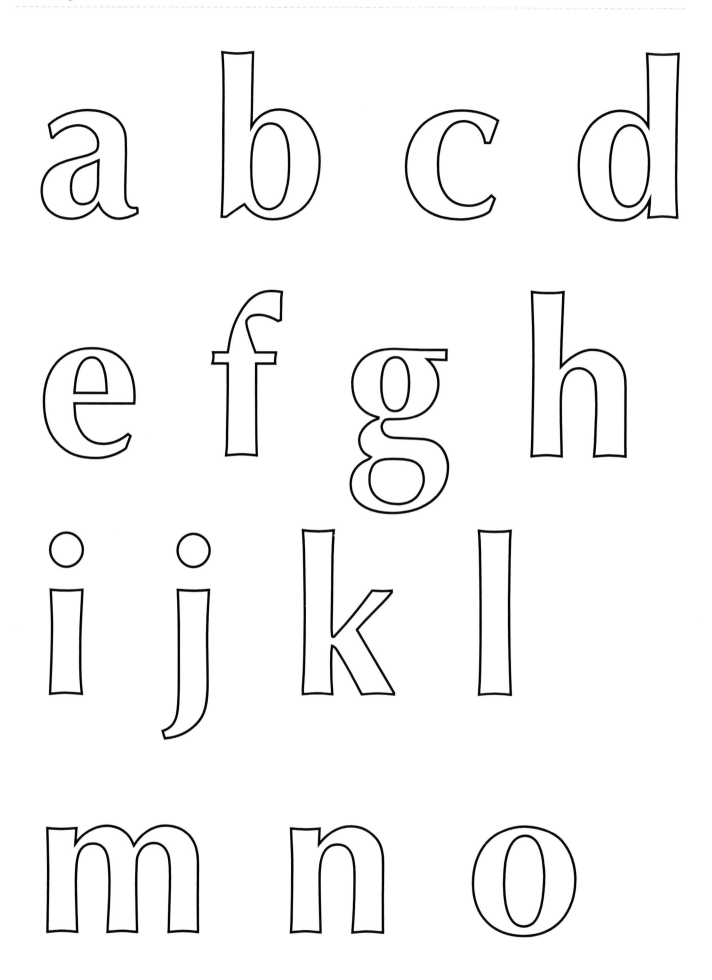

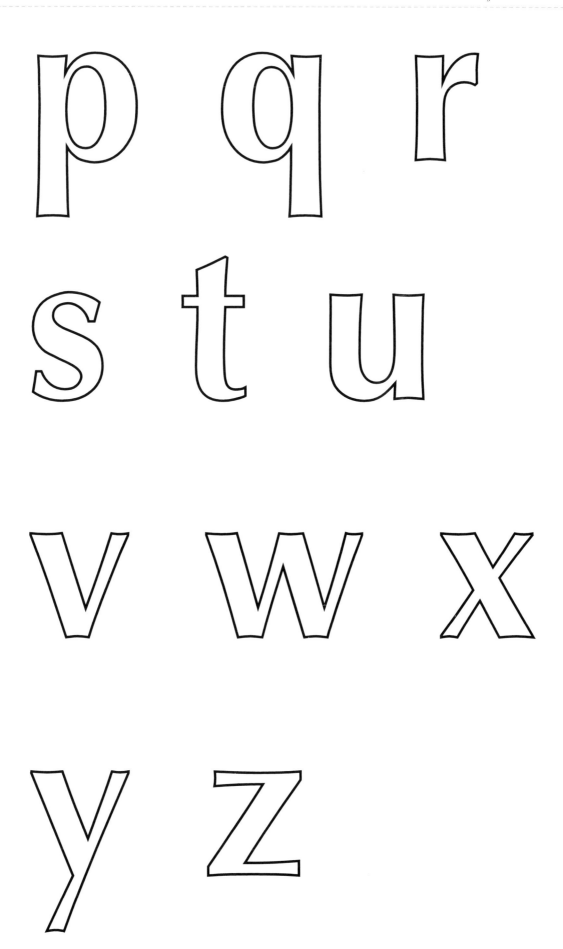

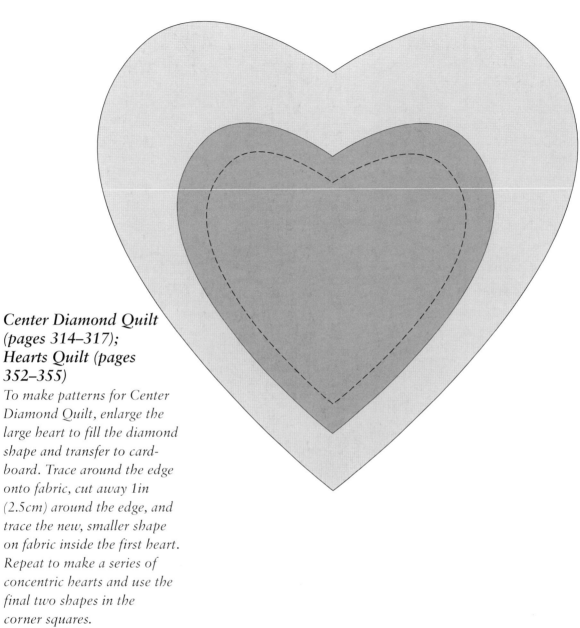

Center Diamond Quilt (pages 314–317); Hearts Quilt (pages 352–355)

To make patterns for Center Diamond Quilt, enlarge the large heart to fill the diamond shape and transfer to cardboard. Trace around the edge onto fabric, cut away 1in (2.5cm) around the edge, and trace the new, smaller shape on fabric inside the first heart. Repeat to make a series of concentric hearts and use the final two shapes in the corner squares.

To make heart appliqués, select a size and transfer to cardboard or template plastic.

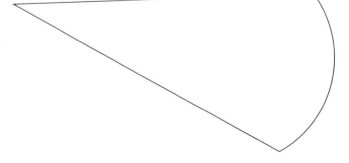

Sashiko Pillow 396–399

To make the chrysanthemum shape for the Sashiko Pillow, enlarge this template and transfer it onto cardboard. Draw around the shape 12 times to make the flower sections.

British Strippy Quilt
(pages 376–379)

This is a quarter section of the quilting template. Trace it on tracing paper four times, so each half mirrors the other. Lay a piece of template plastic on top and cut a channel $^{1}/_{8}$ in (3mm) wide, leaving "bridges" to hold the stencil together.

Hawaiian Wall Hanging (pages 360–363)

Photocopy and enlarge the template as necessary, or transfer design to graph paper and then copy onto larger piece of paper at the desired size. Trace it onto tracing paper and place the diagonal edge of the tracing along the center fold of the paper you are using for your pattern.

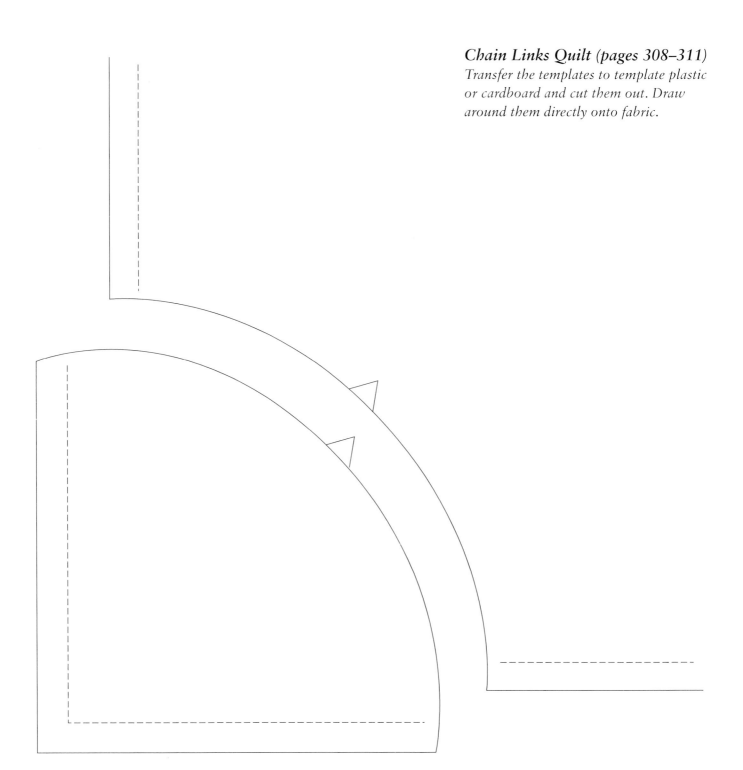

Chain Links Quilt (pages 308–311)
Transfer the templates to template plastic
or cardboard and cut them out. Draw
around them directly onto fabric.

Baby Blocks Playmat (opposite; pages 304–307)
This is a quick and easy way of cutting the huge number of paper
templates that you need for the diamond shapes in this quilt – far easier
than tracing each one individually! Photocopy or trace the whole page
onto the paper you are using for your paper patterns and then cut out
the number of diamond shapes you need.

Mola *(pages 364–367)*
*The three appliqué shapes are reproduced
actual size, so trace the shapes and transfer
them onto cardboard.*

Index

Numbers in italics refer
to the illustrations.

ACKNOWLEDGMENTS

With thanks to David for his patience and to Joshua and Daniel for their timely absence. Also to Sally Brown, who loaned her grandson's favorite quilt, Rebecca Arscott for her stitching skills, and the team at Collins & Brown.

PICTURE CREDITS

The illustrations in this book are published by kind permission of the following:

pages 6–13: America Hurrah Archive, New York City; page 14: The Chase Manhattan Arts Program; page 15: America Hurrah Archive, New York City; pages 16–17: Maggi McCormick Gordon; pages 18–23: America Hurrah Archive, New York City; pages 24–26: Museum of International Folk Art (Doug Brown, Neutrogena Collection), a unit of the Museum of New Mexico, Santa Fé; pages 27–28: America Hurrah Archive, New York City; page 29: Museum of International Folk Art (Doug Brown, Neutrogena Collection), a unit of the Museum of New Mexico, Santa Fé; page 30: America Hurrah Archive, New York City; Museum of International Folk Art (Doug Brown, Neutrogena Collection), a unit of the Museum of New Mexico, Santa Fé; pages 32–43: America Hurrah Archive, New York City; page 44: The Chase Manhattan Arts Program; pages 45-51: America Hurrah Archive, New York City; page 52: Beamish, The North of England Open Air Museum; page 53: America Hurrah Archive, New York City; pages 53–63 America Hurrah Archive, New York City; pages 64–65: The Chase Manhattan Arts Program; pages 66–70: America Hurrah Archive, New York City; page 71: Beamish, The North of England Open Air Museum; pages 72–107: America Hurrah Archive, New York City; page 111: The Chase Manhattan Arts Program; pages 112–116: America Hurrah Archive, New York City; page 117: The Chase Manhattan Arts Program: pages 118–165: America Hurrah Archive, New York City; pages 167–171 Museum of International Folk Art (Michael Monteaux, Girard Foundation Collection and International Folk Art Foundation), a unit of the Museum of New Mexico, Santa Fé; page 172–173: Maggi McCormick Gordon; pages 174–176: America Hurrah Archive, New York City; page 177: Beamish, The North of England Open Air Museum; pages 178–181: America Hurrah Archive, New York City; pages 182–187: Beamish, The North of England Open Air Museum; page 188: Museum of International Folk Art (Doug Brown, Neutrogena Collection), a unit of the Museum of New Mexico, Santa Fé; pages 189–190: Beamish, The North of Engand Open Air Museum; page 191: America Hurrah Archive, New York City; pages 192–195: Beamish, The North of England Open Air Museum; pages 196–197: The Bowes Museum, Co. Durham; pages 199–212: America Hurrah Archive, New York City; pages 214–217: America Hurrah Archive, New York City; page 218: Beamish, The North of England Open Air Museum; pages 219–221: America Hurrah Archive, New York City; page 222: Maggi McCormick Gordon; page 223: Sally Brown; pages 224–227: America Hurrah Archive, New York City; pages 312–313: The Bowes Museum, Co. Durham; pages 322–323: Museum of International Folk Art (Doug Brown, Neutrogena Collection), a unit of the Museum of New Mexico, Santa Fé; pages 330–331: America Hurrah Archive, New York City; pages 344–345: America Hurrah Archive, New York City; pages 368–369: America Hurrah Archive, New York City; pages 370–371: America Hurrah Archive, New York City.

All other photographs are copyright Collins & Brown Ltd.

Whilst every effort has been made to ensure that all pictures have been fully and correctly credited, the publishers would be please to hear of any omissions.

ABOUT THIS BOOK

Quilts are dated in most cases with a 20–25-year approximation unless the date is known positively. Wherever possible, we have included an assumed date and the area in which the quilt is thought to have been made, as well as any other verifiable historical information that is available.

Measurements in this book are given where necessary and relevant. Standard (imperial) is given first, with metric in parentheses. It is not possible to convert precisely, so either one system or the other should be used, never a combination of the two. The templates given at the back of the book can be enlarged or reduced on a photocopier to make a pattern of the right size for your own projects.

There is usally more than one way to execute a technique, and you should always feel free to experiment, but always read the directions for a project through from start to finish before you begin work.